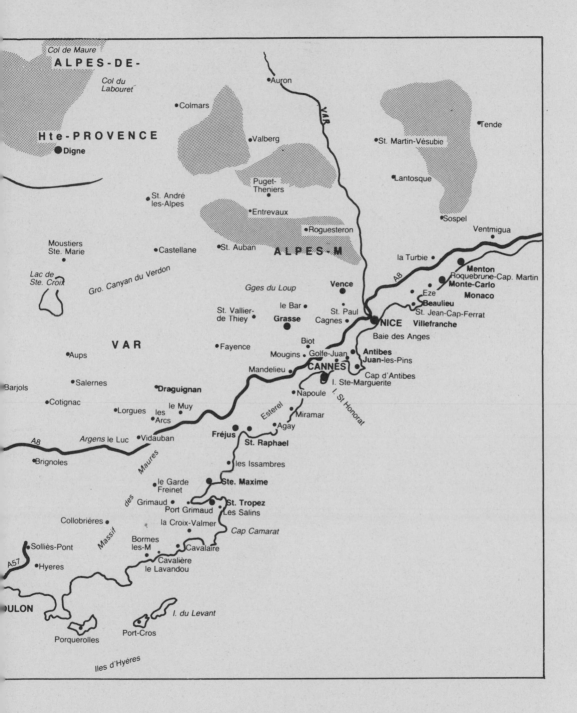

ALPES-DE-

Col de Maure

Col du Labouret

•Auron

•Colmars

•Valberg

•Tende

Hte-PROVENCE

•St. Martin-Vésubie

●**Digne**

Puget-Theniers

•Lantosque

•St. André les-Alpes

•Entrevaux

•Sospel

•Roguesteron

•Ventmigua

Moustiers Ste. Marie

•Castellane

•St. Auban

ALPES-M

la Turbie •

Lac de Ste. Croix

Gro. Canyan du Verdon

Gges du Loup

Vence

A8

Menton
Roquebrune-Cap. Martin

Monte-Carlo

Monaco

Eze

St. Vallier-de Thiey

le Bar

St. Paul

Beaulieu

St. Jean-Cap-Ferrat

VAR

Grasse

Cagnes

NICE

Villefranche

•Aups

•Fayence

Biot

Baie des Anges

•Salernes

Mougins

Golfe-Juan

Antibes

Juan-les-Pins

Barjols

CANNES

•Cotignac

•Lorgues

les Arcs

le Muy

Mandelieu

Cap d'Antibes

I. Ste-Marguerite

Draguignan

Napoule

I. St Honorat

Esterel

Miramar

A8

Argens le Luc

Vidauban

Fréjus

Agay

•Brignoles

Maures

St. Raphael

•les Issambres

le Garde Freinet

Ste. Maxime

des Grimaud

St. Tropez

Collobrières

Port Grimaud

Les Salins

la Croix-Valmer

Cap Camarat

•Solliès-Pont

Massif

Bormes les-M

Cavalaire

A57

•Hyeres

Cavalière le Lavandou

ᑌULON

I. du Levant

Porquerolles

Port-Cros

Iles d'Hyères

The South of France

An Anthology

Still Life : Henri Matisse

The South of France

An Anthology

COMPILED BY

LAURA RAISON

BEAUFORT BOOKS

PUBLISHERS ● *NEW YORK*

Compilation copyright © 1985 by Cadogan Publications Ltd.

Library of Congress Cataloging-in-Publication Data
Main entry under title:
The South of France.
          Bibliography: p.
          1. France, Southern — Literary collections.
          I. Raison, Laura.
PN6071.F68S6 1985   808.8'032448   85-19988

ISBN 0-8253-0334-6

Published in the United States by Beaufort Books
Publishers, New York.

Designed by Julian Rothenstein
Typeset by Words Illustrated (TU)
Printed in Great Britain
First American Edition
10 9 8 7 6 5 4 3 2 1

Contents

Introduction

IMAGINE YOURSELF STANDING, as Petrarch once stood, on the top of Mont Ventoux to the east of the Rhône Valley, and look around you. To the west lies Roman Orange, to the south-west Nîmes, Avignon, city of the Popes, and Arles, perhaps the most typical of all Provençal towns. Turn now to the south, towards Aix-en-Provence and on further to Marseilles and the Mediterranean. On a clear night it is possible to pick out the lighthouses that dot the coast stretching on and out of sight to the Riviera. From Ventoux's high peak one can see, as Petrarch saw, the wide and varied spread of Provence, with its special combination of hills and marshes, mountains and plains; the area most commonly known to travellers as the South of France. It is to this region that, as early as 600 BC, colonists and settlers came, first by boat and later by horse and carriage (now car, train or aeroplane) crossing that invisible boundary where the olive trees begin and Northern Europe becomes the South.

The landscape of Provence, though diverse, is essentially Mediterranean with its vines and olives, pines and cypresses and, to the east, Mimosa and orange trees. On every hill there seems to sleep a sunbaked village where old men drink Pastis and play Pétanque in the shady square and children dart like lizards between doorways calling to each other in endless street games. The air is generally dry and clear, and the colours dazzling. It is not surprising that people, particularly artists, have come in droves to experience this bright world of busy fishing ports, spectacular landscapes and lazy towns. Van Gogh, one of Provence's most illustrious visitors, characteristically saw the region in terms of the blazing colours he loved to use.

..... a view of Arles. Of the town itself one sees only some red roofs and a tower, the rest is hidden by the green foliage of fig trees, far away in the background, and a narrow strip of blue sky above it. The town is surrounded by immense meadows all abloom with countless buttercups — a sea of yellow — in the foreground these meadows are divided by a ditch full of violet irises ..... But what a subject, hein!

Amid all this beauty one also experiences a sense of history. Avignon, Aigues-Mortes, Tarascon, Les-Saintes-Maries-de-la-Mer, Toulon, Antibes, St-Paul-de-Vence, the very names conjure up a procession of gladiators, troubadours, crusaders and Kings — heroes and villains who battled out their lives in the area leaving behind castles or churches, statues and frescoes. Their presence can still be felt even among the present day bustle of commerce and tourism. If one climbs the steep paths of Les Baux (preferably either very early or late in the day) one can still hear the manic laughter of the wicked Lord Des Baux as he threw his victims off the rocks for sport. And in Aigues-Mortes one can experience something of the horror and stoicism of the French Protestants incarcerated in the Tour de Constance; in particular that of Marie Durand, locked up for thirty-eight years, whose mark is still on the wall of her cell; '*Au ciel, resistez*'. But now modern France is also increasingly evident in all but the remoter parts of Provence and the eastern Languedoc. The larger towns are sophisticated and commercialised with fast growing populations and busy roads, and, particularly around Marseilles, there is a vast industrial wasteland of oil refineries and factories.

Nowhere has the problem of cars and people become more out of hand than along France's south-eastern coast — the Riviera. With its spectacular natural beauty the Côte d'Azur has aways attracted travellers; Phoenician, Roman and Saracen in the early days; its tradition of holiday villas was already well established in Roman times, and has of course developed dramatically since then. Centuries later, in 1763, the English novelist Tobias Smollett spent a year in Nice, and in 1834 the politican Lord Brougham first went to Cannes, between them heralding the start of the vogue for English tourism in the area. Thereafter, a stream of visitors from England, America and Russia arrived in search of a pleasant climate, ready to swim, socialise and to gamble. By the turn of the century there were still some relatively undiscovered fishing ports and beaches, but these were about to change forever. In the twenties Scott Fitzgerald gave this wry account of Antibes in a letter to a friend:

..... There was no one at Antibes this summer except me, Zelda, the Valentinos, the Murphys, Mistinguett, Rex Ingram, Dos Passos, Alice Terry, the Macleishes, Charlie Brackett, Maude Kahn, Esther Murphy, Marguerite Namara, E Phillips Oppenheim, Mannes the violinist, Floyd Dell, Max and Crystal Eastman, ex-Premier Orlando, Etienne de Beaumont — just a real place to rough it, an escape from all the world.

Nowadays in summer much of the Riviera is very crowded and expensive, the sweltering roads are jammed and campsites litter the coast. But even at the height of the season the Côte d'Azur has not lost all its charm. The main towns have retained a certain amount of individuality and, if Nice is huge and claustrophobic, Cannes is chic in its way, and Menton remains attractively sleepy. Beside the resorts lies the blue Mediterranean, unchanged since D H Lawrence described it as: 'young as Odysseus in the morning'. Monaco may have become Americanised with its many skyscrapers, but there is a thrill for some in watching the Formula One cars roar around Monte Carlo's twisting streets in May, or in taking a picnic up to La Turbie and looking down at the annual fireworks as they explode over the glittering port of the Principality each August. And when the coast becomes exhausting one can always drive a short distance inland, where myriad hilltop villages wait quietly in the sun as they have waited virtually unchanged for hundreds of years.

I have tried, through this anthology, to create a vivid composite picture of one of France's most beautiful regions, and to enable the reader to discover, through the words of both natives and travellers, the magic essence of the South of France. In the words of one of Provence's favourite sons, the poet Frederic Mistral:

> *..... It is enough. For me, upon the sea of history,*
> *Thou wast, Provence, a pure symbol*
> *A mirage of glory and victory,*
> *That in the dusky flight of centuries,*
> *Grants us a gleam of the Beautiful .....*

LAURA RAISON

Statue of Mistral at Arles : Raoul Dufy

CHAPTER ONE

Towns and Ancient Places

〜〜〜〜〜〜〜〜〜〜〜〜〜〜〜〜〜〜〜〜〜〜〜〜〜〜〜

Charles Maurras, poet, essayist and journalist, born in Martigues and educated at Aix-en-Provence, was an arch-conservative, highly critical of all romantic attitudes.

H E R E I S T H E shipwreck of archaeologists, critics and historians. From time to time there arrive at the gates of Avignon travellers well-versed in these beautiful and serious matters. They have hardly passed the toll gates when they are transformed; their party henceforth numbers only lovers ..... C H A R L E S M A U R R A S (1 8 6 8 - 1 9 5 2) (translated by Heimann)

Lawrence Durrell, English poet and novelist, here contemplates a meeting in Avignon.

Avignon

Come, meet me in some dead café —
A puff of cognac or a sip of smoke
Will grant a more prolific light,
Say there is nothing to revoke.

A veteran with no arm will press
A phantom sorrow in his sleeve;
The aching stump may well insist
On memories it can't relieve.

Late cats, the city's thumbscrews twist.
Night falls in its profuse derision,
Brings candle-power to younger lives,
Cancels in me the primal vision.

Come, random with me in the rain,
In ghastly harness like a dream,
In rainwashed streets of saddened dark
Where nothing moves that does not seem.
L A W R E N C E D U R R E L L (1 9 1 2 -)

Prosper Mérimée, the French dramatist and storyteller whose works included the original Carmen, *travelled extensively, writing reports in his other capacity as Napoleon III's Inspector General of Historical Monuments.* N O T E S D ' U N V O Y A G E D A N S L E M I D I D E L A F R A N C E *was published in 1835.*

A V I G N O N G I V E S T H E impression of a garrison town, (or has the look of a garrison town). All the large buildings are designed in military style, and its palaces, as well as its

~~~~~~

churches look like so many fortresses. Battlements and Machicoutis crown the bell towers, everything points to a tradition of rebellion and Civil War.

PROSPER MÉRIMÉE (1803-1870) (translated by J Karslake)

H E W H O T A K E S leave of Avignon takes leave of his senses.

PROVENÇAL PROVERB

The Countess of Blessington rose from humble Irish birth to rank and fame as a hostess and writer. Thrice married, she was a friend of Byron and in her closing years lived with the dandy Alfred, Count d'Orsay. Her prolific output included sketches from her European travels.

A V I G N O N , 2 0 T H : T H E R E is poetry and romance in the name; or, at least, in the associ-ations it calls up. Petrach, with the power that appertains to genius alone, has invested this place with an interest for all who can appreciate the beauty of his works; and we view Avignon with different feelings to those with which we regard more attractive towns. The approach to Avignon is imposing: the high towers of the ancient palace, with their rich and warm toned hue of brown, rise above the walls of the city; and many a spire and steeple give beauty to the pic-ture, which is crowned by Villeneuve, seen in the distance. The battlemented walls are flanked by square towers, erected at regular distances, and have seven gates.

The Rhône is nowhere seen to greater advantage than here, where it sweeps along with a rapidity and grandeur that glides over it the appearance of being hurried on by some irresist-able influence; like those vessels we read of in fairy tales, that skim the waters with magical swiftness, but cannot retard their course.

The ruins of the ancient bridge, with a chapel in the centre, have a very picturesque effect; and the sound of the rushing, arrowy Rhône, as it is dashed against the stones, has a melan-choly in it well suited to the *triste* character of this silent and nearly deserted place. Mont Ven-toux, which is said to be the highest mountain in France, rises to the north of Avignon, its sides glowing with all the varied hues of vegetation, while its summit is veiled in snow; and on the south, the horizon is bounded by the chain of blue mountains of the Angles and the Issarts.

The *rocher de Don,* which we explored today, commands a fine view of the town and a mag-nificent one of the surrounding country. The plains of Languedoc, rich in mulberry and olive trees, and sprinkled with undulating hills, covered with vineyards, look like a vast garden spread over the country and to the east are seen the abrupt and sterile rocks of Vaucluse, form-ing a fine contrast to the fertile scene they bound.

Never did I behold a more glorious sunset than this evening: the river was crimsoned with its rich reflection, and all the objects around were tinged by its brilliant rays. Who could believe, while beholding it, that this was the gloomy month of November, notwithstanding that the *vent de bise* reminds one it is not summer?

We were much amused this morning by a visit from the poet laureate of Avignon, to present a congratulatory ode on our arrival. The poem was as poor as its author, which is saying not a little; for poverty was stamped on every lineament of his care-worn face, and threadbare garments. He has for many years welcomed every traveller whose appearance indicated the power of remunerating the distinction with a similar felicitation; nay, people are malicious enough to assert, that the same poem, inserting merely a change of name, answers for every English family.

The poor poet retired happy in the possession of our donation; and left us wondering if, as he stated, he lived by his wits, how he could exist on so slender a capital.

THE COUNTESS OF BLESSINGTON (1789-1849)

In 1888 Van Gogh went to Arles, where he painted some of his most beautiful pictures, before committing himself to the Asylum St Paul in St Remy-de-Provence.

FURTHER A VIEW of Arles. Of the town itself one sees only some red roofs and a tower, the rest is hidden by the green foliage of fig trees, far away in the background, and a narrow strip of blue sky above it. The town is surrounded by immense meadows all abloom with countless buttercups — a sea of yellow — in the foreground these meadows are divided by a ditch full of violet irises. They were mowing the grass while I was painting, so it is only a study and not the finished picture that I had intended to do. But what a subject, hein! That sea of yellow with a band of violet irises, and in the background that coquettish little town of the pretty women! Then two studies of roadsides — later — done with the mistral raging.

VINCENT VAN GOGH (1835-1890) (translated by J van Gogh-Bonger)

The Yellow Houses in Arles : Vincent Van Gogh

The author Hilaire Belloc, noted particularly for his writing for children, was born in France and educated in England. He was a keen traveller and wrote many accounts of his journeys. HILLS AND THE SEA *was first published in 1906.*

THE CITY OF Arles is small and packed. A man may spend an hour in it instead of a day or a year, but in that hour he can receive full communion with antiquity. For as you walk along the tortuous lane between high houses, passing on either hand as you go the ornaments of every age, you turn suddenly upon the titanic arches of Rome. There are the huge stones which appal you with the Roman weight and perpetuate in their arrangement an order that has modelled the world. They lie exact and mighty; they are unmoved, clamped with metal, a little worn, enduring. They are nonetheless a domestic and native part of the living town in which they stand. You pass from the garden of a house that was built in your grandfather's time, and you see familiarly before you in the street a pedestal and a column. They are two thousand years old. You read a placard idly upon the wall; the placard interests you; it deals with the politics of the place or with the army, but the wall might be meaningless. You look more closely, and you see that that wall was raised in a fashion that has been forgotten since the Antonines, and these realities still press upon you, revealed and lost again with every few steps you walk within the limited circuit of the town.

Rome slowly fell asleep. The sculpture lost its power; something barbaric returned. You may see that decline in capitals and masks still embedded in buildings of the fifth century. The sleep grew deeper. There came five hundred years of which so little is left in Europe that Paris has but one doubtful tower and London nothing. Arles still preserves its relics. When Charlemagne was dead and Christendom almost extinguished the barbarian and the Saracen alternately built, and broke against, a keep that still stands and that is still so strong that one might still defend it. It is unlit. It is a dungeon; a ponderous menace above the main street of the city, blind and enormous. It is the very time it comes from.

When all that fear and anarchy of the mind had passed, and when it was discovered that the West still lived, a dawn broke. The medieval civilization began to sprout vigorously through the eleventh and twelfth centuries, as an old tree sprouts before March is out. The memorials of that transition are common enough. We have them here in England in great quantity; we call them the 'Norman' architecture. A peculiarly vivid relic of that spring-time remains at Arles. It is the door of what was then the cathedral — the door of St Trophimus. It perpetuates the beginning of the civilization of the Middle Ages. And of that civilization an accident which has all the force of a particular design has preserved here, attached to this same church, another complete type. The cloisters of this same Church of St Trophimus are not only the Middle Ages caught and made eternal, they are also a progression of that great experiment from its youth to its sharp close.

You come into these cloisters from a little side street and a neglected yard, which give you no hint of what you are going to see. You find yourself cut off at once and put separately by. Silence inhabits the place; you see nothing but the sky beyond the border of the low roofs. One old man there, who cannot read or write and is all but blind, will talk to you of the Rhône.

Then as you go round the arches, 'withershins' against the sun (in which way lucky progression has always been made in sacred places), there pass you one after the other the epochs of the Middle Ages. For each group of arches comes later than the last in the order of its sculpture, and the sculptors during those 300 years went withershins as should you.

You have first the solemn purpose of the early work. This takes on neatness of detail, then fineness; a great maturity dignifies all the northern side. Upon the western you already see that spell beneath which the Middle Ages died. The mystery of the fifteenth century; none of its wickedness but all its final vitality, is there. You see in fifty details the last attempt of our race to grasp and permanently to retain the beautiful.

When the circuit is completed the series ends abruptly — as the medieval story itself ended.

There is no way of writing or of telling history which could be so true as these visions are. Arles, at a corner of the great main road of the Empire, never so strong as to destroy nor so insignificant as to cease from building, catching the earliest Roman march into the north, the Christian advance, the full experience of the invasions; retaining in a vague legend the memory of St Paul; drawing in, after the long trouble, the new life that followed the Crusades, can show such visions better, I think, than Rome herself can show them.

HILAIRE BELLOC (1870-1953)

Alan Ross is perhaps best known as editor of the LONDON MAGAZINE.

Arena at Arles

Tartarin de Tarascon in all the bookshops,
Prints by Van Gogh, provençal cottons and garlic.
And Daudet strings it together, fetching
Back the past as easily as his donkey,
The sails of his mill stiff against child's blue,
L'Arlesienne and the bridge painted form straw
Pigment, a half-remembered Chinese etching.

The voice returns, droning *Next, next, translate
A passage, Vansittart, Ross,* politely, *Would it bore you?*
While all the time summer was cramming our nostrils —
Cut-grass, roses, a cricket match going on
Somewhere, far away as our minds
Never much occupied with Daudet and his mill,
But rehearsing desire, scribbling the blank horizon.

Now that afternoon and this gently spill
Two decades together, men repairing the arena
For the Sunday *corrida,* bells ringing out sunset

From St Trophime — or is it the bell
For evening chapel, prep, the long dream:
But the blank has been scrawled on, *graffiti*
Scarring the heart like this scorched stone,
Over which clouds now drift from the Camargue.
Bearers of storm, in which we move suddenly alone.

ALAN ROSS (1922-)

Henry James was born in America but lived much of his life in England: in addition to his many novels and short stories, he composed several travel sketch books, among them A LITTLE TOUR IN FRANCE, *published in 1884.*

THE WEATHER THE next day was equally fair, so that it seemed an imprudence not to make sure of Aigues-Mortes. Nîmes itself could wait; at a pinch I could attend to Nîmes in the rain. It was my belief that Aigues-Mortes was a little gem, and it is natural to desire that gems should have an opportunity to sparkle. This is an excursion of but a few hours, and there is a little friendly, familiar, dawdling train that will convey you, in time for a noonday breakfast, to the small dead town where the blessed Saint Louis twice embarked for the Crusades. You may get back to Nîmes for dinner; the run — or rather the walk, for the train doesn't run — is of about an hour. I found the little journey charming and looked out of the carriage window, on my right, at the distant Cévennes, covered with tones of amber and blue, and, all around, at vineyards red with the touch of October. The grapes were gone, but the plants had a colour of their own. Within a certain distance of Aigues-Mortes they give place to wide salt-marshes, traversed by two canals; and over this expanse the train rumbles slowly upon a narrow causeway, failing for some time, though you know you are near the object of your curiosity, to bring you to sight of anything but the horizon. Suddenly it appears, the towered and embattled mass, lying so low that the crest of its defences seems to rise straight out of the ground; and it is not till the train stops close before them that you are able to take the full measure of its walls.

Aigues-Mortes stands on the edge of a wide *étang,* or shallow inlet of the sea, the farther side of which is divided by a narrow band of coast from the Gulf of Lyons. Next after Carcassonne, to which it forms an admirable *pendant,* it is the most perfect thing of the kind in France. It has a rival in the person of Avignon, but the ramparts of Avignon are much less effective. Like Carcassonne, it is completely surrounded with its old fortifications; and if they are far simpler in character (there is but one circle), they are quite as well preserved. The moat has been filled up, and the site of the town might be figured by a billiard-table without pockets. On this absolute level, covered with coarse grass, Aigues-Mortes presents quite the appearance of the walled town that a school-boy draws upon his slate or that we see in the background of early Flemish pictures — a simple parallelogram, of a contour almost absurdly bare, broken at intervals by angular towers and square holes. Such, literally speaking, is this delightful little city, which needs to be seen to tell its full story. It is extraordinarily pictorial, and if it is a very small sister of Carcassonne, it has at least the essential features of the family. Indeed, it is even more like an image and less like a reality than Carcassonne; for by position and prospect it seems even more detached from the life of the present day. It is true that Aigues-Mortes does a little business; it sees certain bags of salt piled into barges which carry their cargo into actual places. But nothing could well be more drowsy and desultory than this industry as I saw it practised, with the aid of two or three brown peasants and under the eye of a solitary douanier, who strolled on the little quay beneath the western wall. *'C'est bien plaisant, c'est bien paisible,'* said this worthy man, with whom I had some conversation: and pleasant and peaceful is the place indeed, though the former of these epithets may suggest an element of gaiety in which Aigues-Mortes is deficient. The sand, the salt, the dull sea-view, surround it with a bright, quiet melancholy. There are fifteen towers and nine gates, five of which are on the southern side, overlooking the water. I walked all round the place three times (it doesn't take long), but lingered most under the southern wall, where the afternoon light slept in the dreamiest, sweetest way. I sat down on an old stone and looked away to the desolate salt-marshes and the still, shining surface of the *étang;* and, as I did so, reflected that this was a queer little out-of-the-world corner.   H E N R Y   J A M E S   (1 8 4 3 - 1 9 1 6)

The imposing castles of Beaucaire and Tarascon, which for seven centuries have watched each other over the river, are seen here by Marcel Brion, a writer and member of the Académie Français who was born in Marseilles.

T A R A S C O N   A N D   B E A U C A I R E face one another across the Rhône. They are in no sense enemies, as some have said, but rather rivals, the one owing allegiance to the Empire, the other remaining staunchly royalist. For many years now it has been customary for the Rhône watermen to call the left bank 'Empire' and the right bank 'Kingdom'. Like all those great rivers which both join and separate territories — the Rhine is another example — the Rhône marks the division between Provence and Languedoc. But it is also a link between them. And the great suspension bridge between the two towns ensures their unity. Nevertheless, when the fierce mistral sweeps across it those who try to defy the roaring wind run the risk of being borne away.

Alphonse Daudet brought unexpected fame to Tarascon when he made it the birthplace of Tartarin. Tartarin is not a ludicrous character; Daudet, in attributing certain comical qualities to his celebrated hero, was rather generalising than just poking fun at the Provençal: 'All Frenchmen have in them a touch of Tarascon'. The Tarasque is as illustrious as Tartarin. This fabulous, dreaded monster had ravaged the countryside until Saint Martha tamed it. Even the boldest knights could neither tame nor subdue it. Martha was one of those 'Holy Maries' who, according to tradition, came to Provence with their brother, the resurrected Lazarus. She fettered the beast with a silken cord round its spiny neck and then, in obedience to her command, it plunged straight into the Rhône. It has never been seen since — except as a harmless dragon-like effigy of stuffed cardboard at the feast of Saint Martha. It is then escorted in procession through Tarascon by youths and maidens, following the ancient rites codified by good King René — who made a cult of old Provençal customs — in about 1470.

Whether it be authentic or legendary, the Tarasque constitutes a very ancient symbol. Its cult, half worship and half exorcism, is a perfect example of those primitive religions in which the wild forces of nature and man's bestial instincts, incarnated in the form of a monster, were overcome and deprived of their destructive wrath by innocence and purity. It is said that Saint Martha remained in Provence, living at Tarascon until her death; her body was discovered there during the XIIth century. The church which bears her name was built on the spot, around her tomb. The saint's sarcophagus, surrounded by ancient tombs, can still be seen in the crypt of this sanctuary. The loveliest of these other tombs is that of the Seneschal of Provence, Jean de Cossa, a faithful henchman of King René, by whose order he built the beautiful castle which kept guard over the bank of the Rhône. In subsequent centuries it was used as a prison. Now the bolts and bars have been removed and Tarascon castle has become a museum. It gives an excellent idea of the appearance of a princely residence in the XVth century.

Richelieu, who always feared that the feudal spirit would revive, pulled down the fortress of Beaucaire on the opposite bank. Only the triangular keep remains. The ramparts are now a public garden where the Beaucairois enjoy their leisure. Beaucaire is not so loyal to its past as its neighbour Tarascon. It has forgotten its glorious calling and the stories of Saint Louis halting before its gates on his way to the Crusade. A money-making instinct prevails, stimulated by the unrivalled trading opportunities provided by the Rhône. Above all Beaucaire enjoys its reputation for the famous fair held for centuries, at fixed dates, on the enormous plain alongside the river. People from many countries would come to this veritable city of wood and canvas in order to buy and sell their wares.

The hubbub and clamour of the traders bargaining, haggling and swopping in twenty different tongues can be heard no more. The Fair of Beaucaire has declined from the peak of lavish opulence it maintained up to the XIXth century, and no longer attracts foreign traders. Nowadays all one can see under its avenues of planes are the customers of a small town market sauntering somewhat sleepily in the July sunshine from one meagre stall to another.

MARCEL BRION (1 8 9 5 - 1 9 7 4) (translated by S G Colverson)

Les-Saintes-Maries-de-la-Mer ......

I T I S N O T a task I relish, but I feel that I should perhaps warn some future traveller not to expect too much from Les Saintes-Maries-de-la-Mer. The church is magnificent, and of its kind possibly the most beautiful in France, if not the whole of Europe. It is the surroundings, which not so long ago were simple fishermen's dwellings, that I find inexcusable. On my first visit a number of years ago, they had already started building, but the houses, topped by sunbaked roofs and washed in pale colours, were comparatively inoffensive. The stone pavements shone like polished bone, and canvas awnings stretching across the streets gave a pleasant luminosity. Now the place is better not described, and spreads like some hideous parasitic growth between the church and the sea.

One has simply to shut one's eyes to the criminal desecration, and by an effort of will isolate the church — remember the country only as it appears in its wilder stretches. Drive down the straight roads bordered with feathery, golden-brown reeds and, if it's winter, look out over the muddy waters of the empty rice-fields — square patches of dulled taffeta shot with the sky. And always this flatness of landscape, everything beaten down by the wind; only the umbrella pines seem to resist and grow in great clumps like freak toadstools. It is a bleak, beautiful country, an emptiness of strange mirages: migrating drifts of flamingoes, black bulls and white horses — and the immortal saints! RODERICK CAMERON (1975)

Beaucaire is still famous for its fair which sometimes attracted as many as 300,000 people in the Middle Ages. It was destroyed by the advent of the railway in the 19th Century. In 1787 Arthur Young became caught up in the fair traffic on his way to Nîmes.

THE 26TH. THE fair of Beaucaire fills the whole country with business and motion; meet many carts loaded; and nine diligences going or coming. Yesterday and today the hottest I ever experienced; we had none like them in Spain — the flies much worse than the heat. — 30 miles.

The 27th. The amphitheatre of Nismes is a prodigious work, which shews how well the Romans had adapted these edifices to the abominable uses to which they were erected. The convenience of a theatre that could hold 17,000 spectators without confusion; the magnitude; the massive and substantial manner in which it is built without mortar, that has withstood the attacks of the weather, and the worse depredations of the barbarians in the various revolutions of sixteen centuries, all strike the attention forcibly.

I viewed the Maison Carrée last night; again this morning, and twice more in the day; it is beyond all comparison the most light, elegant, and pleasing building I ever beheld. Without any magnitude to render it imposing; without any extraordinary magnificence to surprize, it rivets attention. There is a magic harmony in the proportions that charms the eye. One can fix on no particular part of pre-eminent beauty; it is one perfect whole of symmetry and grace. What an infatuation in modern architects, that can overlook the chaste and elegant simplicity of taste, manifest in such a work; and yet rear such piles of laboured foppery and heaviness as are to be met with in France. The temple of Diana, as it is called, and the ancient baths, with their modern restoration, and the promenade, form parts of the same scene, and are magnificent decorations of the city. I was, in relation to the baths, in ill-luck, for the water was all drawn off, in order to clean them and the canals. The Roman pavements are singularly beautiful, and in high preservation. My quarters at Nismes were at the Louvre, a large commodious, and excellent inn, the house was almost as much a fair from morning to night as Beaucaire itself could be. I dined and supped at the table d'hôte; the cheapness of these tables suits my finances, and one sees something of the manners of the people; we sat down from twenty to forty at every meal, most motley companies of French, Italians, Spaniards and Germans, with a Greek and Armenian; and I was informed, that there is hardly a nation in Europe or Asia; that have not merchants at this great fair, chiefly for raw silk, of which many millions in value are sold in four days: all the other commodities of the world are to be found there.

ARTHUR YOUNG (1741-1820)

Edward Rigby, an English doctor, wrote a series of letters home from his French travels in 1789.

OUR VISIT TO Nismes was in great measure to view the celebrated Roman antiquities in that place and neighbourhood. The first we visited formed part of a stupendous aqueduct called the 'Pont du Gard'. It passes over a deep valley, through which runs the rapid mountain stream the Gardon. The scenery of the spot corresponds well with the magnificence of these ruins. Immense rocks have been piled on one another by nature, and immense arches have been piled on one another by the skill of the Romans. We climbed the rocks and walked to the top of the building, where, though perfectly safe, the view of the great depth below was tremendous. I gathered some *Dyanthus virginianus* on the Pont du Gard. Nismes is also an old city, but the streets are wide, and there are many open spaces in it, now used as promenades. Here are some vestiges of Roman fountains and baths which have been lately repaired, and serve still, as they did under the Romans, to supply the city with excellent water. A part also of a beautiful temple of Diana remains, and an amphitheatre sufficiently preserved to give an idea of its original magnitude, of the kind of spectacles the Romans were fond of, and of the great population which could require such a space for them. But the vast area is now filled with houses, and several streets pass through it. The most perfect monument of Roman architecture, however, is a temple of the composite order, called *la maison carrée*. Besides these, on the summit of a high rock, are the remains of something like an enormously high tower. I persuaded my companions that this was an ancient gazebo, and that was probably the use it served, as it must have commanded an immense prospect. We left Nismes on Tuesday morning, and found the roads crowded with people going to a fair at Beaucaire, about twenty miles off. Here we had another specimen of the populousness of this country. The streets were full of people, every house was a shop, and a long quay was crowded with booths full of different kinds of merchandise. Besides these there were a number of vessels in the Rhône, lying alongside the quay, full of articles for sale, and no less crowded with people, access being had to them by boards laid from one to the other. I observed many articles in cast iron. From Beaucaire the country was, I think, more romantic than any we had passed through. At St Remy, a small town between Beaucaire and Orgon, I bought a few peas of an old woman, who was dressing some in a sieve. They were of a singular kind. She said they were not eaten green, but when ripe they made good soup, *pour les malades*.

DR EDWARD RIGBY (1747-1821)

In her book PLEASURE OF RUINS, *Rose Macaulay alights upon Les Baux.*

IN THE CATEGORY of Ghostly Streets one must put the Provençal mountain stronghold of Les Baux, whose ruins sprawl, a robber's nest, over a spur of the Alpilles, overlooking three valleys, its ruined dwellings, churches and castle cut out of the living rock, towers, walls and boulders inextricably mixed, the whole a fantastic Doré scene of infernal nightmare. Pleasure has been given to many by the legend that Dante made it a model for some of his Circles; unfortunately this tale seems insubstantially based. Still, it is enough in its own right, this shattered mountain citadel hewn out of pale soft limestone, sprawling over its high escarpment, with the crazed air of an extinct moon. Through its ruins runs a little street called the Grande Rue; the ruins are so many and so ruined that, before they were neatly labelled in this century, it was impossible to know which was what, except for the great feudal castle, a few churches, the Hotel de Ville, a palace or two. It is a jumble of medieval houses, with Romanesque or Renaissance façades, of towers scooped out of cylindrical rocks, arches and vaults, battlements, underground passages and chambers, fallen columns with rich carving, great shapeless fragments and massy boulders lying everywhere, the rock-based castle itself tottering and falling, a few tiled roofs and inhabited small houses, where the tiny population makes its living out of guiding tourists: 'of the present inhabitants of Les Baux it were better not to speak' says the guide sold on the postcard stalls. This population is a recent growth. Dumas, in the 1850s, found Les Baux empty but for a few beggars; Prosper Mérimée said that *'une demi-douzaine de mendiants composent toute la population',* but the pleasures of ruined Les Baux were gradually discovered, both by tourists, and by those who made money out of tourists, and in 1906 the number of inhabitants was a hundred and eleven; one gathers that all of these competed fiercely for the profitable job of showing the tourists round, and that blood on occasion flowed among *'ceux des Baux'.* Possibly it still does; but in these days, as the ruins are labelled, guides are less required. The guides, if you employ them, will bore you by telling you about the Courts of Love, the least interesting phenomena of Les Baux's romantic history, though apparently regarded as the greatest pleasure for tourists. For the history of Les Baux *is* romantic; very early it seems to have been a refuge for those who fled from the Visigoths who had captured Arles; three centuries later, we hear of a Count of Les Baux, and through the Middle Ages these enterprising and turbulent counts and seigneurs and princes played their stormy feudal part, terrorizing neighbouring baronies and cities, waging war against Barcelona, acquiring fresh lands by treaty, by intrigue, by marriage, till they had half Provence at heel. They did not lose their heritage until the fifteenth century, when it passed to the royal family of Anjou. It played a war-like part in the wars of religion, and its fortress castle was demolished by Richelieu. After this its inhabitants drifted out of it; at the Revolution it was taken over by the nation, and crumbled year by year into wilder desolation, until the thriving industry of tourism has of late years turned the desolation to profit by making it a show-place. Show-place though it be, it remains fantastically, excitingly grand; a crater of the moon set with thirteenth-, fourteenth-, and fifteenth-century houses, Romanesque churches and chapels, fine renaissance dwellings, with their family arms. Over the ruins towers the extraordinary, huge castle, more than half in ruins and looking most insecure. Below the citadel is Beaumanoire, the Renaissance pleasure garden of which remains one lovely round pavilion. Among the ruins nestles the 'squalid little village' which feeds on them. But neither this nor the placarded labels have wholly taken from Les Baux the strange frightening air of doom that broods among those grotesque shapes. 'You feel,' wrote Theodore Cook half a century ago, 'as if a blood-stained band of medieval cut-throats were lurking behind every crag, or slowly retreating, as you mount, to lure you on to final, irremediable fate'. As well you may, for the Seigneurs des Baux, who must still haunt their eyrie, were precisely this.

Pleasure in Les Baux has been, at least since the romantic revival of the eighteenth century, keen and growing. It had everything that the ruin-tasters could desire — antiquity, abandonment, decay, a magnificent and forbidding site. It was indeed

'an awful pile .....
Waste, desolate, where *Ruin* dreary dwells',

with in addition, the romance of troubadour Provence, courts of love, and all the rest of the medieval feudal trappings beloved of the public. It has inspired novels and poems, not all of which have seen print; no nineteenth-century R A M B L E S I N O L D P R O V E N C E , illustrated with little drawings, was complete without it; and from the walls of Victorian drawing-rooms discreet pale water-colours looked down, entitled in flowing scripts, 'A Robbers' Eyrie in Provence', and painted by great-aunts. Today, though grown vulgar, it still makes its flamboyant dramatic effect. R O S E   M A C A U L A Y (1 8 8 1 - 1 9 5 9)

Nude lying in front of a Mirror : Henri Matisse

The Marseillaise, the battle song of the army of the Rhine, was adopted by the supporters of the 1792 Revolution. Composed by a young army officer, Rouget de Lisle, it quickly became popular with the volunteers who marched to Paris. Now it has become the French National Anthem.

THE MARSEILLAISE

Come, children of your country, come,
New glory dawns upon the world,
Our tyrants, rushing to their doom,
Their bloody standard have unfurled;
Already on our plains we hear
The murmurs of a savage horde;
They threaten with the murderous sword
Your comrades and your children dear.
Then up, and form your ranks, the hireling foe withstand;
March on, — his craven blood must fertilize the land.

Those banded serfs, — what would they have,
By tyrant kings together brought?
Whom are those fetters to enslave
Which long ago their hands have wrought?
You, Frenchmen, you they would enchain;
Doth not the thought your bosoms fire?
The ancient bondage they desire
To force upon your necks again.
Then up, and form your ranks, the hireling foe withstand;
March on, — his craven blood must fertilize the land.

Those marshalled foreigners, — shall they
Make laws to reach the Frenchman's hearth?
Shall hireling troops who fight for pay
Strike down our warriors to the earth?
God! shall we bow beneath the weight
Of hands that slavish fetters wear?
Shall ruthless despots once more dare
To be the masters of our fate?
Then up, and form your ranks, the hireling foe withstand;
March on, — his craven blood must fertilize the land.

Then tremble, tryants, — traitors all, —
Ye, whom both friends and foes despise;
On you shall retribution fall,

Your crimes shall gain a worthy prize.
Each man opposes might to might;
And when our youthful heroes die
Our France can well their place supply;
We're soldiers all with you to fight.
Then up, and form your ranks, the hireling foe withstand;
March on, — his craven blood must fertilize the land.

Yet, generous warriors, still forbear
To deal on all your vengeful blows;
The train of hapless victims spare,
Against their will they are our foes.
But O, those despots stained with blood,
Those traitors leagued with base Bouillé,
Who make their native land their prey; —
Death to the savage tiger-brood!
Then up, and form your ranks, the hireling foe withstand;
March on, — his craven blood must fertilize the land.

And when our glorious sires are dead,
Their virtues we shall surely find
When on the selfsame path we tread,
And track the fame they leave behind.
Less to survive them we desire
Than to partake their noble grave;
The proud ambition we shall have
To live for vengeance or expire.
Then up, and form your ranks, the hireling foe withstand;
March on, — his craven blood must fertilize the land.

Come, love of country, guide us now,
Endow our vengeful arms with might,
And, dearest liberty, do thou
Aid thy defenders in the fight.
Unto our flags let victory,
Called by thy stirring accents, haste;
And may thy dying foes at last
Thy triumph and our glory see.
Then up, and form your ranks, the hireling foe withstand;
March on, — his craven blood must fertilize the land.

ROUGET DE LISLE (c 1792) (translated by John Oxenford)

Mark Twain, the American creator of Huck Finn, was also a globetrotter and wrote of his experiences abroad.

THESE MARSEILLAISE MAKE Marseillaise hymns, and Marseilles vests, and Marseilles soap for all the world; but they never sing their hymns, or wear their vests, or wash with their soap themselves.   MARK TWAIN (1835-1910)

The essence of the Marseillais was epitomised in Marcel Pagnol's famous trilogy Marius, Fanny *and* César *filmed in Marseilles around the early 1930s.*

THERE ARE, AS with every town of strong character, three different aspects of Marseilles; its history, its present appearance, and the myth which people have invented about it. In a normal town these three aspects should have about the same importance. But with Marseilles — like Timbuktu or Samarkand — the myth has been blown up to an enormous size; it is so big and so often repeated that it has become an explicit part of the city's life, and you have to know the myth before you can understand Marseilles. If you can believe it, this myth is based in part upon funny stories. All over France people tell yarns about Marseilles. Marseilles stands for wild exaggeration, for a sort of easygoing bawdiness of the Rabelaisian kind; and in these stories there are nearly always three very earthy characters: Marius, Olive and Titin. These are the perpetual comics of French humour, and they crop up again and again every year in a thousand different situations.

It is not the sort of humour that is easily transmittable in print, because it is highly local, not very witty, and it depends heavily on the manner in which it is told. However, let me try to relate one of the more innocuous specimens just to give you the flavour.

One day Marius was walking down the Cannebière with Olive and Titin and he said, 'Why don't you come out and see my cabin?' (the Marseillas love to have little wooden shacks outside the city where they can grow vegetables and sleep on Sunday afternoons).

'All right,' say Olive and Titin, 'but how does one get there?'

'Take the No. Six tramway as far as it goes,' Marius says. 'Then walk about five kilometres until you get to the beach. Then go along the beach, maybe for another three or four kilometres, until you get to a cabin painted blue with an enormous seashell as large as an elephant standing beside the front door. And there you are. Just kick the door open with your foot and you'll find me inside'.

'But why,' Olive says, 'do we have to kick the door open?'

'Because,' Marius explains, 'your arms will be full of the liquor and food you are bringing'.

It is not, you perceive, overwhelmingly funny, and I don't think you would find the really bawdy yarns much more amusing. But told in the Marseilles accent, which is thick and heavy, with plenty of elaborate gestures and much wine passing across the table, a good humour permeates the atmosphere and Marseilles seems a very droll place indeed.

Then, too, the Marseilles man is supposed to have a tremendous command of swear words. He swells himself out like a turkey, thrusts his chin forward and launches into the most frightful threats at his opponent — but seldom actually fights. During a traffic block I have observed scenes that would make your blood run cold anywhere else. The cop whirls his baton and blows continuously on his whistle. From every angle cars charge in with horns full blast, drivers yelling. Suddenly it is all over and, inexplicably, everybody laughs.

Out of these light matters the myth has been built up: these and the Marseilles accent which turns *demain matin* into *demang matang;* and bouillabaise, the famous fish soup which, to my mind, is a messy, uninspired dish; and the fearsome wind called the mistral, that sometimes howls down the Cannebière; and the red-light district around the opera; and the rackets, and La Marseillaise itself, perhaps the most moving of all national anthems. It was not written by a local man, but was first sung by the five hundred volunteers from Marseilles who went to Paris to take part in the revolution in 1792.

Fortunately this myth has been captured, and almost perfectly, like a fly in amber, in a remarkable trilogy of motion pictures written and directed by the playwright Marcel Pagnol. He wrote the pieces first as stage plays, under the names of *Marius, Fanny* and *César,* and later turned them into three of the most engaging French films ever made. They tell a simple story of family life in the city, of the quarrels between the dominant father and the son who goes away to sea, of the solemn masses celebrated in the church on the hill and the sinful life in the café on the waterfront, and of the endless succession of births, marriages and funerals.

ALAN MOOREHEAD (1910-1983)

André Gide, Parisian critic and novelist, and winner of the 1947 Nobel Prize for Literature, was in Marseilles during the filming of Pagnol's trilogy Marius, Fanny *and* César.

THE EXTERIORS OF Pagnol's *Fanny* are being filmed. The requisitioned cops are hardly enough to hold at a distance the horde of idlers from the Old Port; ropes are strung up. Between two series of shots, the movement of trams and autos resumes, and, despite orders, the area in use is invaded by a throng of gapers, who are again driven back only with great difficulty. Among all these people, not the slightest eagerness to help, if only by not getting in the way of others' work. I imagine a properly disciplined crowd policing itself and taking pleasure in collaborating in an achievement from which it is eventually to profit. I remain there more than three hours, now with the operators, wandering from group to group, now outside the enclosure; and my eyes seek among the crowd, seek in vain, some face at which to glance with pleasure. The youngest already stigmatized by poverty. Among the older ones, every form of egotism: listlessness, craftiness, meanness, and even cruelty. Whoever claims to love humanity is especially attached, mystically, to what it might be, to what, doubtless, it would be without that monstrous atrophy. Whoever claims to love humanity should attack first the causes of that atrophy. I long professed that the ethical question should outweigh the social question; it no longer appears so to me at present; and even, as it happens in such cases, I no longer very well understand what I meant by this. The individual, even today, interests me more than the mass; but first it is important to have favorable conditions for the mass, in order to allow the healthy individual to be produced. Considerations of this nature seem almost silly when expressed in such summary fashion. They would need dialogue, novel or drama.

Much better impression of the sailing and fishing population of Cassis, where I go to join Roger Martin du Gard. In Marseille, indeed, it is not the masses, but the riffraff.

ANDRÉ GIDE (1 8 6 9 - 1 9 5 1) (translated by J O'Brien)

This is taken from the 1926 diary of Evelyn Waugh, caustic English novelist.

EVERYONE IN MARSEILLES seemed most dishonest. They all tried to swindle me, mostly with complete success.   EVELYN WAUGH (1 9 0 3 - 1 9 6 6)

Jean Cocteau was a versatile writer, artist and film-maker, equally at home with the avant-garde and the Académie Française. This rewritten myth, set in Marseilles, first appeared in 1933, but he recast it as a monologue for Edith Piaf in 1955.

FOR FOUR DAYS Achilles has been living in the women's apartments disguised as a woman. But we are not concerned, as you might think, with the Achilles of legend and you are not beginning a Greek tale. The Achilles I'm telling you about was an Arab and his mother belonged to Marseilles; he was twenty and looked fifteen. He was good-looking and his good looks were feminine without being effeminate. I mean that his firm beardless face and slim waist, his slender wrists and ankles allowed this young rascal to wear with dazzling effect the clothes dictated by a fashion whereby women try to resemble ephebes; and when worn by him these fashions became feminine by contrast and endowed him with a charm that was inde-scribable, fabulous (in the proper sense of the word) and equivocal.

Why was our Achilles wearing a woman's dress, stockings and necklaces? Where was he wearing them? For the scrupulous accuracy of our story we have to admit that he was hiding or, more precisely, he was being hidden and shielded from the police. This ruse, arranged by a woman named Rachel, amused her companions greatly and these companions and this Rachel, much more scantily clad than our hero, surrounded him with ritual and acts of kind-ness in a secret room within a place of much ill-fame in Marseilles.

In short Achilles, in spite of his youth, acted as pimp for two girls. One, Rachel, worked in the brothel and the other, Marthe, worked on the Canebière and in the neighbouring streets.

Rachel and Marthe loved Achilles. Achilles loved them. He showed just enough cruel indif-ference to maintain his role in the milieu, a milieu where, except in rare circumstances, affec-tion is not in evidence.

All these nice people were very naïve, in spite of what one might suppose; many customs of high society would have appeared deeply shocking to the members of this little trio who intended no harm and observed the ritual of an age-old tradition.

Misfortune willed it that Achilles allowed himself to be led by Victor (a colleague) into a less official enterprise — a burglary, to be honest — and that, since the police were looking for him, Rachel and her companions had the audacity to dress him as a girl and include him in their troupe. Madame was won over by Achilles' niceness and became an accomplice in the stratagem; for four days Achilles could be found like the Achilles of legend, in women's clothes, in the women's apartments.

Alas, all good things come to an end. Madame anticipated a domiciliary visit and, in spite of the improper aspects of the situation, it was decided that our hero should leave the *Flamboyant* and walk the dark alleyways until further instructions.

His first steps along the street amused Achilles. The disguise made his flight look like a full-dress carnival and the entertainment concealed the drama from him. It concealed it so well that instead of remaining, as agreed, in the darkness of the narrow streets surrounding the market, Achilles took the risk, about eight o'clock in the evening, of appearing, first on the quayside, opposite the boats which go out to the Château d'If, with the gramophone playing, and then, right out on the Canebière.

It was there that he noticed Marthe walking up and down along the pavement. Wishing to avoid her and fearing a scene he rushed headlong towards the road. As he took to his heels an astonished glance from a policeman reminded him that his sprint could not have been in keeping with his actual appearance. He tried to slow down too quickly, stepped back, became entangled in the Marseilles traffic, which is notorious for confusion, and stumbled as a limousine touched him and almost knocked him down.

Within a moment he found himself at the centre of a gesticulating crowd, he was lifted up by the strong-armed chauffeur of the limousine and deposited on the cushions beside an extremely grave gentleman who with one hand told the chauffeur to drive on and with the other indicated to the crowd and the policeman that he was taking responsibility for everything, that the incident was closed, that they could disperse and seek other delights.

The owner of the limousine was called Monsieur Fabre-Maréchol, he was one of the richest men in Marseilles, manufactured olive oil (Maréchol oil) and was returning home from his club. He had just acted, he thought, under the influence of an entirely natural human reflex and gradually, while the vast limousine glided along beside the sea, he wondered, as he looked at his victim's suggestive profile and figure, if his human reflex was not, rather, an example of our remarkable aptitude for making contact with chance, for leaping astride the miracle which all men summon in secret and which is demanded by the least imaginative people even when they think they are accepting the inevitable.

Monsieur Fabre-Maréchol patted Achilles' hands and asked him if he was hurt, if he was still suffering from his fall.

When it was a question of inventing a story Achilles was never at a loss. He played the scene marvellously. He sighed, said he was a silly girl, made out that he was a poor girl called Lily, turned his head away when speaking of his fall, so that this fall might look like attempted suicide, wiped away a tear, spoke of his loneliness and his disgust for the means of livelihood available to young people in Marseilles when their families were dead, in short, he moved the worthy Monsieur Fabre-Maréchol to the point when this very worthy man wondered, without daring to believe it too much, whether destiny had not just touched him with a snowy finger and if the sentimental heart which he concealed beneath his paterfamilias-cum-businessman's jacket had not just, at last, found a reason to start beating.

Monsieur Fabre-Maréchol had a wife, two daughters and a son, all unbearable; he was one of those charming men of whom people say: he's stupid but he has a first-class wife, daughters and a son.

These first-class characters were at that moment on holiday at Pourville. Monsieur Fabre-Maréchol was enjoying bachelor life and sighed as he thought of the pied-à-terre which he kept empty and which he hoped to use one day for some dream. Casual romances would have shocked his sensitive soul; he dreamed vaguely, waited, built up ideas, hoped, I say, and now, suddenly and as though some fairy had waved a wand, there was a young woman in his car, a young bird-woman, a young face as sweet, as blonde, as anonymous as Melisande.

Monsieur Fabre-Maréchol deemed this conquest worthy of pursuing into the still virgin pied-à-terre. It was in this way that Achilles, instead of prowling dangerously about before the

Memories of the Ballets Russes — P Picasso/Igor Stravinsky : Jean Cocteau

eyes of the police, landed in a luxurious milieu prepared lovingly and carefully by a rich businessman, where he could gild an idol and worship it.

Achilles' plan was not complex: 'If he touches me,' he calculated, 'I'll fly at him, I'll knock him down, relieve him of his wallet and run away.'

But Monsieur Fabre-Maréchol decided differently. And gradually, confronted by the septuagenarian's respectful attitude, Achilles modified his plans. They changed from rapid to long-term. After a few hours it was a question of actually installing Lily, placing her among her furniture, having her cooking done by the old concierge and waiting for the moment when, through his care and attention, Monsieur Fabre-Maréchol would manage to break the ice, succeed in overcoming legitimate modesty and experience the consummation of his desire.

'You realize,' Achilles had said, 'you're not like the others. I wouldn't want to give you false hopes and put on an act. You speak to my heart ..... I shall wait until my heart responds ..... ' It can be seen that he knew how to behave and that, as the phrase goes, he could be allowed out on his own.

I add, and this is the finishing touch, that Monsieur Fabre-Maréchol, intoxicated with love and trust, asked if she did not have some girl friend who could act as maid, and that our hero, following blindly the plot of Italian *opera-buffa,* suggested and obtained the services of Marthe.

I leave to the imagination Marthe's surprise, the couple's giggles and the strange scenes that the poor businessman would have interrupted if he had not been afraid of intruding and had not exhibited incredible tact in the timing of his visits.

The extraordinary situation lasted. The couple took good care of each other. Marthe went out and told Rachel. The police lost interest.

Monsieur Fabre-Maréchol hoped.

For a week his hope had even been tinged with a slight impatience, for he saw with some fear that the date of his family's return was coming closer and he dreaded, with justification, the imbroglios of a double life.

Marthe felt this impatience. She immediately advised the young man to relax slightly, to show a little abandon and suggest for example an 'outing', which would flatter the old man's vanity. This outing was very dangerous. Achilles risked it. People saw them together and talked. Questions were asked at the club. Fabre-Maréchol blushed, lowered his eyes, defended himself weakly and accepted the unkindness.

Things became so tense, so strained, that Marthe, who was more nervous, less oblivious, decided that they must be brought to an end. They must buy a gun (can one ever tell?) and risk what the apaches call *une mise en l'air,* that is a sudden attack which would leave the poor businessman gagged, bound and alone one night amidst the ruins of his dream.

This plan made Achilles very gloomy. He agreed about the value of bringing things to an end but he liked this existence and he did not see how he would easily take up any other, which would be strangely complicated by fresh police inquiries.

For the dénouement the couple selected an evening when Fabre-Maréchol proudly took his conquest to a kind of dancing-club. Marthe would await their return, with the gun in her soubrette apron pocket, they would attack the defenceless old man, immobilize him and beat a retreat.

The dance-hall was full of people and noise. Nobody dared approach the mysterious little table where Fabre-Maréchol was relishing his triumph. Achilles, who was no longer concentrating on his role, presented a strange sight to the spectators. 'If I were Maréchol, I would have my suspicions about that girl's way of life,' stated a very beautiful young woman who lorded it over a table where the town bigwigs were crowded together.

The fact was that Achilles, beneath his make-up and false eye-lashes, his feathers and tarlatan, was assuming a boyish look that was less and less disguised. He no longer heard the orchestra, no longer saw the lights, no longer caught the multicoloured balls. His heart sank into vague sorrow, he was not skilful enough to deal with the feelings that made him rebel against his base ingratitude, he relapsed into strange fantasies, saw himself dragging Maréchol into the car, throwing himself at his feet, confessing everything, begging him to be kind, to keep him as a son; then there were other images. He was constantly prowling about, his hands in the pockets of a short jacket. He had to avoid the police, he had to disappear into Chinese shops, wait and wait, slip out, start walking again down the Rue de la Rose, the Rue Saint-Christophe, through the sinister docks. No! He would confess the truth to Maréchol! Maréchol wouldn't drive him out, he'd understand, forgive. He was kind, tender-hearted ....

He jumped: and Achilles found himself in the dance-hall once more, brushed against by the dancers, contemplated by Maréchol, who was slightly drunk, inspected by a hundred pairs of eyes. 'Let's go', he said.

It was at the top of the marble staircase leading down into the foyer that the catastrophe took place, with the fearful mischievous quality of lightning. Achilles, absorbed by recollections, gave as little as possible to his role of elegant woman, and had just had his fur coat placed round his shoulders when, at the bottom of one of the flights of the vast staircase, he recognized Victor, his accomplice in the burglary, wearing the uniform of a page. The rest, I repeat, happened so fast that I must resort to a kind of slowing down in order to describe it to you.

After shouting 'Victor!' and giving a strident whistle obtained with outlandish effect by the insertion of ring-laden fingers between scarlet lips, Achilles, as though mounted on speed and death, jumped astride the marble balustrade, leaving behind him the wide-open mouths of the maître d'hôtel and Fabre-Maréchol. The poor boy, victim of a crook's reaction, caught up in his dreams and his skirts, had forgotten his fetters. There was a cry and suddenly, from one second to the next, this celestial slide was transmuted into something terrible, fatal, immobile, red, pale, definitive, given over to the solemn silence of ruins.

The crowd rushed forward. Fabre-Maréchol, his eye-glasses in disarray, went down step by step, with fixed gaze, towards a scarecrow of cock feathers and tarlatan, a flat little creature, crushed on the ground and, due to a funereal disorder, about whose sex there could be no doubt.

A white tablecloth was placed over the body, but everyone had had time to relish the spectacle of the businessman, his eyes fixed on the telltale indecency. A derisive murmur therefore followed Maréchol as, still respected by the police, he staggered towards his car. The murmur was even more derisive, it can be understood, when the wretched man took with him Victor, sole link between the possible and the impossible, a strange Antigone in the uniform of a page.

In the car, while Maréchol's head rolled on his chest as though decapitated, Victor talked and talked. 'Don't be upset', declared this optimist. 'Achilles wasn't the only one in the world. You'll get over it. Like me, now, I'm telling you, I don't look anything; but when I'm dressed as a woman, my word! You'd take me for Marlene Dietrich!'

They arrived, went upstairs, rang the bell. Marthe, strained to breaking-point, was waiting for it to ring. As she was about to open her mouth ..... 'Don't bother,' said Victor. 'Don't bother, Monsieur knows everything'.

Monsieur knew nothing, understood nothing. For the last hour he had been living in a fateful world, that topsyturvy world where even the smallest signs no longer have any meaning, where the broken heart wondered how it could beat.

In a state of collapse, slumped in an armchair, he looked in turn, uncomprehending, at Victor, Marthe, the furniture, the haunted décor that had been assembled in the vague hope of living there happily.

A great tear trickled down the side of his nose, lodged in the bristles of his grey moustache, hesitated, continued its way into his beard. Marthe saw this tear and was taken in. Victor had just told her what had happened. 'Oh,' she cried, 'the bastards! They were in league together!'

She seized the revolver, aimed and fired.

The scandal at the court and the way the papers juggled with the details of the trial are well known.

When questioned by the magistrate Marthe said that she ought to feel sorry for her action, since Monsieur Maréchol was a decent man and that she couldn't understand why he had wept, but that in fact she wasn't sorry at all, as she couldn't live without Achilles and that poor gentleman couldn't have lived either, 'because he was in love with a ghost'.

JEAN COCTEAU (1889-1963) (translated by M Crosland)

Alexandre Dumas, creator of the Three Musketeers, *journeyed a great deal in the South of France and wrote a book of his travels entitled* VOYAGE DANS LE MIDI DE LA FRANCE.

TEN MINUTES AFTERWARDS, we were rolling along on our route to Martigues, where we arrived at day-break.

I never saw a more original looking spot than this little town; situated between the lake of Berre and the canal of Bouc, and erected, not upon the shore of the sea, but upon the sea itself. Martigues is to Venice, what a charming peasant girl is to a fine lady; it only requires, however, the caprice of a king to convert the village beauty into a queen.

Martigues, it is said, was built by Marius. The Roman general, in honour of the prophetess Martha, who attended him, as everyone knows, gave it the name which it still retains. The etymology, perhaps, is not very exact; but etymology, as is well known, is, of all hothouses, the one which forces the most extraordinary flowers.

The most striking feature about Martigues, is its joyous appearance, its streets intersected with canals, and strewn with cyanthas and the pungent sea-weed; its crossways, where boats ply, like coaches in ordinary streets. Then, at every step, dwarfs of ships rise into view, with their tarred bottoms and dried nets. It is a vast boat, in which everyone is engaged in fishing; men with nets, women with lines, children with their hands; they fish in the streets, they fish under the bridges, they fish from the windows; and the fish, always plentiful and always stupid, thus allow themselves to be captured in the same spot, and by the same means, for the last two thousand years.

And yet, what is very humiliating for the fish, is, that the simplicity of the inhabitants of Martigues is such that, in the Provençal patois, their name, *Le Martigao,* has passed into a proverb. *Lé Martigao* are the Champenois of Provence; and as, unfortunately, they have not had born unto them the smallest resemblance of a La Fontaine, they have preserved their primitive reputation in all its purity.

That fellow was a Martigao, who, wishing to cut off a branch of a tree, took his bill-hook, ascended the tree, seated himself on the branch, and cut away between himself and the trunk.

That was a Martigao, who, entering a house in Marseilles, saw for the first time a parrot, approached it, and addressed it familiarly, as is the custom towards the feathered tribe.

'Sacrè cochon!' replied the parrot, in the gruff voice of a drunken musqueteer.

'A thousand pardons, sir,' said the Martigao, taking off his hat; 'I took you for a bird'.

These were three Martigao deputies, who, sent to Aix to present a petition to Parliament, made out immediately on their arrival the residence of the chief president, and gained admission into the hotel. Conducted by the usher, they traversed some passages, whose splendour astonished them; the usher introduced them into the cabinet leading to the audience-chamber, and, pointing to the door, bade them enter, and retires. The door, however, which the usher had indicated was hermetically sealed by a heavy piece of tapestry, according to the custom of the time; so that the poor deputies, observing neither key, nor handles, nor egress, through the large folds of the curtain, pulled up, much embarrassed, and ignorant what to do. Thereupon they held a council, when the most intelligent of the three, after a minute's silence, observed: 'Let us wait till somebody goes in or out, when we will do as he does'. The advice appeared good, was adopted, and the deputies waited.

The first who appeared was the president's dog, who, without further ceremony, dived under the curtain. The three deputies went down on all-fours, passed through like the dog, and as their petition was granted, their fellow-citizens never doubted for a single moment that to the suitable way in which it was presented, rather than to the justice of their claims, they were indebted for their prompt and complete success.

There are many other stories told, not less interesting than the preceding; for instance, that of the Martigao who, after having for a long time studied the mechanism of a pair of snuffers, to assure himself at last of the utility of that small utensil, snuffed the candle with his fingers, and duly deposited the snuff in the receiver. But I am afraid that some of these charming anecdotes must lose much of their value in their transition. Here, however, they possess a racy flavour of the soil, while from the time of its foundation, which we have traced to Marius, Martigues has supplied anecdotes and cock-and-bull stories for every town; with a liberality, according to our host, which is beginning by degrees to grow wearisome.

ALEXANDRE DUMAS (1 8 0 2 - 1 8 7 0 (translated by Offices of the National Illustrated Library)

Joseph d'Arbaud, a native of the Langue d'Oc region, describes the Plain from Aix to Avignon thus.

..... FAULTLESS AND UNSPOILED. There is no untidiness, no harshness, nothing that jars; nor is there any hint of weakness about the smooth, bold contours, rising towards the sun, of Mount Olympus of Trets and Mount Sainte-Victoire. These are the facade of the distant mountain ranges of the Étoile and the Sainte-Baume. Sainte-Victoire is the heart of the Aix countryside, its temple and altar, its spirit and substance. Transparent and ethereal, vibrating with life at daybreak, kindled to fire at sunset, cloud-capped majestically in stormy weather — it is a soul made visible, a living face that reflects every change of weather or season. It casts a veritable spell over the countryside and it ennobles and cheers all who see it .....

JOSEPH D'ARBAUD (1 8 7 4 - 1 9 5 0) (translated by S G Colverson)

In 1846 Charles Dickens published his TRAVELS IN ITALY *in which he describes Aix thus.*

THE TOWN WAS very clean; but so hot, and so intensely light, that when I walked out at noon it was like coming suddenly from the darkened room into crisp blue fire. The air was so very clear, that distant hills and rocky points appeared within an hour's walk; while the town immediately at hand — with a kind of blue wind between me and it — seemed to be white hot, and to be throwing off a fiery air from the surface.

CHARLES DICKENS (1 8 1 2 - 1 8 7 0)

Roy Campbell, South African poet and translator of French and Spanish literature, published a collection of his poems in 1941 entitled SONS OF THE MISTRAL.
Fishing Boats in Martigues

Around the quays, kicked off in twos
The Four Winds dry their wooden shoes.

ROY CAMPBELL (1 9 0 1 - 1 9 5 7)

THE 31ST. TO Aix. Many houses without glass windows. The women with men's hats, and no wooden shoes. 　　　　　　ARTHUR YOUNG (1 7 4 1 - 1 8 2 0)

Paul Arène, novelist and poet of Provençal life, dictated this description of his home town, Sisteron, to his son Jean des Figues.

PICTURE TWENTY NARROW streets sheer as staircases, thickly carpeted with box and lavender to make them less dangerously slippery; and all jumbled together like the streets in an Arab village. They were flanked by gloomy houses built of cold stone and so tall that they almost met at the top, leaving only a narrow ribbon of sky visible. They were so old that, but for the equally ancient great pointed arches spanning the street about every ten paces, their façades would have collapsed and their roofs would have bent forward to kiss one another. In the local dialect these streets were called *androne*s. Sometimes where there was very little space between the ramparts a third house would perch itself — God knows how! — on the arch between the other two and across the street. These sheltered spots, called *couverts* offered ideal shelter to vulgar philanderers on rainy days.

PAUL ARENE (1843-1896) (translated by S G Colverson)

Toulon, France's second port, lies in a perfect natural harbour surrounded by fort-topped hills.

TOULON IS A large, well-built city, the great naval arsenal for the Mediterranean. Here are two harbours *(Rades),* the outer and inner, both well secured. In the inner were many vessels, and on one side a number of ships of war, unrigged, and regularly moored alongside each other. Several vessels were landing melons from the Isle of Hières; we bought some very large and excellent ones for sixpence each, which, we were told, was much above the common price. We saw no cockades here, nor any marks of rejoicing on account of the Revolution. Toulon, of course, is a government town, its principal inhabitants holding offices connected with the marine.

Did I describe Toulon? if not, let me say that it is a well-built fortified city, situated on a most beautiful bay of the Mediterranean. It is one of the King of France's principal harbours for ships of war, and is at this time well filled with very noble vessels. The stores are kept in the arsenal, which few foreigners, and particularly not the English, are permitted to see. Everything appears in good order and well arranged, and there is a quay on which in the evenings are crowds of well-dressed people walking. This city, being inhabited principally by officers and others holding place under the King, did not exhibit the same revolutionary signs. Elsewhere, in every city, town, and village we had passed, every hat was adorned with a Revolution cockade, and our ears were saluted from every quarter with 'Vive la Nation, et les Tiers États'. At Toulon there were no cockades to be seen, no acclamations to be heard, none but the usual appearances of French mirth, which are ever seen in the smiles of the women, and the lively manner in which the men with them sit round their doors to converse, and enjoy the pleasures of their delightful evening air. DR EDWARD RIGBY (1747-1821)

In 1929, the ailing D H Lawrence stayed with friends in a hotel in Bandol, from where he visited Toulon.

N E W Y E A R C A M E in with a crash of storm, then we had snow and ice, unheard of here — and the mountains behind are still white with snow, the wind bites. But the sun blazes and is warm all day. I lie in bed and watch him rise red from the sea, and I must say I think the sun is more important than most things, particularly casual people. Yesterday we went to Toulon in the bus — a port, all sailors and cats and queer people — not unattractive: and this afternoon we went out on the sea in a motor-boat, the four of us — a blue sea, bright sun, but a cold little tiny wind — and I had no idea the mountains behind us were so deep in snow, a long low range of white.   D H L A W R E N C E   (1 8 8 5 - 1 9 3 0)

Michel de l'Hôpital, chancellor of France in the 1560s, described Fréjus thus.

W E A R R I V E D A T Fréjus, which is nothing more now but a poor little town. Here are grand ruins of an ancient theatre, foundered arcades, baths, aqueduct, and scattered remains of quays and basins. The port has disappeared under sand, and is now nothing but a field and a beach.   M I C H E L D E L ' H O P I T A L   (1 5 0 5 - 1 5 7 3) (translated by S Baring Gould)

Hugh Macmillan, a Scottish minister who wrote on religion and natural history, frequently travelled in France.

N O T H I N G C A N B E more charming than the situation of Fréjus, with the graceful outlines and changing hues of the Esterels forming its eastern horizon, and bright glimpses of the sea constantly shining through its olive and pine woods. Over all the place, too, broods the dreamy atmosphere of the past. One seems to live there in an old forgotten world, as remote as possible from this busy exciting age. The ghost of departed Rome still haunts the spot, and imparts the wondrous magic of its history to every feature of the landscape and to every quaint ruin around. No other part of Provence retains so many traces of Roman occupation; and by means of the surviving relics it would not be difficult to construct in imagination a picture of the town as it was in the days of Julius Caesar, its founder, after whom it was named Forum Julii.
                    H U G H M A C M I L L A N   (1 8 3 0 - 1 9 0 3)

Stendhal was the pseudonym of the novelist and critic Henri Beyle, born in Grenoble. He was a great traveller, and spent his last years as French consul in Trieste. This account of Grasse comes from his J O U R N A L .

A S W E A P P R O A C H E D Grasse, the colour of the leaves on the olive trees took on a deeper green; the trees themselves were as large as willows. The fig trees are often eight inches around the trunk, exactly like the trees on the road to Portici. That is because Grasse is sheltered from the north by a mountain that is bare on top. At last I have seen rose bushes cultivated in the open. The wind was from the south and rolling up enormous clouds; I fear we shall have rain.

Suddenly I saw Grasse, flat against a little hill and surrounded by other hills covered with olive trees that looked as though they were about to hurl themselves down on the town. This town is completely Genoese in character. Never have I seen anything in miniature more reminiscent of Genoa and its coastal towns.

We were high above the sea which seemed to be two miles away. On arriving in Grasse, we found a terrace filled with great trees, far more beautiful than the trees of Saint-Germain. On the right and on the left, mountains literally covered to their summits with tufted olive trees and, down below, a vast expanse of sea which, as the bird flies, does not seem to be more than two miles away.

I was told that this town is filled with clubs which makes it very unpleasant for a stranger. No regular café. I had the greatest trouble in finding a way to read the latest number of the *Débats*.

Narrow streets as in the towns on the shore around Genoa. The farming would make one think we were in Sestri or Nervi, but with a total absence of architecture and cafés and the bad odour in the streets where they are always making a little manure heap after the execrable custom I had met in Aubagne and in Luc.

They do not need an aqueduct here. At the highest part in town a fine stream of water rises out of the ground. I spent a long time gazing at this sight from the top of the parapet that overlooks the source. There is no luxury here, I was told. A man with a fortune of a hundred thousand francs wears a threadbare coat; and Grasse numbers several millionaires, all as poorly dressed as the rest of its citizens. On the other hand, the lower middle class who, today (Sunday), throng the magnificent terrace, all look very well-to-do.

The prettiest site on this terrace, the one where, if we were in Italy, there would be any number of cafés, is occupied by the general hospital. I admit the need for a hospital, but it should be built outside of the town and the present building restored to civilization. If the inhabitants were wealthy, this would be the place for them to meet and enjoy themselves.

S T E N D H A L (1 7 8 3 - 1 8 4 2) (translated by E Abbott)

Two Trees : Paul Cézanne

CHAPTER TWO

Rural Life

Harold Monro is chiefly remembered as the founder and editor of the P O E T R Y R E V I E W.

At a Country Dance in Provence

Comrades, when the air is sweet,
It is fair, in stately measure,
With a sound of gliding feet,
It is fair and very meet
To be join'd in pleasure.
Listen to the rhythmic beat:
Let us mingle, move and sway
Solemnly as at some rite
Of a festive mystic god,
While the sunlight holds the day.
Comrades, is it not delight
To be govern'd by the rod
Of the music, and to go
Moving, moving, moving slow?
Very stately are your ways,
Stately—and the southern glow
Of the sun is in your eyes:
Under lids inclining low
All the light of harvest days,
And the gleam of summer skies
Tenderly reflected lies.
May I not be one of you
Even for this little space?
Humbly I am fain to sue
That our arms may interlace.
I am otherwise I know;
Many books have made me sad:
Yet indeed your stately slow
Motion and its rhythmic flow
Drive me, drive me, drive me mad.
Must I now, as always, gaze
Patiently from far away
At the pageant of the days?—
Only let me live to-day!
For your hair is ebon black,
And your eyes celestial blue;
For your measure is so true,
Slowly forward, slowly back—

I would fain be one of you
Comrades, comrades!—but the sound
of the music with a start
Ceases, and you pass me by.
Slowly from the dancing ground
To the tavern you depart.
All the earth is silent grown
After so much joy, and I
Suddenly am quite alone
With the beating of my heart.

HAROLD MONRO (1879-1932)

The film-writer and dramatist Marcel Pagnol, famous for his satirical comedies, spent most of his childhood in Provence.

THERE NOW BEGAN the most beautiful days of my life. The house was called the New Bastide, but it had been new for a very long time. It was a tumbledown old farmhouse, which had been patched up thirty years earlier by a city gentleman, who sold tent-canvas, floor-mops and brooms. My father and my uncle paid him an annual rent of eighty francs (that is to say, four *louis d'or),* which their wives considered rather a lot. But the house looked like a villa, and there was 'water available at the sink': that is to say, the enterprising broom-merchant had had a big tank built on to the back of the house, as large and almost as tall as the building itself. All you had to do was to turn on the copper tap that was set above the sink to see the cool, clear water flow .....

This was an extraordinary luxury, and it was only later that I grasped the miracle of this tap. The whole region, from the village fountain to the peaks of *L'Etoile,* was as dry as dust; within a radius of twenty kilometres there were only a dozen wells (most of them dry from May onwards) and three or four 'springs' — a 'spring' being a crack in the rock, at the bottom of some small cave, which would weep in silence into a beard of moss.

That's why, whenever a peasant woman walked into our kitchen to bring us eggs or chick-peas, she would shake her head with awe as she stared at the gleaming Tap of Progress.

There was also, on the ground-floor, a vast dining-hall (quite five yards by four) which boasted a small fireplace made of genuine marble.

A curving staircase led to the four rooms on the first floor. By an artful modern contrivance, the bedroom windows were fitted with movable window-frames between the glass-panes and the shutters, and these frames were covered with a fine wire-mesh to keep the insects out .

Lighting was provided by paraffin lamps and some emergency candles. But as we had most of our meals out on the terrace, under the fig tree, there was above all the Hurricane Lamp.

Miraculous Hurricane Lamp! My father extracted it one night from a big cardboard box, fil-led it with paraffin, and lit the wick. A flat, almond-shaped flame spurted out and he covered it with an ordinary chimney. This he enclosed in an egg-shaped globe which was protected by a nickel-plated grille topped by a metal lid. This lid was a windtrap: it had holes in it which inhaled the night-breeze, made it coil around itself and pushed it dead on the impassive flame which devoured it ..... Whenever I looked at it, hanging from a branch of the fig-tree, burning brightly and as serene as an altar-lamp, I'd forget all about my grated cheese soup and decide to dedicate my life to science ..... That almond of fire still illuminates my childhood, and I found the sight of the Planier lighthouse, when I visited it ten years later, much less astonishing.

Anyhow, just as the Planier beacon lures quail and lapwings, it attracted all the insects of the night. As soon as one hung it up on its branch, it was surrounded by a swarm of fleshy moths, whose shadows danced on the table-cloth: consumed by a hopeless love, they would fall, cooked to a nicety, onto our plates.

There were also enormous wasps, called *cabridans,* which we brained with our napkins, knocking the jug over sometimes, and the glasses invariably. There were also capricorn-beetles and stag-beetles, which shot out of the night as if catapulted, making the lantern tinkle before diving into the tureen. The shiny, black stag-beetles bore on their heads huge flat pincers with two antlered branches. This fabulous tool was of no use to them because it could not be articulated, but it was most convenient for attaching string harnesses, thus enabling the tamed stag-beetles to drag the enormous weight of the flat-iron very easily over the oil-cloth.

The 'garden' was nothing more than a very old, overgrown orchard, fenced in by wire-netting, most of which had been gnawed away by the rust of time. But by christening it a 'garden', we confirmed the status of the 'villa'.

Moreover, my uncle had bestowed the title of 'housemaid' on a bemused-looking peasant-wench who came to wash the dishes in the afternoon and sometimes to do the laundry, which gave her an opportunity of washing her hands. We were thus linked, three times over, to the upper class, the class of distinguished bourgeois.

In front of the garden spread poorly cultivated wheat and barley fields, divided by age-old olive trees.

Behind the house, the pinewoods formed sombre islands in the vast *garrigue* which stretched over mountains, valleys and tablelands right up to the mountain-range of Sainte-Victoire. The *Bastide Neuve* was the last building on the doorstep of the desert, and one could walk for forty kilometres without coming across anything but the squat ruins of three or four mediaeval farm-houses and a few deserted sheep-pens.

We went to bed early, exhausted by the day's play, and little Paul had to be carried upstairs, limp as a rag-doll: I would catch him just in time as he fell from his chair, gripping in his clenched hand a gnawed apple or half a banana.

Every night as I went to bed, half-asleep, I'd resolve to wake up at dawn, so as not to lose a minute of the miraculous morrow. But I didn't open my eyes before seven o'clock, as vexed and querulous as if I had missed a train.

Then I'd call Paul, who'd start to grunt plaintively and turn to face the wall; but he could not resist the window which suddenly shone resplendently as the wooden shutters banged open, while the song of the cicadas and the scents of the *garrigue* rushed into the expanding room.

We went downstairs stark naked, carrying our clothes in our hands.

My father had fixed a long rubber hose to the kitchen-tap. It stuck out of the window and ended in a copper nozzle on the terrace.

I would spray Paul, then he would drench me. This method was a brainwave of my father's, for the abhorred 'washing' had become a sport; it lasted till my mother shouted out of the window: 'Stop it! When the tank's empty, we'll be obliged to leave!'

After this appalling threat, she would conclusively turn off the tap.

We quickly washed down our bread and butter with milky coffee and then the great adventure began.

We were forbidden to leave the garden, but no watch was kept on us. My mother believed the fence to be impassable — and my aunt was cousin Pierre's slave. My father often went into the village 'shopping' or up into the hills to collect herbs. As for Uncle Jules, he spent three days a week in town, for he had only twenty days' holidays and had spread them over two months.

Thus left to ourselves most of the time, we would climb up to the nearest pinewoods. But these explorations, knife in hand and ears cocked, usually ended in a headlong flight towards the house, following some unforeseen encounter with a boa constrictor, a lion, or a troglodyte bear.

Our earliest sport was hunting the cicadas which sucked the sap of the almond trees as they sang. To begin with, they escaped us, but we had soon acquired such skill and efficiency that we came home surrounded by a halo of music, for we brought back dozens of them which went on chirping in our jolting trouser-pockets. Then came the capture of butterflies, the two-tailed sphynx with its large, blue-bordered white wings that left a silvery dust on your fingers.

For several days we threw Christians to the lions: that is to say, we flung handfuls of small grasshoppers into the diamond-studded cobwebs woven by big, black, velvety spiders with yellow stripes. Their captors swaddled them in silk in a matter of seconds, daintily drilled a hole in their victims' heads and sucked at them for a long while with a gourmet's delight. We would break off these innocent games to feast on the gum of almond trees, a reddish gum like honey. This was a sweet and marvellously sticky delicacy, but strongly disapproved of by Uncle Jules who claimed that this gum would 'eventually stick our guts together'.

My father, anxious to see us pursue our studies, advised us to give up our futile games. He recommended the minute observation of the habits of insects and, to begin with, those of the ants, in whom he saw the models of good citizens.

That's why, next morning, we spent a long time tearing up the dry grass and the *baouco* around the main entrance to a fine ant-heap. When the place was nice and tidy within a radius of at least two yards, I managed to slip into the kitchen while my mother and my aunt were picking almonds behind the house, and stole a big glass of paraffin and a few matches.

The ants, with no evil forebodings, marched to and fro in double file, like stevedores on a ship's gangway.

I first made sure that nobody could see us, then I poured a big dose of paraffin into the principal opening. The head of the column broke up in great confusion, and scores of ants came up from below; they ran hither and thither, completely bewildered, and those who had big heads opened and closed their strong mandibles, looking for the invisible enemy. I then shoved a paper spill into the hole. Paul coveted the honour of setting light to it, which he did very efficiently. A red, smoky flame rose, and our studies began.

Unfortunately, the ants turned out to be too easily combustible. Instantly blasted by the heat, they disappeared in a blaze of sparks. These little fireworks were rather amusing but too short-lived. Moreover, after the sublimation of the extra-mural workers, we vainly awaited the exit of the mighty subterranean legions and the noisy explosion of the queen, on which I had firmly counted; but no more appeared, and all that remained before our eyes was a small, smoke-blackened funnel, sad and solitary like the crater of an extinct volcano.

However, we soon consoled ourselves for this failure with the capture of three big *pregadious,* or praying mantises which, clothed entirely in green, were wandering on the green twigs of a verbena bush: fine subjects for scientific observation.

Papa had told us (with a certain agnostic glee) that the so-called 'praying' mantis was in fact a fierce and pitiless creature; that it could be considered 'the tiger among insects', and that a study of its habits was deeply engrossing.

I therefore decided to study them, that is to say, in order to provoke a fight between the two biggest ones, I presented them to each other at very close quarters, with claws at the ready.

This enabled us to advance our studies by observing that these creatures could live without claws, then without legs, and even without half their heads ..... After a quarter of an hour of these innocent joys of childhood, all that remained of one of the champions was its upper half which, after devouring its opponent's head and torso, unhurriedly got to work on the lower limbs which were still twitching nervously. Paul, who was kind-hearted, went to steal a small tube of seccotine ('makes even iron stick') and attempted to glue the two halves together to make them one again, to which whole we could then solemnly give back its freedom. He could not bring this generous operation to a happy end, for the top half managed to escape.

But there still remained the third tiger in the glass jar. I decided to confront it with ants, and this happy initiative allowed us to enjoy a delightful spectacle.

I briskly up-ended the jar, and placed it over the main entrance of a busy ant-heap. The tiger, being taller than the jar was wide, stood up on its hind-legs and swivelled its head about with a tourist's curiosity. Meanwhile, a horde of ants foamed out of the tunnel and attacked its legs so effectively that it lost its calm and began to dance, at the same time thrusting its two pincers right and left: with each thrust it picked up a cluster of ants which it lifted to its jaw, from which they dropped, snapped in two.

As the thickness of the glass distorted the beauty of the spectacle, and as the tiger's uncomfortable posture irked its movements, I though it my duty to remove the jar. The *pregadiou* fell into its natural position, its pincers folded and its six feet on the ground. But at the end of each foot four ants implacably clung on, their jaws locked, their claws clutching the gravel: thus over-powered by these Lilliputians, the tiger was as helpless as Gulliver.

Meanwhile the *pregadiou's* pincers attacked each of the mooring-parties in turn and wrought havoc among the personnel. But even before the truncated insects fell from the snapping jaws, others had taken their place, and the *pregadiou* had to start all over again.

I wondered how this situation could evolve, since it seemed stabilized — I mean, fixed in an immutable cycle — when I noticed that the reflexes of the grabbing pincers were no longer as swift nor as frequent as before. I concluded that the *pregadiou* was beginning to lose courage because of the inefficiency of its tactics and that no doubt it would change them. And, indeed, after a few minutes, the lateral attacks stopped altogether.

The ants promptly abandoned its neck, chest and back, and it remained upright and motionless, its pincers in prayer and its thorax held almost straight up on its six long, faintly twitching legs.

Paul said to me: 'He's thinking'.

His thoughts seemed to me rather prolonged, and the ants' disappearance intrigued me; so I lay down flat on my belly and discovered the tragic truth.

Under the three-pronged tail of the pensive tiger, the ants had enlarged the natural orifice: one stream filed in, another filed out, as if it were the door of a big store on Christmas Eve. Each one carried away its booty: the diligent housewives were removing the inside of the *pregadiou.*

The unfortunate tiger, still motionless and, with a kind of introspection, apparently attentive to what was going on inside him, had no means of indicating his torture or despair, being by nature unequipped with facial or vocal expression. His agony therefore was unspectacular. We realized that he was dead only when the mooring-parties let go of his legs and began to carve up the thin envelope which had contained him. They sawed off the neck, cut up the chest into neat slices, peeled the legs and elegantly dismantled the terrible pincers, as a cook does with a lobster. The lot was then dragged underground and stored away in the depths of a warehouse, in a different arrangement.

All that remained on the ground were the lovely green wing-sheaths, which had fluttered so gloriously above the green jungle and had terrorized quarries and enemies alike. Scorned by the housewives, they sadly confessed that they were inedible.

That is how our studies of the 'habits' of the praying mantis and of the 'diligence' of the toiling ants came to an untimely end.

'Poor beast!' Paul said to me. 'He must have had an awful bellyache!'

'Serves him right', I said. 'He eats grasshoppers alive, and cicadas too, and even butterflies. Papa told you: he's a tiger! I don't care a hang about a tiger's belly-ache'.

MARCEL PAGNOL (1895-1974) (translated by R Barisse)

Still Life : Paul Cézanne

Émile Zola was born in Paris but brought up at Aix-en-Provence. His most autobiographical novel, L'OEUVRE, *depicts his country childhood and his two friends Paul Cézanne (whom he calls Claude Lantier) and Baptiste Baille (Dubuche). Zola himself is Sandoz.*

T H E N O T H E R M E M O R I E S came back to them, causing their hearts to swell, of the fine days of fresh air and sunshine they had lived down there, away from school. While they were still children, in the sixth form, the three inseparables had a passion for long excursions. They took advantage of every holiday, they discovered new places, becoming bolder as they grew up, until finally they roamed over the whole countryside on outings that sometimes lasted several days. They slept wherever night happened to overtake them, in a hole in the rocks, on a stone-paved threshing-floor, still scorching from the sun, where the beaten wheat straw made them a soft bed, in some deserted hut whose floor they covered with a heap of thyme and lavender. These were escapes from the world, an instinctive sanctuary in the breast of nature, the unconscious love of children for trees, streams, mountains, for the limitless joy of being alone and free.

Dubuche, who lived at school, only joined the others during the holidays ..... But Claude and Sandoz never tired, and one would wake the other every Sunday at four in the morning by throwing stones at his shutters. Especially in summer they yearned for the Viorne [Arc], the river whose thin trickle waters the low meadows around Plassans. They learned to swim when they were scarcely twelve; and they loved to dabble in pools where the water was deep, to pass whole days, naked, drying themselves in the hot sand only to plunge in again, to live in the water, on their backs, on their bellies, searching the grasses along the river banks, submerging themselves to the ears, and watching the hiding places of the eels for long hours. This trickle of pure water which kept them moist under the hot sun prolonged their childhood, gave them the gay laughter of runaway kids when, as young men, they returned to town in the oppressive heat of the July evenings. Later they took up hunting, but hunting as it is practised in that game-less land, six leagues of stalking to kill half a dozen warblers, tremendous expeditions from which they often returned with empty pouches, or with an imprudent bat brought down when they unloaded their guns at the entrance to the town. Tears came to their eyes at the memory of these orgies of walking: they saw again the white roads, interminable, covered with a layer of dust like a thick fall of snow; they followed these roads, happy to hear the scuffle of their heavy boots, then they cut across the fields, over the red earth tinged with iron, where they trudged on and on; and a blazing sky, not a speck of shade, nothing but olive and almond trees with scanty foliage, and each time they came home, the delicious relaxation of weariness, the triumphant boast of having walked farther than the last time, the joy of being at last unconscious of their steps, of plodding mechanically ahead, spurred on by some bloodcurdling marching song which was, to them, as soothing as a dream.

Already Claude carried, between his powder-horn and his box of cartridges, a sketch-book in which he drew bits of landscape; while Sandoz always had a book of poetry in his pocket. It was a romantic frenzy, wingèd verses alternating with barrack-room obscenities, odes tossed to the luminous vibrations of the burning air; and when they happened on a spring, four willows that made a spot of grey against the intense colour of the earth, they let themselves go the limit, they acted plays that they knew by heart, their voices swollen to a bellow for the heroes, thin and quavering as the sound of a fife for the ingénues and the queens. On such days they let the sparrows alone. In this far-away country district, in the sleepy dullness of a small town, they had thus, from the age of fourteen, lived isolated, swept by a fervent passion for literature and art. At first the gigantic conceptions that appear on the immense stage of Hugo in the midst of the eternal strife of opposites enchanted them, caused them to make grand gestures, to watch the sun set behind ruins, to see life pass by under the false and superb illumination of the fifth act. Then Musset came to overwhelm them with his passion and his tears, they could hear their own hearts beating in him, a more human world was opened to them that overcame them by pity, by the eternal cry of distress that they would ever after hear mounting on all sides. They were not really hard to please, they exhibited the gluttony of youth, a prodigious appetite for reading, swallowing impartially the best and the worst, so anxious to admire that often the most execrable works threw them into the same exaltation as a true masterpiece.

And as Sandoz now said, it was the love of long tramps, it was this hunger for literature, that saved them from the deadening influence of their surroundings. They never entered a café, they professed a loathing for the streets, claiming that they withered away in them like eagles in a cage, while their comrades were already soiling their schoolboy sleeves on little marble tables and playing cards for the drinks. This provincial life that caught hold of children while they were still young, the local club, the newspaper spelled out laboriously to the last advertisement, the everlasting game of dominoes, the same stroll at the same hour on the same street, the final degeneration under this millstone that ground one's brains flat, infuriated them, caused them to revolt, to clamber up the nearby hillsides in order to find some hidden refuge, to shout verses under the driving rain without seeking shelter, because of their hatred of towns. They planned to camp out on the banks of the Viorne, to live like savages, to do nothing but swim, taking along five or six books, not more, which would be ample for their needs. No women would be allowed there, they suffered from timidities, awkwardnesses,which they idealized in their own minds as the chastity of superior young men. For two years Claude had been consumed with love for a milliner's apprentice, whom he followed every day at a distance; but he had never had the courage to speak to her. Sandoz had visions of ladies he would meet while travelling, of lovely damsels who would appear suddenly in some unknown forest, who would yield themselves to him for a day, and who would vanish like ghosts at twilight. Their only gallant adventure still made them laugh, it seemed so silly: serenades played to two young girls, when they were members of the school band; nights passed in playing the clarinet and the cornet under a window; horrible dischords that frightened the neighbours until the memorable evening when the exasperated parents had emptied all the chamber-pots in the house on their heads.

E M I L E   Z O L A   (1 8 4 0 - 1 9 0 2) (translated by G Mack)

In a letter to her friend Marguerite Moreno, the writer Colette describes her life in the South with her lover Maurice Goudeket.

Y E S T E R D A Y M O R N I N G , A M O N G other quarry, we caught two eight-liter crayfish. They were monsters which would cost twenty francs each at the market. And a beautiful lobster ..... this morning, a terrible creature from the depths, with a bristling body some thirty centimeters in diameter. He had destroyed a good piece of the net, imagine! Paws half a meterlong, as terrible as his body. We didn't know what to cook him in, so we're going to put him in an old wash-basin .....

Saint-Tropez, August 11, 1929

A string of storms, for two days running, an unhoped-for manna, has made the countryside sparkle. It's magnificent. But how have I ever been able to work here? My patio is a madcap of flowers! Maurice works in the garden, with astonishment and clumsiness, and keeps asking a hundred questions. Whenever the cats see us pick up a rake they come dashing to join us. When, Marguerite, shall we all retire to the country? You have peacocks, yes, but I have zinnias as large as end tables, and eggplants that are indecent!

Saint-Tropez, September 12, 1929

My daughter has arrived ..... She will have had marvelous and ruinous vacations: a month of English countryside and London. A fortnight in Limousin, three weeks at Saint-Jean-de-Braye, and the rest here in Provence. She is exultant. Just think! She has been traveling alone all the time! A twelve-kilo portable phonograph follows her everywhere like a shadow. She has boy's shirts and the breasts of a young Negress. And she swims underwater like a little shark. And drives any car — except the Talbot, which I preserve at the top of my voice .....

C O L E T T E   (1 8 7 3 - 1 9 5 4) (translated by R Phelps)

〰〰〰〰〰〰〰〰〰〰〰〰〰〰〰〰〰〰〰〰〰〰〰〰〰〰〰

Ezra Pound, American poet and critic, drew inspiration from the troubadours: this poem is from the Provençal original of Arnaut Daniel.

Alba

When the nightingale to his mate
Sings day-long and night late
My love and I keep state
In bower,
In flower,
'Till the watchman on the tower
Cry:

'Up! Thou rascal, Rise,
I see the white
Light
And the night
Flies.'

EZRA POUND (1885-1972)

Alphonse Daudet, novelist, was born in Nîmes. He wrote this sad little tale while living near Fontvieille, on the edge of the Alpilles, in the windmill which became, after his death, a Daudet museum.

THE GIRL FROM ARLES

ON THE WAY down to the village from my windmill you pass a farmhouse, built near the road at the far end of a large courtyard planted with African lotus trees. It is a real Provençal farmer's house with its red tiles, its wide expanse of irregularly placed windows, its lofty wind-vane and its pulley for hoisting the bundles of hay, brown wisps of which cling everywhere .....

Why did this house fill me with such a feeling of horror? Why did the sight of its large closed gateway make my heart contract? I could not have said why, yet this house caused shivers to run down my spine. It looked too silent ..... No dogs barked as you passed, even the guinea-fowl used to run to hide noiselessly. Never the sound of voices from inside. Nothing, not even the sound of a mule-bell ..... But for the white window curtains and the smoking chimneys, you would have thought the place uninhabited.

Yesterday, at the stroke of midday I was returning from the village, and, to avoid the sun, I was walking close to the wall of the farm in the shade of the trees ..... On the road in front of the farmhouse some workmen were silently loading a cart with hay. The large door had been left open. As I passed I glanced inside and I saw at the back of the court-yard — with his elbows on a broad stone table and his head in his hands — a big white-haired old man. He was wearing breeches that were in tatters and a jacket that was too small for him. I stopped.

'Ssh! It's the master,' one of the men whispered to me. 'He's been like that since the death of his son.'

Just then a woman and a little boy, dressed in black and carrying big, gilt prayer-books, passed close to us and entered the farm .....

The man added:

'The mistress and the younger son coming back from Mass. They go every day since the boy killed himself ..... Ah, monsieur, what an affliction! ..... His father still wears the dead boy's clothes; nobody can stop him wearing them ..... Get along there!'

The cart began to move off. Wishing to know more, I asked the driver if I could get up beside him. And it was up there, on top of the hay, that I learnt the whole of this heart-breaking story .....

His name was Jan. He was a fine country lad, twenty years old, open-faced, well-built, as gentle as a girl. Because of his good looks, the women used to follow him with their eyes, but he had eyes only for one of them — a girl from Arles, all in velvet and lace, whom he had met one day beside the Lice in Arles. At first everybody at the farm was not pleased. The girl was said to be flighty and her parents were not local people. But Jan was determined to have his girl from Arles. He used to say:

'I will die if she is not mine.'

The situation had to be accepted. It was agreed they should be married after the harvest.

Well, one Sunday evening, the family were just finishing dinner in the courtyard. It was almost a wedding feast. The fiancée was not there, but many glasses had been drunk in her honour ..... Then a man appears at the door and in a trembling voice asks to speak to the farmer Estève, by himself. Estève gets up and goes out on to the roadway.

'Master,' says the man, 'you are marrying your son to a hussy who has been my mistress for two years. What I say I can prove: see these letters! Her parents know and they had promised her to me, but ever since your son has kept pestering her, her fine ladyship and her parents don't want anything more to do with me .... But I'd have thought, after what these letters show, she couldn't become the wife of another man.'

Estève looks at the letters.

'That settles it,' he says. 'Come in and have a glass of muscatel.'

The man replies:

'Thank you, but I am not thirsty, only full of sorrow.'

And he goes away.

The father goes back in, his face betraying nothing; he takes his place again at the table; and the meal continues merrily .....

That evening, Estève and his son went out together into the fields. They stayed out a long time. When they came back, the mother was still waiting for them.

'Wife,' said the farmer, leading his son to her, 'take him to you! He is very unhappy ..... '

Jan never mentioned the girl from Arles again. But he loved her still; more even, since they had proved to him she had lain in the arms of another. It was simply that he was too proud to say anything; that is what killed him, poor boy! ..... Sometimes he would pass whole days sitting alone in a corner. Other times he would go out on to the land and do furiously, by himself, the work of ten labourers ..... In the evening, he would take the road to Arles and walk on and on until he saw the slender steeples of the town rising against the sunset. Then he would turn back. Never did he go any further.

Seeing him like this, always sad and alone, the people at the farm did not know what to do. They began to dread some disaster ..... Once, during dinner, his mother looked at him, her eyes full of tears, and said:

'All right! Listen, Jan, if you still want her, you shall have her ..... '

His father flushed and looked down, overcome by the shame of it.

Jan shook his head and went out .....

From that day his attitude changed. He pretended to be always cheerful, in order to reassure his parents. He was seen again at dances, in taverns, at bull-brandings. At the fair at Fontvieille it was he who led the farandole.

The father kept saying:

'He's got over it.' The mother still had her forebodings and watched her boy more than ever ..... Jan slept with his younger brother, quite near the silkworm rearing-house; the poor old woman had a bed made for her next to their room ..... The silkworms might need her, in the night.

Then came the feast of St Eloi, patron of farmers.

Great rejoicings at the farm ..... There was Châteauneuf for everybody, and mulled wine flowed like water. Fireworks followed, bonfires in the yard, and coloured lanterns hung on all the trees ..... Long live St Eloi! Everybody danced the farandole until they dropped. The younger son burnt his new smock. Jan himself actually looked happy; he danced with his mother; the poor woman wept for joy.

At midnight they went to bed. Everybody was ready to fall asleep on their feet ..... Everybody except Jan. His younger brother told later that all night Jan lay sobbing ..... Yes, he was still taking it very badly, poor lad.

Next day, at dawn, his mother heard somebody pass through her room, running. She knew at once something was wrong.

'Jan? Is that you?'

Jan does not reply; he is already on the stairs.

Quickly the mother gets up.

'Jan! Where are you going?'

He goes up to the loft. She follows him.

'Jan, my boy, answer me. What are you doing?'

She gropes for the latch, her old hands trembling ..... A window opening, a body falling on to the paving-stones of the yard and all is over.

The poor boy had said to himself:

'I love her too much ..... I am going to go away from it all .....' Ah, what misery the human heart can bear. But there is one burden too heavy for it — to realize we cannot stop loving the woman we have come to despise.

That morning, the people of the village wondered who was crying out so, up at Estève's farm.

There, in the yard, in front of the dew-covered, blood-covered stone table, the mother, naked from her bed, was crying for her child, lying dead in her arms.

ALPHONSE DAUDET (1840-1897) (translated by F Davies)

The poet Frédéric Mistral was a leading light in the revival of Provençal language and literature. Here he describes the stony plain of the Crau in his tour de force MIRÈIO.

> The Crau was motionless and silent.
> In the far distance its expanse
> Lost itself in the sea, and the sea in the blue air.
> The swans, the lustrous scoters,
> The flamingoes with fiery wings,
> Were coming, alongside the meres,
> To greet the last fair gleams of dying light.

FREDERIC MISTRAL (1830-1914) (translated by C M Girdlestone)

Here is the legend of the Crau.

BETWEEN MARSEILLES AND the outlets of the Rhône there is a circular plain, about 100 stadia distant from the sea, and about 100 stadia in diameter. It has received the name of the Stony Plain, from the circumstance of its being covered with stones the size of the fist, from beneath which an abundant herbage springs up for the pasturage of cattle. In the midst of it are water, salt-springs, and salt. The whole both of this district and that above it is exposed to the wind, but in this plain the black north, a violent and horrible wind, rages especially: for they say that sometimes the stones are swept and rolled along, and men hurled from their carriages and stripped both of their arms and garments by the force of the tempest. Aristotle tells us that these stones being cast up by the earthquakes designated *brastai,* and falling on the surface of the earth, roll into the hollow places of the districts; but Posidonius, that the place was formerly a lake,which being congealed during a violent agitation, became divided into numerous stones, like river pebbles or the stones by the sea-shore, which they resemble both as to smoothness, size, and appearance. Such are the causes assigned by these two [writers]; however, neither of their opinions is credible, for these stones could neither have thus accumulated of themselves, nor yet have been formed by congealed moisture, but necessarily from the fragments of large stones shattered by frequent convulsions. Aeschylus having, however, learnt of the difficulty of accounting for it, or having been so informed by another, has explained it away as a myth. He makes Prometheus utter the following, whilst directing Hercules [along] the road from the Caucasus to the Hesperides.

'There you will come to the undaunted army of the Ligurians, where, resistless though you be, sure am I you will not worst them in battle; for it is fated that there your darts shall fail you; nor will you be able to take up a stone from the ground, since the country consists of soft mould; but Jupiter, beholding your distress, will compassionate you, and overshadowing the earth with a cloud, he will cause it to hail round stones, which you hurling against the Ligurian army, will soon put them to flight!'

Posidonius asks, would it not have been better to have rained down these stones upon the Ligurians themselves, and thus have destroyed them all, than to make Hercules in need of so many stones? As for the number, they were necessary against so vast a multitude; so that in this respect the writer of the myth seems to me deserving of more credit than he who would refute it. Further, the poet, in describing it as fated, secures himself against such fault-finding. For if you dispute Providence and Destiny, you can find many similar things both in human affairs and nature, that you would suppose might be much better performed in this or that way; as for instance, that Egypt should have plenty of rain of its own without being irrigated from the land of Ethiopia; that it would have been much better if Paris had suffered shipwreck on his voyage to Sparta, instead of expiating his offences after having carried off Helen, and having been the cause of so great destruction both amongst the Greeks and Barbarians. Euripides attributes this to Jupiter:

'Father Jupiter, willing evil to the Trojans and suffering to the Greeks, decreed such things.'

S T R A B O   (? 6 3 B C - 2 3 A D)   (translated by H C T Hamilton)

Landscape with Bare Trees : Paul Cézanne

Horses on the Camargue

In the grey wastes of dread,
The haunt of shattered gulls where nothing moves
But in a shroud of silence like the dead,
I heard a sudden harmony of hooves,
And, turning, saw afar
A hundred snowy horses unconfined,
The silver runaways of Neptune's car
Racing, spray-curled, like waves before the wind.
Sons of the Mistral, fleet
As him with whose strong gusts they love to flee,
Who shod the flying thunders on their feet
And plumed them with the snortings of the sea;
Theirs is no earthly breed
Who only haunt the verges of the earth
And only on the sea's salt herbage feed —
Surely the great white breakers gave them birth.
For when for years a slave,
A horse of the Camargue, in alien lands,
Should catch some far-off fragrance of the wave
Carried far inland from his native sands,
Many have told the tale
Of how in fury, foaming at the rein,
He hurls his rider; and with lifted tail,
With coal-red eyes and cataracting mane,
Heading his course for home,
Though sixty foreign leagues before him sweep,
Will never rest until he breathes the foam
And hears the native thunder of the deep.
But when the great gusts rise
And lash their anger on these arid coasts,
When the scared gulls career with mournful cries
And whirl across the waste like driven ghosts:
When hail and fire converge,
The only souls to which they strike no pain
Are the white-crested fillies of the surge
And the white horses of the windy plain.
Then in their strength and pride
The stallions of the wilderness rejoice;
They feel their Master's trident in their side,

And high and shrill they answer to his voice.
With white tails smoking free,
Long streaming manes, and arching necks, they show
Their kinship to their sisters of the sea —
And forward hurl their thunderbolts of snow.
Still out of hardship bred,
Spirits of power and beauty and delight
Have ever on such frugal pastures fed
And loved to course with tempests through the night.

ROY CAMPBELL (1901-1957)

J H Smith describes the spectacular marshes of the Camargue in the Rhône Delta.

LIKE AN OCEAN it stretches on and away to the horizon or the fantastic boundaries of the mirage. Here the dead soil blossoms in shining crystalline flowers of salt, fatal to all other blooms; there wide marshes gleam with shallow ponds, set about with tufts of rushes and thinly screened with lines of tamarisks. Indefinable odors, breathing of the sea or breathing of the swamps, drift listlessly to and fro, and above us the cloudless blue is marked with triangles of cormorants, long files of rosy flamingoes, and circling flights of white sea-gulls. Little by little the stillness becomes conscious of invasion. Distant bellowings and neighings make themselves heard. Louder and nearer they grow, mingled with shouts. A vast, dark mass approaches, the *manade* of some rich farmer. The ground quivers beneath the march of scores of glossy black bulls, followed by hundreds — perhaps thousands — of cows and heifers. Around them hover the mounted guards armed with tridents; and in the midst of the great migration the swarthy proprietor, calm but alert, rides his powerful white horse with his pretty wife on the crupper. Another moment and the trampling host has passed. The shouts diminish; the bellowings die away. Stillness resumes her throne; and presently the ducks and herons, the partridges and bustards, recovering their courage, issue forth again, and — lonely as the bitterns amid the ruins of Nineveh — fill the desert places with mournful cries, answered only by the far low plaint of the sea.

St Gilles should be called the capital of the Camargue, for, though a town, it seems equally desolate, and hardly less poetic, than the marshes before it. There are people within its gate, but they do not appear to live. Outside the old city, like the ring of wood around the hollow of an ancient willow, is a new and busy place; but beyond the wall reigns the spirit of antiquity, and the people — even the children — move about like shadows.

J H SMITH (c 1889)

Rêverie d'un Gardien

Where are the clear light of the dawn and the gallop
Of horses neighing in the wind of the morning?
The fire throws on to the shining pewter of the dresser
Its soft warmth and the reflection of the flame.

The cat, asleep on my knees, is purring;
Listening to the flutter of the wind amongst the brands,
I think of all the fruits that I have crushed in my mouth,
I sit thinking of all the paths on which I have gone astray.

My youth has gone as went the swallows
When they saw the mists come towards them above the sea,
And the bowl is cracked and the wine is bitter
And in the failing body the soul sits solitary.

There was a time when in the little streets with white walls
Proudly I galloped in the midday heat,
Lance in hand, the belt above the haunches.

There was a time when we left the corrals at the break of day.
The girls clustering round the doors of the cabins
With their clear laughter wished us their good-days.

But, grave, rolled in our woollen burnouses,
In the breath of the dawn we pressed the bulls along,
The rising sun shining on their horns.

Pride of the strong, swelling pride of the chieftains,
Thirst of the conqueror swooping down on conquered towns .....
All these were ours when we galloped before the door.

A-gallop, invincible, we swept into the arena
And the girls from the balconies clapped their hands for us.

Then when came evening before the calm of the night
Erect in our stirrups we drove out of that oval
Pressing before us the panting bulls

And the blood of the horses bathed our spurs.

JOSEPH D'ARBAUD (1874-1950) (translated by Ford Madox Ford)

Still-Life with Tahitian Hat : Henri Matisse

In *Frederic Mistral's* P O U È M O D O U R O S E *he describes the Mistral, the fierce wind of Provence.*

...... The mistral hurricane
Is still blowing. The trees, greeting it
With groans, bend and shake
As if to tear themselves from their trunks. The wind
Holds back the Rhône, become smooth as a mirror.
Against water and wind the strong teams,
Nose down, march northward
With a regular step. Like a mighty bagpipe,
The resounding storm astounds the animals
And makes them prick up their ears.
The exasperated waggoners raise their hands
To their hats and plush caps,
And, with lips awry, let fly against the mistral
A torrent of full-mouthed oaths ......
...... And with a clicking
Of whips, they drive on their heavy horses ......
F R E D E R I C   M I S T R A L   (1 8 3 0 - 1 9 1 4) (translated by C M Girdlestone)

Mistral

At four the dawn mistral usually
A sleep-walking giant sways and crackles
The house, a vessel big with sail.
One head full of poems, cruiser of light,
Cracks open the pomegranate to reveal
The lining of all today's perhaps.

Far away in her carnal fealty sleeps
La Môme in her tiny *chambre de bonne.*
'*Le vent se lève ..... Il faut tenter de vivre.*'

I have grave thoughts about nothingness,
Hold no copyright in Jesus like that girl.
An autopsy would fuse the wires of pleading.
It is simply not possible to thank life.
The universe seems a huge hug without arms.
In foul rapture dawn breaks on grey olives.
Poetry among other afflictions
Is the purest selfishness.

I am making her a small scarlet jazz
For the cellar where they dance
To a wheezy accordion, with a one-eyed man.
Written to a cheeky begging voice.

> *Moi je suis*
> *Annie Verneuil*
> *Dit Annie La Môme*
> *Parfois je fais la vie*
> *Parfois je chome*
> *Premier Prix de Saloperie*
> *De Paris à Rome*
> *Annie La Môme*
> *Fléau du flic le soir*
> *Sur La Place Vendôme,*
> *Annie Verneuil*
> *Annie La Môme*

Freedom is choice: choice bondage.

Where will I next be when the mistral
Rises in sullen trumpets on the hills of bone?

LAWRENCE DURRELL (1912-)

---

*Francesco Petrarch, Italian lyric poet and scholar of great influence during the Renaissance,
wrote idealised poems to his Laura, whose tomb was discovered in Lyons in 1535.*

Non al suo amante più Diana piacque

Diana did not please her lover more
When by some chance quite naked
He saw her standing in cold water,

Than the wild hill girl,
Washing a light cloth in the bright air,
Pleased me.

The sky is burning. I am shaking with cold.

FRANCESCO PETRARCH (1304-1374) (translated by N Kilmer)

In his fascinating book LOVE, DEATH AND MONEY IN THE PAYS D'OC *Le Roy
Ladurie analyses a 14th century story of a young village boy Jean-l'ont-pris, written by Jean-
Baptiste Castor Fabre. Here is an extract about the boy's early life.*

I WAS LEFT with my grandmother, who, refusing to be cast down by so many misfortunes,
went back to making matches, working herself to death and inculcating in me a knowledge of
the ways of the world befitting a child of good family. My poor little grandmother! Alas! Jean-
l'ont-pris will never be able to repay his debt to her!

But that reminds me, now that my own story is about to begin, I should tell you where that
name of mine comes from, for, however bourgeois it may seem to you, I would not change it
for that of Hobgoblin. You see, when the band of men in blue took away my father, I would
be about three years old, and I was called Jean. In order to make me speak, the inhabitants of
the village would always be saying to me: 'Jean, where's your father? Jean, where's your papa
now? Jean, what became of Truquette the merchant?' And I would answer: *'Ils l'ont pris, ils l'ont
pris'* ['They have taken him away']; and so the name Jean-l'ont-pris stuck.

But let's go back to the lessons my grandmother gave me in how a man of my station should
comport himself in the world. Poor as I was, I was none the less the son of Monsieur Truquette,
which meant that a certain consideration would be shown me that would not be shown, as you
know, to the children of riff-raff. I won't bore you with all the sweet things my grandmother
would say to me, or with all the little pet names she gave me: my chicken, my lamb, my darling,
my prince, my king, my emperor; the riff-raff say such things to their children even more often

than the nobility; but she taught me politeness, and the rules of elegant behaviour, which are much more important and which not everybody is capable of teaching.

'You see, my son', she would say to me, 'if you wish to show where you come from, remember what your grandmother has taught you.

'First, you must always wear your hat, when you have one, at a rakish angle and don't raise it for anyone, especially for important people, unless they have done so before you; otherwise you will be considered an incompetent who is obliged to them, whereas if you keep your hat on your head, it means: "So much for you, Jean de Paris!" You don't have to pull it down over your eyes, like a bad payer, nor straight on your head, like a bumpkin, but wear it pulled down over your right eye, like this, watch how I do it with these three packets of matches, like that, yes! No more, no less.

'You are still young now, so if you are in good company, and you have to blow your nose, you will raise your little gown at the front, then you will hold your pretty little nose with the shirt, you will blow as hard as you can, to get the snot out completely, and you will let your clothes drop in such a way that no one sees what has become of the jelly.

'When you pass the time of day with someone who is worth bothering with, you will make a loud kiss in the hollow of your hand. Then you will step back, bow, scraping the ground with both feet like a hen.

'If you are invited to a castle, you must put on airs, say that your pot is on fire at home and that, thank God, you have no need of anyone else's. In this way, people will beg you to come, and will consider themselves very happy to have you in their house. If there are ladies present, don't forget to pinch their thighs and slap their knees, then drink their health, clink their glasses, put your five fingers cleanly into the salt and sprinkle their food with it. In this way you will be considered a well-brought-up young man who knows all there is to know about the customs and manners of people of fashion'.

It would soon send you to sleep, my lord, if I recounted all the wonderful things my grandmother told me to turn me into a respectable fellow. It may be that I am one; but all her rigmarole was never much use to me. The hat you see on my head is the first I have ever worn in my life; I always wore a cap until now. I have never had a little gown that I could lift so that I could blow my nose on my shirt; I have seen ladies in my time, but, whatever my wishes were on the matter, if I have ever eaten a morsel in their company, let it choke me. It is true that once I had occasion to sup at the Château de La Boissière, but it was in the cellar with the gamekeeper and his wife, and she was no more a lady than I'm a bishop. So you see, all my grandmother's hopes and fine words got me nowhere. Because, in her youth, she happened to have eaten, danced and even slept with people of high station, she must have imagined, I suppose, that her whole family enjoyed such a right. She took no account of the fact that Jean-l'ont-pris was not a girl and that boys, however pretty they may be, do not always enjoy such a privilege. Unfortunately, my grandmother was a bit hasty on this matter; but one can forgive anything in a person of that age, especially when it concerns someone one loves.

As soon as I was a bit older, I let her talk on and took charge of my own education.

ABBÉ J-B CASTOR FABRE (14th Century) (translated by A Sheridan)

These documents from Arènes give an interesting picture of life in a big house in the Middle Ages.

O N 2 0 J U L Y 1557 an enquiry was held: .....
The Son and heir, the new lord, François de Salsen was under age when his Father and Mother died. Later when he came of age he had to join the Army; as soon as he returned and wished to run his affairs he realised he had been the victim of exploitation by unscrupulous relatives. The castle, fields and woods had been plundered and were scarcely recognisable. Testimony was required as to their condition in the first instance to reconstitute the inheritance in its entirety; to this end the entire countryside had been brought to testify.
The testimony of the countryside, what is it if not the voice of the people? .....
Jehan de Salsan and his wife Marguerite de Grémat, of good lineage, led a respectable life, and provided great hospitality .....

Both celebrated family anniversaries worthily; they usually invited the clergy and religious orders from the town of Alais as well as people of quality, and provided them, as they would their normal visitors, with several rooms furnished with seven or eight beds and decorated with beautiful tapestries. There was nothing that was not in good order in their house, one would have to look far to find a castle as well provided with coffers great and small; there were also a number of clothes chests, benches, dressers, tables, chairs and stools; it was accessible and so open that the local people were familiar with the kitchens, where they could see the dinner service, beautiful pewter dishes and many painted plates.

All this was said, not without a certain pride, by the witnesses, as if the honour pertaining to their former Lord and Master had been their own; but what they added carried even more weight and they voiced it unanimously and with special feeling.

Jehan de Salsan had always lived in their midst 'he always resided at Arènes managing his lands himself. It was a very beautiful and spacious estate consisting of fields, vines, gardens, grapes, statues, enclosures, woods etc. cultivated by his servants, family and domestic servants for which purpose they were provided with suitable tools. For his personal use he mounted a nice quiet horse valued at 12 crowns.

CHARLES DE RIBBE (b 1898) (translated by J Karslake)

Zelda Fitzgerald, wife of the American novelist Scott Fitzgerald, gives this picture of a quiet time in her troubled life: she was staying at St Raphael at the age of 23.

T H E D E E P G R E E K of the Mediterranean licked its chops over the edges of our febrile civilization. Keeps crumbled on grey hillsides and sowed the dust of their battlements beneath the olives and the cactus. Ancient moats slept bound in tangled honeysuckle; fragile poppies bled the causeways; vineyards caught on jagged rocks like bits of worn carpet. The baritone of tired medieval bells proclaimed disinterestedly a holiday from time. Lavender bloomed silently over the rocks. It was hard to see in the vibrancy of the sun.

ZELDA FITZGERALD (1900-1948)

I STILL LOVE the Mediterranean, it still seems young as Odysseus, in the spring.

D H LAWRENCE (1885-1930)

Allen Tate, the major American poet, stayed in Provence for some years. Here is one of his best poems.

The Mediterranean

Quem das finem, rex magne, dolorum?

Where we went in the boat was a long bay
A slingshot wide, walled in by towering stone —
Peaked margin of antiquity's delay,
And we went there out of time's monotone:

Where we went in the black hull no light moved
But a gull white-winged along the feckless wave,
The breeze, unseen but fierce as a body loved,
That boat drove onward like a willing slave:

Where we went in the small ship the seaweed
Parted and gave to us the murmuring shore,
And we made feast and in our secret need
Devoured the very plates Aeneas bore:

Where derelict you see through the low twilight
The green coast that you, thunder-tossed, would win,
Drop sail, and hastening to drink all night
Eat dish and bowl to take that sweet land in!

Where we feasted and caroused on the sandless
Pebbles, affecting our day of piracy,
What prophecy of eaten plates could landless
Wanderers fulfil by the ancient sea?

We for that time might taste the famous age
Eternal here yet hidden from our eyes
When lust of power undid its stuffless rage;
They, in a wineskin, bore earth's paradise.

Let us lie down once more by the breathing side
Of Ocean, where our live forefathers sleep
As if the Known Sea still were a month wide —
Atlantis howls but is no longer steep!

What country shall we conquer, what fair land
Unman our conquest and locate our blood?
We've cracked the hemispheres with careless hand!
Now, from the Gates of Hercules we flood

Westward, westward till the barbarous brine
Whelms us to the tired land where tasseling corn,
Fat beans, grapes sweeter than muscadine
Rot on the vine: in that land were we born.

ALLEN TATE (1899-1979)

Peter Quennell, English poet, historian and biographer, watches the flamingoes returning over the Mediterranean to the Camargue.

UP THE GULF of Beaulieu, arriving from Italy, came a column of slowly travelling birds — not in extended order as wild geese fly, when they travel at night above the Scottish lowlands, but linked one by one in a gently undulating chain like the floating tail of a vast celestial kite, the drifting streamer that might follow an archangel or a loose ribbon attached to the Chariot of Venus. They were flamingoes making for the marshes of the Camargue, where, amid the lagoons and the reed-beds and the salt pastures of wandering black cattle, they are still permitted, even in the twentieth century, to lead their harmless unnecessary lives, and brighten the mud-banks on which they descend with a scattering of delicate rosy feathers ..... They were flying in unison; and every rhythmic pulse of their wings momentarily revealed the rosy under-surface; so that the celestial streamer not only changed its shape — an exquisite arabesque forming and reforming through a variety of beautifully broken curves — but, at the same time, was constantly changing its time as it traversed the brilliant background of the heavens, now greyish, faintly flushed with rose, now the vivid rose of an unclouded summer dawn.

PETER QUENNELL (1905-)

Lord Byron, the great English Romantic, uses the image of the Rhône in his epic poem CHILD HAROLD'S PILGRIMAGE.

Now, where the swift Rhône cleaves his way between
Heights which appear as lovers who have parted
In hate, whose mining depths so intervene,

That they can meet no more, though broken hearted:
Though in their souls, which thus each other thwarted,
Love was the very root of the fond rage
Which blighted their life's bloom, and then departed: —
Itself expired, but leaving them an age
Of years all winters, — war within themselves to wage:

Now, where the quick Rhône thus hath cleft his way,
The mightiest of the storms hath ta'en his stand:
For here, not one, but many, make their play,
And fling their thunder-bolts from hand to hand.

LORD BYRON (1788-1824)

In this piece, the same river is addressed by the American creator of Hiawatha.

To The River Rhône

Thou Royal River, born of sun and shower
In chambers purple with the Alpine glow,
Wrapped in the spotless ermine of the snow
And rocked by tempests! — at the appointed hour
Forth, like a steel-clad horseman from a tower,
With clang and clink of harness does thou go
To meet thy vassal torrents, that below
Rush to receive thee and obey thy power.
And now thou movest in triumphal march,
A king among the rivers! On thy way
A hundred towns await and welcome thee;
Bridges uplift for thee the stately arch,
Vineyards encircle thee with garlands gay,
And fleets attend thy progress to the sea!

HENRY WADSWORTH LONGFELLOW (1807-1882)

Memories of Toulon — The Toulon Barber : Jean Cocteau

CHAPTER THREE

Heroes
and Villains

Berenger-Feraud illustrates what he considers the dominant characteristics of the Provençal with these two seventeenth century examples.

THE PROVENÇAL CHARACTER ..... was a mixture of cunning and naiveté, of suspicion and childish credulity. But above all it was constantly dominated by the desire to turn everything that happened into a joke once the moment of public emotion, all too often tragic, had passed. The joke was usually direct, frequently earthy and expressed more often than not in the most farcical way. So it was for instance in 1650 when the Count of Alais sent his son-in-law, the Duke de Joyeuse, to Marseilles. The townspeople, tired of the nobleman's presence, spread a rumour that the plague had brokn out in the city. For several days all funeral processions were routed under the Duke's windows. He was so terrified that he promptly left and by this stratagem the people of Marseilles rid themselves of an irksome authority.

In 1649 Louis de Valois, Governor of Provence, incurred the hatred of the common people, having enjoyed great popularity. The inhabitants of Aix showed their antipathy towards him and his wife by dressing up, masked, during the procession of the Holy Eucharist where there were already many grotesque objects. A jester represented the Count and so arranged his clothes that he could raise the flaps of his coat with strings. Near him was a woman dressed as the Countess. They were accompanied by people dressed up as president, councillor and officials and finally by a choir made up of four peasants, clothed in long robes which were red on one side and yellow on the other, who sang an uncomplimentary ditty about the Count and his wife. Each couplet ended with a refrain ..... during the refrain the individual impersonating the Count revolved round and round as he waltzed, pulling the strings of his coat to reveal his bare bottom.

L B J BÉRENGER-FERAUD (1900 -) (translated by J Karslake)

Henry Swinburne was a great traveller both in Europe and further afield. He died, in fact, on a trip to Trinidad.

THE PROVENÇAL IS all alive, and feels his nerves agitated in a supreme degree by accidents and objects that would scarce move a muscle or a feature in the phlegmatic natives of more northern climes; his spirits are flurried by the slightest sensations of pleasure or of pain, and seem always on the watch to seize the transient impressions of either; but to balance this destructive propensity, nature has wisely rendered it difficult for those impressions to sink into their souls; they easily receive, but as easily discard and forget, thus daily offering a surface smoothed afresh for new pains and pleasures to trace their light affections upon. But this by no means excludes warm attachments and solid friendships; when time and habit afford leisure for the impression to penetrate deep enough, it will, no doubt, acquire and retain as firm a hold in their breast as in any other, and perhaps be stamped with still greater warmth and energy.

HENRY SWINBURNE (1752-1803)

〰〰〰〰〰〰〰〰〰〰〰〰〰〰〰〰〰〰〰〰〰〰〰〰

Ford Madox Ford, originally surnamed Hueffer, was an English novelist. This passage comes from his discussion of the ethos of the bullfight in his book P R O V E N C E.

IN PROVENCE — AND of course in Spain — the bull-fight continues still its triumphant progress at the sword-ends of actors who alone today are as beloved as the boy who in Antipolis a couple of thousand years ago danced and gave pleasure. The bull-fight too may die out in the whole general collapse; it is an immensely expensive mass-art — though its essentials are neither the expense nor the immense crowds; its essentials are swiftness and skill in wielding a thin spike of steel against a furious and alert monster. For still today the most admired matadors are not those who offer the most display of agility. They are those who with the classic nonchalance of the *hidalgos* who first practised this art — and who alone have the right to the name *toreador* — stroll about the arena, their sword beneath the arm, or sit on a chair till the moment comes to deliver to the bull who has meanwhile been worked into position by the servants, the *coup de grâce.* For that no lists are needed; no tiers on tiers of humanity ..... no limelight, no publicity ..... Nothing but a smooth place, some shade-trees, the arms, the man and the bull.

Yes, the great, shining *corridas* whether of Nîmes or Pampeluna or Perpignan or Madrid and St Sebastian may go, though it seems unlikely since that art has lasted two thousand years in these places.

But the art will not go, the courage, the skill; the alertness. In every village of Provence there is a bull-ring and on every Sunday of the year when the days are warm enough all the young men of courage face, without arms, the wild bulls of the Camargue doing nothing more deadly to them than affix rosettes beneath their horns or on each shoulder ..... And they face the charging bull, place a foot between the horns and spring right over the beast, or vault over him with a jumping-pole, or catch him as he charges with their two hands on his horns and somersault across his back ..... It is just a sport, like cricket, but without advertisement, carried on so obscurely that you might well say it was secret ..... a sport in the blood of the people, carried on by the sons of the barbers, the furriers, the peasants, the bakers ..... It is as it were the *conte-fable* as against the high and renowned *gestes* of the troubadours. It is considered that, before a man should have wherewith to pay for his seat at the *mise à mort,* he must have worked bulls himself .....

FORD MADOX FORD (1873-1939)

The troubadour Raimbaut d'Orange, who began his writing in 1147, evidently saw himself in the role of the anti-hero; he gives this account of his charms.

> I've been silent for a long time now,
> but God doesn't want me to keep
> my deficiencies a secret any longer,
> and this fills me with grief and horror.
> So listen, knights, and see
> if indeed I don't lack something.

You may rest assured on one score:
I've lost those things which make
men gayest — hence my shame;
and I don't dare say who did it.
But you can see I speak the truth
when I admit to such chagrin.

The reason I so willingly confess
the cause of my endless grief
is that I want to relieve, without
delay, all husbands of any fear,
anxiety or worry which might have
made them look at me askance.

Though I seem likable and pleasant,
I'm really thin, nasty and cowardly
(with or without my armor),
leprous and foul smelling,
a vile, niggardly host, and the worst
soldier you have ever seen.

So any man is clearly a fool
to worry if I court his wife;
why should he drive me off,
since no harm
could ever come to him
from my endless wretched sighs?

For even without this deficiency
(which makes me tear out my beard in rage)
I have so much else on which to preen myself
— other evil sins into which I've fallen —
that to no woman whole in body
would I be worth a moment's thought.

And if I'm allowed to do so, I'll sing,
for this I will never abandon.
Let every husband grow a pimple
on his snout if he gets angry
when I wish to hide my grief
behind a mask of gaiety.

I've commended myself to ladies
so that I may have some joy,
which I'm powerless to realize
in bed; so I'll grow fat
merely from desiring
and looking — I seek nothing else.

I'd like the countess at Monrosier
to hear of my perfect joy.

RAIMBAUT D'ORANGE (d 1 1 7 3) (translated by I Farnell)

The town of St Gilles on the Camargue takes its name from an old legend .....

BETWEEN ARLES AND Aigues Mortes lies the abbey of St Gilles, medieval pilgrimage spot of European renown but now dusty and deserted. When it was first built, the Rhône flowed near by and the town was a busy seaport, the busier for the incessant traffic in pilgrims whom the fame of the Saint, still invoked against fire, epilepsy, madness and fear, brought in its train. But now the river has changed its course, and the lagoons which enabled vessels to approach from Italy, Spain and the Levant have evaporated. Only the legend of St Gilles remains to re-create for us the glorious past.

St Gilles the Athenian was, according to a medieval L I F E , 'the flower of youth in his country, his head covered with golden curls, his skin white as milk, his nose and ears of perfect shape, teeth like pearls, and a lovely mouth, he was thin and graceful, supple and strong.' In early manhood he came to Arles and thence as a hermit to the spot which now bears his name; here he was fed with milk by a white stag which presented itself every day at the thicket in which the Saint had made his habitation. One day the stag was chased by the dogs of the king out a-hunting, and fled to the protection of St Gilles; and the dogs dared not approach the thicket but sat round it in a circle, baying. Whereupon a huntsman who was in the King's following shot an arrow into the thicket; and then the King dismounted and came up to it, and saw the holy man, his hand pierced by the arrow, sheltering the stag. The King was touched by the sight, and built a monastery so that St Gilles might rule over it; but it was to his cave that the peasants used until recently to come when disaster threatened the country-side.

W BRANCH JOHNSON (1 9 2 7)

St Martha was, according to legend, the founder of Avignon.

WHEN THE HOLY Maries and their companions were, by the will of God, cast upon the shore of the Mediterranean, near to the spot where stands today the village of 'Les Saintes Maries de la Mer,' Martha was directed by her brother Lazarus to go northward towards the river Rhône. She walked for a long while, following the course of the river, her feet torn by the reeds and pebbles of the way; and, for relief from her sufferings, she looked down always at the cross which she held sometimes before her, sometimes pressed close to her breast.

Coming, one evening, upon a dreary plain, she saw, far off, a wild growth of sombre wood-land. The crimson sun was disappearing behind the black boughs, and Martha seemed to hear, coming thence, the sound of weeping and of groans. These mournful echoes awoke a great pity within her, and she hastened her steps towards the border of the wood.

And now there passed two shepherds, pale and emaciated, who were hastening along the path, driving before them a troop of ill-fed sheep. At the sight of the stranger, who was seeking to make her way through the thicket of stunted oak trees, one of them threw his staff before her feet, and, with a gesture of fear, seemed to invite her to retrace her steps.

But the cries became more heart-rending. The saint brushed the suppliant aside and crossed the threshold of that threatening forest. White and aerial as a heavenly vision, she glided across the shadowy spaces, beneath the vaults of the giant trees, whose leaves hung motionless as though frozen with horror; along tortuous ways, beside rugged colonnades of primaeval trunks. Her steps echoed down the darkening paths. Suddenly the twilight gave place to night, but still the saint walked on through the darkness, guided by the cries which rang in her ears.

And suddenly, in the utter blackness of the wood, there appeared before her a luminous cross from which, bathing Martha in its beams, there shone out a white light that revealed to her the accursed place. It was a vast glade, formed by a marsh, greenish in aspect, surrounded by stunted trees and dead bushes that stretched out their spectral arms in fear-inspiring shapes. And, by the strange light of the miraculous cross, Martha perceived a living being, a woman, all in disarray, whose clenched hands were tearing her face, and whose eyes were shedding tears of blood.

A mother it was, whose wild clamours were waking the echoes of the forest of Nerluc, a mother who was wringing her hands as she stared into the water, gloomy and green as a pest-stricken meadow, upon whose slimy surface, instead of flowers, there floated hideous human remains.

At the sight of Martha the woman ceased from her cries. Stupefied she gazed upon this white apparition, this luminous cross that was flooding in fantastic moonlight the twisted trunks of the dead trees; and she took into her hands the saint's tunic. Then she pointed out a ripple that showed itself in the water of the marsh, and continued her sobs and groans.

The saint fell forward in prayer; the cross of light moved to above her head, and her face began to shine like a beautiful lily bathed in the morning's tears and gilded by the rays of the setting sun. Three times her voice invoked a name that the echoes of the forest had never before retold, and that the afflicted mother knew not as yet. She raised her right hand, armed with the rough cross that had protected her during her long journey, and, behold, from the depths of the gloomy pool, a sudden bubbling troubled the greenish water, and there emerged a monstrous head, covered with tangled hair, whence shone two phosphorescent eyes like burning embers, a body covered with scales, bristling with sharp spikes; and the mother uttered a wild cry, the cry of a mad woman, to see, upon the dragon's back, a beautiful naked child, smiling calmly and serenely in his sleep.

The monster swam towards the bank; and, as it passed, the breath that came from its bloody jaws blackened the water and withered leaves that floated around it.

With the steel claws which armed its feet it clung to the firm earth, and gazed, fear-stricken, at the luminous cross; then stretched its gigantic body at the feet of the saint. The mother had already borne off her treasure, and was fleeing towards the border of the wood, her cries of joy breaking the silence of the night.

Martha untied the cord that encircled her waist, passed it round the beast's neck, and, quite docile, it followed her more quietly than the most submissive dog. And still the heavenly beacon shone, and wherever the monster's breath had withered the branches, they were quickened into new life by its healing beams.

When Martha emerged from the forest, she saw before her an eager throng in whose midst the happy mother was holding up her child towards the heavens where the first stars were twinkling out. The dragon stopped, then fell blinded by the light of the cross which was shining with glorious brilliancy; and again Martha invoked the sacred name of the Saviour.

'Jesus, Jesus, Jesus!!! ..... By Thy power banish down to hell the spirit of evil dwelling within this beast, and save, by the cross, the souls that are around me.'

Immediately, with a hoarse roaring, the beast stiffened as though blasted with lightning, and it stammered the awful, unknown name whose virtue had triumphed over the dragon of the forest of Nerluc.

It was thus that St Martha slew the monster that was called the Tarasque, and brought the Christian faith to Tarascon.

PERCY ALLEN (1869-1933)

As with many of the troubadours, it's hard to tell whether Gaucelm Faidit was a hero or a villain!

NOW GAUCELM FAIDIT was of a town named Uzerche of the diocese of Limousin, and he was the son of a burgher, and sang worse than any man in the world, yet made many a good melody, and many a good canzone. And he became a jongleur, because at dice he had lost all that he had. And he was a man of open hand, and a full gluttonous eater, and a wine-bibber, wherefore he grew beyond measure fat. And for a right long time was he ill-fortuned in the getting of gifts and fame, for it was even twenty years and upwards that he journeyed through the world, and he and his songs received the while small favour of any.

And he took to wife a wanton, who long time went with him from court to court, the which hight Guillelma Monia, and was passing fair and skilled, but became even as big and fat as he. And she was of a rich town named Alest, in the march of Provence, and of the lordship of Lord Bernart of Andusa. And my lord, the Marquis Boniface of Montferrat, gave him goods, and raiment and equipment, and set him in great fame, both him and his songs.

MEDIAEVAL LIVES OF THE TROUBADOURS

Song on the Fourth Crusade

Now be to us a guide
The Lord, who for us died,
For whom the noble-hearted,
'Mongst whom I long abide,
I leave, and much beside —
Love, honour, wealth, and pride;
If sad from these I've parted,
I pray He may not chide.
Farewell, sweet Limousin,
And those that dwell therein:
Fair dames of gentle bearing,
Stout knights that honour win,
Neighbours and next of kin!
Sad on my way I'm faring,
And bitter tears begin
To shed, with groans despairing.

Now Anti-Christ doth haste
Fair countries to lay waste,
And Vice, her foes dismaying,
Sweet Virtue hath abased;
Her hand on princes placed,
Good from their hearts hath chased,
And avarice on them preying,
Foully their names disgraced —
He, who o'er France doth reign,
Base gold had liefer gain,
Norman or Frenchman plunder,
Than Seifeddin constrain
To yield up what hath lain
Too long his foul yoke under
Such Kings full long in pain
Will groan or great the wonder.

GAUCELM FAIDIT (c 1160 - 1215) (translated by I Farnell)

The turbulent family of Les Baux was described by John Addington Symonds in these words:

THE REAL TEMPER of this fierce tribe was not shown among troubadours or in courts of love and beauty. The stern and barren rock from which they sprang and the comet of their scutcheon are the true symbols of their natures. History records no end to their ravages and slaughters. It is a tedious catalogue of blood — how one prince put to fire and sword the whole town of Courthézon; how another was stabbed in prison by his wife; how a third besieged the castle of his niece and sought to undermine her chamber, knowing her the while to be with child; how a fourth was flayed alive outside the walls of Avignon. There is nothing terrible and savage belonging to feudal history of which an example may not be found in the annals of Les Baux.   JOHN ADDINGTON SYMONDS (1840-1893)

In 1309 the Papacy moved from Rome to Avignon where, in the hundred years that followed, a Babylon of corruption and debauchery emerged. Petrarch wrote of the town's moral disintegration in a letter from Avignon.

AVIGNON IS THE home of infidelity. The future life is regarded as an empty fable, and hell likewise. The resurrection of the body, the world's promised end, Christ's coming to sit in judgment, are treated as old wives' tales. License to sin is taken as liberal open-mindedness. The city is the habitation of demons. Prostitutes swarm on the papal beds. Aged striplings, white-haired, wide-gowned, foul-minded, abandon themselves to every lust. Satan urges them with every stimulant for failing powers. Husbands of ravished women are driven from their homes to keep them quiet; they are forced to take back wives pregnant by the courtiers, and then, after childbirth, to return them to their unholy unions. Everyone knows this, but few dare speak, or they are deterred by shame.

There was an old cleric, lustful as a goat; for fear of ghosts, or perhaps of mice, he dared not sleep alone. He made new marriages daily, and his embraces were full of novelty, though his years were many and his mouth contained only seven teeth. In his corps of fowlers was one his equal in lust, who spread his snares in every street, especially in the houses of the poor, bestowing money here, there ornaments and rings, and caresses too. He would sing — for he was an excellent cantor, who had transferred his art from the altar to dances and lupanars. 'I knew him; he was pointed out by everyone, with stories of the victims he brought to the wolfish fangs of the old man.' One story of many: he had allured by his promises a poor girl to do the bidding of the old man. But when the time came she was revolted by his age and ugliness, saying that she had come for a high prelate, not an old deformed priest. At last he put on his red hat, crying: 'Cardinalis sum!' And thus he triumphed, with his hat on.

FRANCESCO PETRARCH (1304-1374) (translated by Morris Bishop)

Maurice Agulhon describes the formation and existence of powerful youth groups throughout Provence's history.

THE YOUTH, WHATEVER the official definition, was a body which had its own leaders, its own functions and its own revenues to implement them .... We know of many documents which refer to the levying of taxes from Pelota and revelry (Charivaris) as being among the prerogatives of festival officials .....

Besides these taxes they may have had other revenues. At least so it was in the Languedoc as Emile G Léonard shows us: in his native village in the time of Louis XV in each house, he says, one or more colonies of silkworms were raised. The young people collected the mulberry leaves but they also shared in the profits of the harvested cocoons, from whose sale they were able to dress the virgin in the church in rich clothes, or to defray the cost of their dances.

In the 17th Century Frédéric Mireur said 'the youth of Draguignan formed five or six separate groups, each having an elected head, it own funds, its particular locality for dances and its own complement of musicians,' and he goes on to say: 'the sons of good family gathered round the Prince of Love, Clerks of the Law Courts round the King of the Lawyers and so on down to journeymen; then he adds 'they danced a lot in Draguignan, the bourgeoisie to the strains of the violin, the common people ..... to the fife and drum'.

This segregation sometimes led to brawls as the following document illustrates (confirming Mireur's study). During the 1634 carnival at Le Luc, Angelin Ainesy mortally wounded Honoré Truc, a young vineyard worker. Why? Well, you must understand that 'the young from the best families in that place held their functions separately from the peasants and manual labour-

Antipolis : Pablo Picasso

ers'. So at 8 o'clock in the evening of the 17th January 1634 as they went down the road to the strains of the violin, the murderer to be and his group met up with a large party of labourers and vineyard workers armed with swords and staves and playing serenades on fife and drum. When they saw the bourgeois the labourers and peasants ordered their drummer to stop playing the serenade and beat to arms. Naturally Ainesy ordered the drummer to stop, a peasant, on the contrary, ordered him to beat louder, and battle was joined. As the peasant Truc violently manhandled Jean Armatric, a lawyer, one of the bourgeois band, and threatened 'to tear off his nose with his teeth,' Ainesy drew a dagger and struck. Truc was not to survive.

Among Toulon's records of public auctions and proclamations during 1774-79 there is no lack of restrictive and repressive municipal legislation relating to traditional youthful demonstrations. They recur almost annually at Carnival time towards the end of winter. It was forbidden to throw firecrackers, to shout in the street, to go about masked, to form chains to obstruct and tease passers-by etc.

Sometimes they seem to be specially aimed at the working class; for instance, 30th March 1779: all naval ratings, sailors, carpenters, masons, shoemakers, bakers etc. are strictly forbidden to assemble and congregate in the streets and squares from the onset of dusk. If more than three people gather together they will be arrested, taken to prison and punished as disturbers of the peace.   MAURICE AGULHON (1 9 6 8) (translated by J Karslake)

One of the indisputable heroes in the history of Provence was Good King Réné of Anjou, who is described by Sir Walter Scott in his novel ANNE OF GEIERSTEIN.

RÉNÉ WAS A prince of very moderate parts, endowed with a love of the fine arts, which he carried to extremity, and a degree of good humour, which never permitted him to repine at fortune, but rendered its possessor happy, when a prince of keener feelings would have died of despair. This insouciant, light-tempered, gay and thoughtless disposition, conducted Réné, free from all the passions which embitter life, and often shorten it, to a hale and mirthful old age. Even domestic losses, which often affect those who are proof against mere reverses of fortune, made no deep impression on the feelings of this cheerful old monarch. Most of his children had died young; Réné took it not to heart. His daughter Margaret's marriage with the powerful Henry of England was considered a connexion much above the fortunes of the King of the Troubadours. But in the issue, instead of Réné deriving any splendour from the match, he was involved in the misfortunes of his daughter, and repeatedly obliged to impoverish himself to supply her ransom.   SIR WALTER SCOTT (1771-1832)

In 1720 there was a terrible outbreak of the plague in Provence, with between 40 and 50 thousand people dying in Marseilles alone. Méry, a Marseillais of a later generation, describes the scene and the heroic work of saintly Bishop Belzunce.

THE PHYSICIANS SENT to Marseilles by the Government on arriving found in the place over 20,000 dead and nine to ten thousand sick or dying. The frightful spectacle so affected them that they could hardly eat. In traversing the town, in places they could hardly step without encountering heaps of corpses. The plague-stricken felt a flicker of hope on seeing doctors approach, but this soon died out. Fathers and mothers dragged their children into the streets, and abandoned them after placing a jug of water at their side. Children exhibited a revolting lack of feeling. All generous sentiments had been paralysed by the hand of death. The mortality was so great and rapid in its march that the corpses, piled up before the houses, and in the church porches, indeed everywhere, empested the air. In the heat, the bodies rapidly putrified and dissolved, falling apart in strips. All were naked; the sick were covered by a few rags. Women half-clothed appealed for a drop of water, pointing to the fetid rill that trickled down the gutter; and as no one attended to them, they used their failing powers to crawl to it, often with their babes at their breasts, to dip their lips in the foul stream. Death was preceded by frightful spasms. The number of deaths increased to such an extent that it was not possible to bury the dead. Bewilderment took possession of men. Those of the inhabitants who had not been infected wandered about, not knowing whither to go, but avoiding one another. Others converted their houses into fortresses, as though disposed to maintain a siege; others fled to their country villas; others went on board ship; but the plague pursued them everywhere.

In these days of calamity, the heart of man was shown in all its nakedness, and revealed all its baseness, ignoble inclinations, as well as its virtues and devotion. Those especially belonging to the lowest social beds, who live in fear of the laws, gave themselves up to frightful excesses. The galley slaves, to whom was entrusted the burial of the dead, drew the tumbrils heaped with corpses with a mocking callousness; murdering the sick so as to rob them; flinging those ill along with those dead together, indifferently, into the pits dug to receive the bodies. The civic functionaries, the employés, even priests, deserted their posts, and the monks of S Victor enclosed themselves within their fortress. But there were others, who presented a striking contrast to these men. Priests came hurrying to the empested town from all parts to shut themselves in within this circle of death. Their zeal was stimulated by the sublime self-devotion of Belzunce, bishop of Marseilles. The fear of death never chilled his charity. He hurried through the street, seated himself by the dying, bowed over them to hear their confessions, and the plague spared him as he executed these acts of humanity.

FRANÇOIS MÉRY (1797-1866) (translated by S Baring Gould)

Here is a sad little song from Menton.

Oh, Isabel! Fair Isabel!

Oh Isabel! fair Isabel!
Dost hear the sound of the wedding bell?
At wedding now I ne'er can be,

But at the dance I'll dance merrily.
Then if to the dance you come tonight,
Array thy form in sunny white.

The maiden fair first hastes away
To deck herself that very day:
If fair she looked in robe of blue,
Thrice fairer now in azure hue.
At the first roll of startling drum,
Into the dance all see her come;
At second roll of yon drum so dread,
They see the maiden fall down dead!

'Oh, Isabel! fair Isabel!
Who did this deed 'fore all men tell!'
'Alas! none did this deed to me —
I die — I die for love to thee!'
'Then if you died of love for me,
Soon will I die for love of thee!'
He bent, he fell, close by her side —
Kissed her cold lips, and gently died.

MENTONESE SONG (translated by E Sparks)

In Aigues-Mortes stands the Tour de Constance where many religious prisoners were held. In 1730 a young protestant girl Marie Durand was brought to the tower. She was to stay there for 38 years. Her graffito is still on the wall: 'Résister'.

MARIE HAD BEEN affianced to a pious young man, Matthieu Serre, and on the false report that the marriage had taken place the bridegroom-elect was also seized and taken to Brescou to join her father, on June 28th. Marie was not actually arrested until some weeks later, when on the authority of a royal *lettre de cachet,* she was taken from her home, and on the 25th of August lodged in the Tour de Constance. To the dejected company of women whom she found in that hall of gloom the arrival of Marie Durand, though only fifteen years of age, came like a ray of sunshine into their prison life. She especially devoted herself to the aged and sick.

Although all correspondence was interdicted, the prisoners contrived both to send and receive letters. This was sometimes due to the compassion of the governor or his lady, or ..... to a desire on their part to make use of the prisoners' friends. On the 19th of September, Etienne Durand wrote from Brescou to his daughter, 'The author of nature has permitted that I should experience trials, which still increase. But, thanks be to God, I have always found consolation in placing my confidence in Him. We pray for all, even for our enemies; God give them grace to see the wrong they do to us and to themselves. Your betrothed is well; he lies with me in a good bed, and I hope that if he is patient and prudent he will, like me, have some liberty in the fort.' In the same envelope there was a letter from Matthieu Serre himself. 'My darling, I write these lines to assure you of my regard, and to testify my extreme sorrow at our separation. I could neither eat nor drink till my dear intended father-in-law cheered me by the hope of a speedy reunion, and of good days yet to come for you and me. I sigh for the moment when we three shall see one another again, and I assure you that I have the honour to be your most affectionate servant, SERRE.'

The prisoners in the Tour de Constance were sometimes permitted to ascend to the platform on the top of the tower, where they could breathe a purer air. From this platform their eyes fell on the blue expanse of the Mediterranean stretching southward from the fortified city below, whilst to the north they saw the rich plain of Languedoc, bounded by the Cevennes, many a familiar summit of which they could make out. But Marie's eyes would search for a dark point scarcely discernible on the south-west horizon, the fortress which contained her father and her affianced husband. There is reason to believe that the inmates of the two prisons never met again. The father was set at liberty in 1743, being then more than eighty years of age. Serre, after languishing twenty years in the fort, reflecting honour upon his bonds by his patience and constancy, was released in 1750. 'You have, Sir,' wrote St Florentin to the intendant Lenain, 'long given a good report of the conduct of M Matthieu Serre, who has been a prisoner twenty years on the charge of marrying the sister of a preacher. The king wills that he should be set at liberty, and I send you the royal order to that effect.' But the liberty granted was but a tyrant's grace; Serre was banished from Languedoc, without being permitted to see her whom he had loved in the happy days of his youth, and who still had eighteen years to wear out in her tower.

The view from the platform is thus described in the Diary, "We ascended to the terrace, above which is a turret surmounted by an iron lantern. The appearance of the town from this elevated spot is curious, with its nine gates, its little streets, all at right angles, and the houses lower than the walls. A wide canal, coming from the east, winds round the town, connecting it with the Mediterranean, which is separated from us by a narrow belt of common land and low sandbanks. We found the concierge an intelligent man, ready to answer questions, and giving out his knowledge in a clear deliberate manner. He showed us some of the shoes and one or two other of the relics discovered in the meurtrière ..... but most of these had been taken away by admiring visitors. He told us that in summer, parties of the descendants of the prisoners, or of other victims of the persecution, come for the day, and take possession of one of the halls, where they pray, sing Psalms, and regale themselves. 'And why not?' he asked; 'have we not liberty, equality, fraternity?'"

When Marie Durand had been eight months in the tower, her brother Pierre's mother-in-law, Isabeau Sautel, was sent to join the company of prisoners. She had opposed her daughter's marriage, and when at last she gave her consent she refused to show any sympathy towards the newly married couple. It is remarkable therefore that one of the crimes for which she was condemned was consent to her daughter's marriage. A year later Marie Durand received intelligence of her brother Pierre's martyrdom.

Marie Durand was not released until the 14th of April, 1768, when she was discharged by a letter of grace. In August of that year there still remained five prisoners; the last two were set free in December. On the 11th of that month St Florentin wrote to the intendant: 'The king is pleased to accord favour to Chassefière and Suzanne Pagès, the only prisoners in the Tour de Constance. I send you the two orders necessary for their release, and I pray you to see to the execution of the same.' On the 26th the intendant sent the two orders to the governor of Aigues-Mortes, and the same day, which was Monday, the great gate rolled once more upon its hinges, and the two women passed out. They were in a state of complete destitution. Paul Rabaut wrote, in January, 1770, to Etienne Chiron: 'I have handed to the two last prisoners the four louis you gave me, which I understand would be the last they are to receive. One of them, Suzanne Pagès, although still young, is unable to gain her living, having a broken leg with an open wound.' She had been in the tower more than thirty years.

When Marie Durand regained her liberty she returned to the home of her childhood. She had left it a blooming girl, full of life's bright hopes; she returned blanched, withered, crippled. It was a marvel, as one of the party who visited her home, remarked, how they could ever get her up to Le Bouchet. She found her cottage dilapidated and her orchard cut down. Her niece and the widow Goutez, who had been released before her, were waiting for her under the old roof. Here Marie survived for some years, and we may picture the three friends, with some congenial neighbours, sitting, during the long winter evenings, over the wood embers under that wide open mantel, reviewing, with mournful pleasure, the sad story of the past, and blessing God for the quiet days which had succeeded to so many stormy years. The Walloon Church of Amsterdam allowed Marie a pension of 200 livres, which she generously shared with a neighbour, Alexandre Chambon, who had returned from the galleys of Toulon at the age of seventy-three. Marie died in September 1776.   C H A R L E S   T Y L O R   (1 8 9 3)

Engraving of the Massacre in Avignon in 1791

Avignon also had its share of bloodshed during the Revolution .....

IN THE EARLY autumn terrible news came from the old papal town of Avignon. Avignon, together with a small adjoining province, formed a little foreign State, right in the middle of the south of France: a State which had been sold to the Pope by its rulers, centuries before. The Popes had once resided in Avignon during a long exile from Rome, and when they returned to Rome, had been allowed to retain possession because their rule caused France no inconvenience. But when the Revolution came, the case was altered; the little State became a refuge for the disaffected and a centre of disturbance. About half its inhabitants petitioned to be rejoined to France, while the other half wished to remain under the Pope; the two sides fought, and both committed atrocities.

This could not be allowed to go on and, after long hesitation, the Constituent Assembly decreed, in September 1791, that Avignon should be re-joined to France. Owing to the delays of the Minister, Delessart, the decree had not yet been carried out in October, but every one knew of it.

On the 16th of October, Lescuyer, an unpopular member of the revolutionary party in Avignon, was lured by some opponents into a church, filled with a large gathering of men and women. He was there set upon and slowly put to death with clubs and stones and the scissors of the women. The same evening some of his friends, under the leadership of a man called Jourdan, arrived in Avignon and took vengeance for the murder. They arrested a large number of the Papal party, quite indiscriminately, both men and women, and shut them up in the Pope's old castle. In the night they brought them out one by one, slaughtered them, and flung their bodies, sometimes with life still in them, down the shaft of an open tower once used as an ice-house. Sixty-one persons perished in this manner.

The Assembly shuddered over the massacre at the ice-tower and at first talked of bringing the murderers to justice. But there were difficulties in the way; it seemed unfair that one party should suffer for its crimes and not the other, and Brissot and the Girondins were reluctant to let good 'patriots' who had acted under provocation be punished. Arrests were made, but some months later the idea was started that the amnesty of September ought to be extended to cover the massacre. Vergniaud and Lasource, an eloquent Protestant pastor who had joined the Girondins, persuaded the Assembly to take this view (19th March 1792); the accused were released, and some of the leaders in the massacre afterwards made friends with the principal Girondins.

ED BRADBY (1926)

In October 1793, after the outbreak of the Revolution, Toulon was handed over by local Royalists to the protection of the English navy. Between the French royalists and the English the harbour was rendered almost impregnable until a young captain called Bonaparte was given a free hand to try to break the siege. S Baring Gould, a vicar and prolific author, wrote several studies of the South of France, its geography and history.

IN OCTOBER, 1793 a disorderly mob of soldiers and revolutionary cut-throats, under the command of the painter Carteaux, after having dyed their hands in the blood of six thousand of their countrymen, whom they had massacred at Lyons, invested Toulon, which had shut its gates against the revolutionary army, and had thrown open its port to the English. The town was crowded with refugees from Marseilles, and its bastions were occupied by a mixed multitude of defenders, Sardinians, Spaniards, French, and English, united in nothing save in common hatred of the monsters who were embrued in blood.

The investing army was divided into two corps, separated by the Faron. On the west was Ollioules, where Carteaux had established his headquarters. The commander-in-chief, ignorant of the first principles of military science, and allowing his wife to draw out the orders for the day, and sign them as Femme Carteaux, had planted his batteries where they could do no injury to the English fleet. The siege had begun in September; it dragged on through October. There was organisation neither in the host nor in the commissariat. The army was composed partly of troops detached from that of Italy, mainly volunteers set at liberty by the taking of Lyons, and a horde of Marseillais ruffians, animated by hopes of murder and plunder.

In the midst of this confusion Bonaparte arrived before Toulon, and appearing before Carteaux had the audacity to point out to him the rudimentary errors he had committed. Carteaux was furious, but his claws were clipped by the Commissioners, who, satisfied of his incompetence, dismissed him, and Dugommier, an old officer, was placed in command. On November 25th a council of war was held, and the Commissioners placed the command of the artillery in the hands of Bonaparte.

In compliance with his instructions, the whole force of the besiegers was directed against the English redoubt Mulgrave, now Fort Caire, on the Aiguillette. An attempt to carry it by assault was made on the morning of December 17th. The troops of the Convention were driven back, and Dugommier, who headed the attempt, gave up all for lost. But fresh troops were rapidly brought up in support, another onslaught was attempted, and succeeded in overpowering the Spanish soldiers, to whom a portion of the line was entrusted; whereupon the assailants broke in, turned the flank of the English detachment, and cut down three hundred of them.

The possession of this fort rendered the further maintenance of the exterior defences of Toulon impracticable. Its effect was at once recognised by the English commander, and during the night the whole of the allied troops were withdrawn from the promontory into the city.

Meanwhile, another attack had been made, under the direction of Napoleon, on the rocky heights of Faron, which were carried, and the mountain was occupied by the Republicans, who hoisted the tricolour flag.

The garrison of Toulon consisted of above ten thousand men, and the fortifications of the town itself were as yet uninjured; but the harbour was commanded and swept by the guns of the enemy from l'Aiguillette and Faron. Sir Samuel Hood, in command of the English squadron, strongly urged the necessity of recovering the points that had been lost; but he was overruled, and it was resolved to evacuate the place.

When the citizens of Toulon became aware of this decision, they were filled with dismay. They knew but too well what fate was in store for them if left to the hands of their remorseless fellow-countrymen. Accordingly the quays were crowded with terror-stricken men and women imploring to be taken on board, whilst already the shot from Napoleon's batteries tore lanes among them, or his shells exploded in their midst. With difficulty, as many as could be accommodated were placed in boats and conveyed to the ships. Fourteen thousand were thus rescued; but Napoleon directed shot and shell among the boats, sinking some, and drowning the unhappy and innocent persons who were flying from their homes.

The prisoners now broke their chains and added to the horror, as they burst into the deserted houses, robbing and firing and murdering where resistance was offered. Next day the troops of the Convention entered the town. During the ensuing days, some hundreds of the inhabitants who had not escaped were swept together into an open place, and without any form of trial were shot.

Barras and Fréron issued a proclamation that all who considered themselves to be good citizens were required to assemble in the Champ-de-Mars under pain of death. Three thousand responded to the order. Fréron was on horseback, surrounded by the troops, cannon, and Jacobins. Turning to these latter, he said 'Go into the crowd and pick out whom you will, and range them along that wall.'

The Jacobins went in and did as desired, according to their caprice. Then, at a signal from Fréron, the guns were discharged, and the unhappy crowd swayed; some fell, others, against the wall, dropped. Fréron shouted, 'Let those who are not dead stand up.' Such as had been wounded only rose, when another volley sent them out of life.

Salicetti wrote exultingly: 'The town is on fire, and offers a hideous spectacle; most of the inhabitants have escaped. Those who remain will serve to appease the names of our brave brothers who fought with such valour'. Fouché, Napoleon's future Head of Police, wrote: 'Tears of joy stream over my cheeks and flood my soul. We have but one way in which to celebrate our victory. We have this evening sent 213 rebels under the fire of our lightning'. 'We must guillotine others,' said Barras, 'to save ourselves from being guillotined.' Executions went on for several days, and numbers of the hapless remnant perished. But even this did not satisfy the Convention. On the motion of Barrère, it was decreed that the name of Toulon should be blotted out, and a commission, consisting of Barras, Frèron, and the younger Robespierre, was ordered to continue the slaughter. Such as were able bought their lives. One old merchant of eighty-four offered all his wealth save eight hundred livres; but the revolutionary judge, coveting the whole, sent him under the guillotine, and confiscated his entire property.

Whilst the butchery was in progress, a grand dinner was given in celebration of the taking of the town. Generals, representatives of the people, sans-culottes, galley-slaves, 'the only respectable persons in the town,' as the commissioners said, sat down together, the commissioners occupying a separate table.

Toulon again gradually refilled with people, and under the Directory it was constituted the first military port of France. From Toulon Bonaparte organised his expedition to Egypt.

S BARING GOULD (1834-1924)

At a soirée in Avignon the Countess of Blessington was introduced to Mademoiselle Sombreuil, a celebrated heroine of the Revolution.

8 t h – W E H A D a good specimen of a provincial *soirée* last night, at Madame de L's, where all the *beau monde* of Avignon were assembled. Eight o'clock for an evening party, sounded strangely to our ears, that being about the hour we sit down to dinner in London; but here, it is the general hour of reunion. The Hotel de L is a very fine one; the rooms spacious and taste-fully furnished, remarkably well lighted, and containing several good works of art. One card table was set out for some of the elderly guests; but the rest amused themselves with music and conversation; both very good of their kind. We had duets, which were sung in a style of excel-lence that would not have shamed first-rate professional performers; and which had a peculiar charm for me, as indicating the perfect harmony not only of the voices, but of the lives of the singers; for nothing but the habit of very frequently practising together, could have rendered their notes so beautifully attuned.

Indeed, it was gratifying to observe the extreme cordiality that subsisted between the per-sons assembled, — all, with the exception of ourselves, old friends and neighbours, who are in the habit of meeting every evening during the winter, at each other's houses. The French possess the talent of conversation in a rare degree; their apprehension and comprehension are quick, their flow of words ready and vivacious, and their manners are distinguished by a desire to please, that half accomplishes its aim. They are, for the most part, well informed on the general subjects of interest. With the light literature of their own country they cultivate a familiar acquaintance; but their knowledge, though versatile, is rarely profound. They can talk agreeably on most topics, but instructively on few. They have the address of bringing into exhibition the whole stock of their knowledge, leaving nothing unseen; like those small deal-ers, who display the greater part of their wares in the windows of their shops, reserving no store on their shelves. In fine, they are witty, playful, and brilliant, but rarely, if ever, thought-ful, and never thoroughly erudite. Of humour, they appear to be not only deficient, but ignor-ant. A *bon mot,* an epigram, or a lively sally, they comprehend at a glance; but broad or sly humour, which is so well understood, and duly appreciated in England, has no attraction for them. I refer, of course, to the many; there may be, and, I doubt not, are, very numerous excep-tions to be found in the more studious and reflecting of both sexes; but these classes seldom enter society.

But to return to the *soirée* of Madame de L; among many distinguished persons who were assembled, the individual who the most particularly excited my attention was Madame de Vil-lume, the celebrated Mademoiselle Sombreuil, whose celebrity is among the most honoura-ble that ever was acquired by woman — the heroic discharge of the duties of a daughter in the face of danger and of death. Her father was *gouverneur des Invalides* at the commencement of the Revolution; and displayed a firmness and courage, as well as a devotion to his sovereign, worthy of example. He was arrested and cast into prison soon after the memorable 10th of August; and on the 2nd of September was on the point of being massacred by the sanguinary assassins who immolated so many noble victims; when his young and lovely daughter threw herself between him and them, and clasping him in her arms, offered her fragile person as a shield against their weapons. Her youth, her beauty, and her self-abnegation, touched even the callous hearts of the murderous band; but even their mercy was marked by a refinement in cruelty not to be surpassed by the most atrocious examples handed down from the dark ages. They consented to spare the life of her father provided she would, on the spot, drink a goblet of the human gore fast pouring from the slaughtered victims around!

She swallowed the fearful draught: and saw her father led back to prison; whence, in June, 1794, he was consigned to the scaffold, by the revolutionary tribunal: more cruel than the sanguinary band from whose vengeance his daughter had rescued him. Madame de Villume is wife to the General of that name, and is as remarkable for the exemplary discharge of all the duties of life as of those of her filial ones. She is still strikingly handsome, though her countenance is tinged with a soft melancholy that denotes the recollection of the bitter trials of her youth. Her complexion is peculiarly delicate, her hair fair, and her features small and regular; her manners are dignified and gentle, and her voice soft and sweet. She is exceedingly beloved at Avignon, and universally treated with a respectful deference, that marks the profound admiration which her filial piety has excited. I was told that she shrinks from the slightest allusion to her youthful trials, and cannot bear to look on red wine; which is never brought into her presence.

THE COUNTESS OF BLESSINGTON (1789-1849)

Monte Carlo, usually associated with wealth, fame and glamour, is also famous for its high suicide rate — a consequence of gambling.

A L L T H E L O W E S T types of humanity, the Lazaroni, the North American Indians, the half-caste Peruvians and Mexicans, resort to it with passion, and the unintellectual and those without mental culture throughout Europe will naturally pursue it as a form of excitement. It is therefore just as well that there should be places provided for these individuals of low mental and moral calibre to enjoy themselves in the only way that suits them, but again, the pity is that one of the fairest spots of Europe, this earthly paradise, should be given over to harlots and thieves, and Jew moneylenders, to rogues and fools of every description. The entire principality lives on the tables, the prince, the bishop, the canons, the soldiery, the police, the hotel-keepers, those who have villas, the cabdrivers, the waiters, the boatmen, all are bound together by a common interest — the plunder of such as come to Monte Carlo to lose their money. The institution must be kept going, every scandal must be hushed up. If a case of suicide occurs, in ten minutes every trace disappears, and no public notice is given of what has occurred. It is against the interest of every one connected with the place, with Nice also and Mentone, to allow such an event to transpire.

If any trust may be reposed in the assertions of Captain Weihe, a German naval artillery officer who has resided at Monte Carlo for three seasons, the cases are far more numerous than is supposed. According to him, directly a man has shot or hung himself, he is whisked away by the police and the body concealed till it is ascertained that no one is particularly

La Marche à la Roulette

interested in his fate. Then, at the end of the season, the bodies of the suicides are packed in cases that are weighted, and the boatmen sink them far out at sea between Monte Carlo and Corsica.

According to the same authority, the bodies were formerly thrust into the holes and cracks in the limestone on which the Casino and the tributary buildings of Monte Carlo stand, but the condition in consequence became so insanitary that the place had to be cleared of them, and a large body of workmen was imported from Italy and employed on this work, and the corpses removed were disposed of at sea. Captain Weihe asserts as a matter of his own knowledge or observation that from the upper part of the rift of Pont Larousse, in 1898, sixty corpses, from the lower by Villa Eden ten or twelve, were removed.

S BARING GOULD (1834-1924)

Self Portrait : Paul Cézanne

CHAPTER FOUR

Art
and the Artists

The French philosopher Jean-Jacques Rousseau visited the Pont du Gard with Madame de Larnage, one of the many women with whom he became romantically involved.

... I T W A S T H E first work of the Romans that I had seen. I hoped to see a monument worthy of the hands that had raised it; and for the first time in my life my expectations were surpassed by the reality. It belonged only to the Romans to produce such an effect. The aspect of this simple and noble work struck me all the more that it was in the midst of a desert where the silence and solitude increased its effect ..... I walked along the three stages of this superb construction, with a respect that made me almost shrink from treading on it. The echo of my footsteps under the immense arches made me think I could hear the strong voices of the men who had built it. I felt lost like an insect in the immensity of the work. I felt, along with the sense of my own littleness, something nevertheless which seemed to elevate my soul; I said to myself with a sigh: "Oh! that I had been born a Roman!" ..... I remained several hours in this rapture of contemplation. I came away from it in a kind of dream, and this reverie was not favorable to Madame de Larnage [the latest of the numerous objects of Rousseau's sentimental attachments]. She had been careful to warn me against the attractions of the young women of Montpellier — but not against the Pont de Gard.

JEAN JACQUES ROUSSEAU (1 7 1 2 - 1 7 7 8) (translated by B Steinman and S R Watson)

The beautiful cloisters of St Trophime at Arles date back from the 12th Century. The detailed carvings on the pillars and capitals depict scenes from the Old and New Testaments.

T H E   C O L D   G R E Y stone of the cloister of Saint-Trophime. The morning sun bright through the arches, a woman walks along, her image flashing bright and dark in sun and shadow. Thin high double columns support tiny darkened capitals, whispered reminders of ancient stories of saints and demi-gods and gods. The stone is so grey and full of shadows that even the brilliant sunlight on the grass of the cloister courtyard seems chilled. A cypress grows, its textured vertical bark, its slanting irregular growth a reproach to the narrow straight immobility of the columns. Where once monks hauled water, poured it through pierced containers to maintain the plants and lawn of their cloister through the hot and rainless summer, the invention of a rubber tube to transport the water, of a spinning two-armed machine to spray it about, frees men for other tasks, for idleness. In place of monks tourist couples wander, restless, freed for a hasty wandering incomprehending look at the dark grey stone, the arcane chipped hard-to-perceive capitals, too darkened now with the city's life. Material here to keep eyes and mind occupied for years of cloistered confinement, hard to take in anything in a few minutes, a quarter of an hour. The beardless youthful martyrs, the old nodding saints, the sacred histories. But look, there where Christ is being born, just on the other side of the narrow capital: a shepherd and his flock, and two goats reaching upward, balanced on their hind legs, to pull down toward themselves the higher branches of the tree, stretching their long necks to reach the highest, freshest leaves.

ROBERT BERNEN (1 9 8 1)

James Pope Hennessy records his impression of the great Roman bridge in his excellent book A S P E C T S   O F   P R O V E N C E .

I W A S N E V E R at the Pont du Gard till 1949. That provincial suspicion which makes one distrust too famous sights, that vanity which urges one to try to discover new or unknown places for oneself, had deterred me. This spring of 1949 I and a companion were revisiting Provence by bus, a disastrous enterprise. In a long experience of crowded and dirty French buses, I have never seen one so crushingly overloaded as that which we caught that evening. We almost fell out of the bus at Remoulins, which proved to be a huddle of three or four houses and some old women on a road. The bus lurched off, leaving us, our small handcase, and a bamboo rod on the tarmac in the evening light. We had been told that we should have to walk to the viaduct, and for a moment I did not know which way to go. Then glancing over my shoulder, I saw suddenly that we were already in the presence of the Pont du Gard, which looked still and very yellow between the black foliage of trees in the setting sun. The viaduct was half a mile away, and by some optical trick due perhaps to the perfection of its architectural proportions, it appeared far smaller than I had anticipated, almost miniature. It had, too (and this it retains on closer acquaintance), a quality of inevitability about it, as though it had grown there and had not been built: "The Pont du Gard seems, more than anything else, the completion of a landscape that had been left unfinished by mistake."

J A M E S   P O P E   H E N N E S S Y   (1 9 1 6 - 1 9 7 4)

Built in the 14th Century, the Papal Palace in Avignon presents an image of absolute impregnability. In the words of the 19th Century French novelist Prosper Mérimée:

J U S T L O O K A T the Royal Palace, the most outstanding of all the buildings, yet you would think it was an Asiatic tyrant's citadel rather than the abode of the vicar of the God of peace. Built on sheer rock, the massive towers rise to a prodigious height. Art would appear to have played no part in this vast edifice; everywhere comfort and even convenience have been sacrificed to impregnability. Not only the thickness of the walls, but their height, the ditches which surround them seem to defy attack by main force; but surprise attack has also been anticipated. The palace has been as heavily fortified within as without. Towers and high battlements dominate the main courtyard on all sides. The would-be assailant in possession of the gate and courtyard has achieved nothing as yet; he will have to undertake yet another siege. Finally when all these defences have been breached there is another tower to overcome. The gate is shattered; the enemy rushes the staircase; he is about to break through to the Pope's chosen sanctum. Suddenly the staircase comes up against a blank wall. Above there is a sort of platform only accessible by ladder, it is manned by soldiers who cut down one by one those who thought victory already theirs.

P R O S P E R   M É R I M É E   (1 8 0 3 - 1 8 7 0) (translated by J Karslake)

Pont St Benezet, Avignon's famous bridge, originally had twenty two arches but there are only four left now. Legend goes that it was built towards the end of the 12th Century by a young shepherd boy.

OVER THE RHÔNE at Avignon in southern France there stand four arches — all that remains of a beautiful twelfth-century bridge. In its day it was the dean of medieval bridges, for its builder was St Bénezèt, who, legend says, was the leader of the French Brotherhood of Bridgebuilders. And legend has many other things to say of this structure — among them the following:

One day the good people of the town of Avignon were dozing in church, when suddenly the Bishop's sermon was interrupted by a youthful shepherd lad who had entered the church unnoticed but was now running excitedly toward the altar. In amazement the Bishop stopped and stared at the youth, who, waving his arms toward the congregation, was beginning to say something. What he had to say was, he declared, a divine message: God had sent him to build a bridge over the Rhône! The people grew restless; the Bishop was openly incredulous; however, the lad became more and more insistent. At length, to bring the absurd affair to an end, the Bishop declared that he would believe the story if the shepherd could move a certain huge stone in the neighbourhood to the spot on the river bank where God wished the bridge to be built. Eagerly the lad consented to this superhuman task and dashed out to the stone, followed by the Bishop with his curious flock. The boy knelt earnestly in prayer beside the stone for a few minutes; then he rose, encircled the stone with his arms, and lifted it as easily as he would a pebble. Lightly he carried it over the river's edge and placed it where the abutment of the bridge is now. "A miracle it is — God's miracle!" cried the Bishop, kneeling in awe before the humble shepherd. And so elated were the townsfolk that they proceeded forthwith to raise, by subscription, money for the bridge.

B STEINMAN and S R WATSON (1941)

For many years Alphonse Daudet excited the indignant fury of the people of Tarascon who were deeply insulted by his amusing novels about the infamous scoundrel Tartarin and his fellow Tarasconians.

IT WAS SEPTEMBER, and it was Provence, when the vintage was coming home, five or six years ago.

From the high wagonette, drawn by the rough horses of the Camargue, that carried us at full speed — Mistral the poet, my son, and myself — towards the Tarascon station and the fast train to Lyons and Paris, the closing day struck us as divine, as it burned itself pale; a day suffused, exhausted, and fevered; passionate, like the fine faces of some women there. There was not a breath of air, in spite of our rattling pace. The rank rushes, with their long ribbony leaves, were straight and stiff by the wayside; and on all the country roads, snowy white with the white of dreams, where the motionless dust creaked beneath the wheels, passed a slow procession of wagons laden with the black grape, nothing but the black, followed by young men and girls, all tall and well set up, long-legged and dark-eyed. Clusters of black eyes and of black grapes;

you could see nothing else in the tubs and hods, under the slouched felt hats of the vintagers, and the head-cloth, of which the women kept the corners tight in their teeth. Here and there, in the angle of a field, against the white of the sky, rose a cross with a heavy bunch suspended as a votive offering to each of its arms. "*Ve* — look!" dropped from Mistral, touched and showing it, yet smiling with almost maternal pride in the candid paganism of his people; after which he took up his tale again — some scented, golden story of the Rhône-side, such as the Goethe of Provence sows, broadcast from those ever-open hands of his, of which one is poetry and the other reality.

Oh, miracle of words, magic concord of the hour, the scenery, and the brave rustic legend that the poet reeled off for us all along the narrow way, between the fields of mulberry and olive and vine! How well we felt, and how fair and light was life! All of a sudden my eyes were darkened, my heart was compressed with anguish. "Father, how pale you are!" said my son; and I had scarcely strength to murmur, as I showed him the castle of King René, whose four towers in the level distance watched me come, "There's Tarascon!"

You see, we had a terrible account to settle, the Tarasconians and I! Clever people as they are — like all our people there — I knew their backs were up; they bore me a black grudge for my jokes about their town and about their great man, the illustrious, the delicious Tartarin. I had often been warned by letter, by anonymous threats: "If ever you come through Tarascon, look out!" Others had brandished over me the vengeance of the hero: "Tremble; the old lion has still his beak and claws!" A lion with a beak — the deuce!

Graver still, I had it from a commandant of the mounted police of the region that a bagman from Paris, who, through a sorry identity of name, or simply as a 'lark', had signed 'Alphonse Daudet' on the register of the inn, had found himself assailed at the door of a café, and threatened with a bath in the Rhône. Our honest Tarasconians have in their blood this game of the ducking.

'Willy-nilly, they shall take the jump from the big window of Tarascon into the Rhône,' is the sense of an old Provençal catch of '93, which is still sung there, emphasized with gruesome comments on the drama of which King René's towers were at that time witness. So, as it was not quite to my taste to take a header from the big window, I had always in my journeys south given a wide berth to the good city. And now, this time, an evil fate, the desire to go and put my arm about my dear Mistral, the impossibility of catching the express at another point, threw me straight into the jaws of the beaked lion.

In vain Mistral tried to reassure me. 'Oh, come! don't mind! I'll talk to the crowd;' while my boy, a young medical student of the Paris hospitals, took his bistoury out of his instrument case, and prepared resolutely to rip something up. All this only deepened my gloom.

It was a strange thing, but perceptibly, as we drew nearer to the city, there were fewer and fewer people on the way, and we met fewer of the vintagers' carts. Soon we had nothing before us but the white, dusty road, and all around us, in the country, the space and solitude of the desert.

'It's very queer,' said Mistral, under his breath, rather uneasy. 'You'd say it was a Sunday.'

'If it were a Sunday you'd hear the bells,' added my son, in the same tone; for there was something oppressive in the silence that lay upon city and suburb. There was nothing, not a bell, not a cry, not even the jingle of a country cart, clear in the resonant air; yet the first houses of the outer town stood up at the end of the road — one of the oil-mills, the custom-house, newly whitewashed.

We were getting in. And hardly had we advanced into the long street when our stupor was great to find it deserted, with doors and windows closed, without a dog or a cat, a chick or a child — without a creature: the smoky portal of the blacksmith disfeatured of the two wheels that it usually wore on either flank: and the tall trellis-screen, with which the local doorway protects itself against flies, taken in, departed, like the flies themselves, like the exquisite puff of garlic which, at that hour, should have proceeded from the local kitchen.

Tarascon without the smell of garlic! Is that the sort of thing you can fancy?

Mistral and I exchanged looks of awe, and really it was not for nothing. To expect the howl of a delirious people, and to find the place a Pompeii — as silent as death! Farther on, where we could put a name on every dwelling, on all the shops familiar to our eyes from childhood, this impression of the empty and the forsaken was still more startling.

Closed was Bézuquet, the druggist, on the bit of a Square; closed likewise was Costecalde, the armorer, and Rébuffat, the pastry-cook, "the famous place for caramels." Vanished the scutcheon of Notary Cambalalette, and the sign, on painted cloth, of Marie Joseph Escour-baniès, manufacturer of the Arles sausage; for the Arles sausage has always been turned out at Tarascon. I point out in passing this great denial of historic justice.

But, in fine, what had become of the Tarasconians?

Now our wagonette rolled over the Long Walk, in the tepid shade, where the plane-trees interspaced their smooth white trunks, and where never a cicada was singing: the cicadas had flown away! Before the house of our Tartarin, all of whose shutters were closed — it was as blind and dumb as its neighbours — against the low wall of the bit of a garden, never a black-ing-box, never a little shoeblack to call out, 'A shine, Mossoo?'

'Perhaps there's cholera,' one of us said.

At Tarascon, sure enough, on the arrival of an epidemic the inhabitant moves out and encamps under canvas, at a goodish distance from the town, until the bad air has passed by. At this word cholera, which throws every Provençal into a blue 'funk', our coachman applied the whip to his steeds, and a few minutes later we pulled up at the steps of the station, perched on the very top of the great viaduct which skirts and commands the city.

Here we found life again, and human voices and faces. The trains were up and down, in and out, on the net-work of rails; they drew up with the slamming of doors, the bawling of stations: 'Tarascon; stop five minutes; change for Nîmes, Montpelier, Cette.' Mistral went straight off to the superintendent, an old servant who has never left his platform for five-and-thirty years.

'Well, now, Master Picard, what's the matter? Your Tarasconians — where are they? What have you done with them?'

To which the other, greatly surprised at our surprise: 'Where are they? You don't know? Don't you read anything, then? Yet they've advertised it enough, their island, their Port Taras-con. Well, yes, then, my dear fellow, they've gone, the Tarasconians; gone to plant a colony;

Tartarin the illustrious at their head, carrying off with them the symbol of the city — the very Tarasque.'

He broke off to give orders, to bustle along the line, while at our feet, erect in the sunset, we saw the towers, the belfries and bells, of the forsaken city, its old ramparts gilded by the sun to the superb tone of a 'browned' pasty, and giving exactly the idea of a woodcock pie of which the crust only was left.

'And tell me, Monsieur Picard,' asked Mistral of the superintendent, who had come back to us with his good smile — no more uneasy than that at the thought of Tarascon 'on the go' — 'was this emigration *en masse* some time ago?'

'Six months.'

'And you've had no news of them?'

'None whatever.'

Cracky! as they say down there. Some time later we had news indeed, detailed and precise, sufficiently so to enable me to relate to you the exodus of this gallant little people under the lead of its hero, and the dreadful misadventures that fell upon it. Pascal has said, 'We need the agreeable and the real; but this agreeable should itself be taken from the true'. I have tried to conform to his doctrine. My story is taken from the true — put together from letters of the emigrants, from the *Memorial* of the young secretary of Tartarin, and from depositions published in the authorized law reports — so that when you come across some Tarasconade more extravagant than usual, I'll be hanged if I invented it!

ALPHONSE DAUDET (1 8 4 0 - 1 8 9 7) (translated by F Davies)

Peire Vidal, whose poetry is among the finest of the troubadours', probably lived from 1175-1212.

NOW PEIRE VIDAL was of Toulouse, and was the son of a furrier. And he sang better than any man alive, and was a good troubadour. And he was one of the maddest of men, for he weened that all he willed came verily to pass. And no man in the world was so apt as he in the making of poems and of sweet melodies; and none so mad as he in his talk of arms, and love, and in the slandering of others. And in good sooth did a knight of Saint Giles cause his tongue to be cut out, because he made believe that he was his wife's lover; but Sir Hugh of Baux caused him to be healed of his hurt, and doctored, and, when he was healed, he passed beyond the sea, and brought home with him a Grecian woman, who was given him to wife in Cyprus.

And they had made believe to him that she was the niece of the Emperor of Constantinople; and that, through her, he should of right have the empire. Wherefore, in the making of ships, he spent all he could gain, for he weened he could win him the empire. And he bore the Imperial arms, and styled himself Emperor and his wife Empress.

And he was wont to love whatsoever good ladies he set eyes on, and to seek their love; and all made assent unto his prayers, wherefore, though one and all beguiled him, he weened he was each lady's lover, and that each one was dying for his love. And whither he went he brought with him rich chargers and rich armour, and a throne and a royal tent, and deemed himself one of the doughtiest knights in the world and the most beloved of ladies.

Now Peire Vidal, even as I have told you, loved all good ladies, and weened they loved him likewise. And it chanced that he loved Azalais, wife of Lord Barral of Marseilles, the which lord bore Peire Vidal greater good will than any man alive, for his fair poems, and for the great drolleries that he spoke and did. Moreover, they named one another 'Rainier', and Peire Vidal had ever free access to him at all hours and beyond all other men. And Lord Barral knew full well that Peire Vidal loved his wife, and made merry over it, and over all the follies that he spoke and did. And all men did as much; the lady also made jest of it, as did all other ladies whom he loved, each one speaking him fair, and promising all that it pleased him to ask of them. And he, so wise he was, gave ear to all they said. And, when Peire Vidal and the lady fell out together, Lord Barral it was that made peace betwixt them, and made her promise all that was asked of her.

Now it happened upon a day that Peire Vidal knew that Lord Barral had arisen from his bed, and that the lady was alone in the chamber; so he entered into the chamber, and drew near unto my Lady Azalais' bed, and finding her asleep, knelt down before her, and kissed her on the mouth. And she felt the kiss, and weened it was her lord, and laughing uplifted herself. And when she beheld Peire Vidal the fool, she began to cry out, and to raise great uproar. And hearing this, her maidens hastened unto her from within, saying 'What ails you?' And Peire Vidal went out in haste, and the lady bade call Lord Barral, and made her plaint unto him, because that Peire Vidal had kissed her, and weeping prayed him to avenge her. Then Lord Barral, even as a man of worth and sense, made light of the matter, and fell to laughing and to chiding his wife, for that she had noised abroad what the fool had done. Nathless his rebukes did not so avail him as to hinder his wife from noising abroad the matter, and from striving to bring ill upon Peire Vidal, and from making great threats against him. Then Peire Vidal, from fear thereof, entered into a ship and went to Genoa; and there he tarried until he passed beyond the seas with King Richard, for he was in sore fear lest my Lady Azalais should seek to compass his death. There he abode long time, and there he made many a good song, in the which he minded him of the kiss he had stolen of her.

MEDIAEVAL LIVES OF THE TROUBADOURS (c 1 3 0 0) (translated by I Farnell)

In 1854 Frédéric Mistral, then an unpublished poet of 25, formed a literary society to revive the Provençal language and folklore. It was called the Félibrige after an old Provençal song.

Félibre (To Frédéric Mistral, Neveu)

Of all the immortality-concoctors
Who cook their would-be by their midnight lamps —
They blame me that I shun my fellow-doctors
To haunt the quays, the markets, and the camps.

Yeats on his intellect could pull the blinds
Rapping up spooks. He fell for freaks and phoneys.
Weird blue-stockings with damp, flatfooted minds,
Theosophists and fakirs, were his cronies.

I, too, can loose my Pegasus to graze,
Carouse with drunken fiddlers at the Fair,
And with the yokelry on market days
Jingle in spurs and sheepskins round the square.

They say it is a waste of time. I differ.
To learn should be as easy as to look.
You could not pass examinations stiffer,
Nor sweat a deeper learning from the book —

Than to be passed for native by the million
When chiming in at horsefairs with my bid.
This taught me the Gallego and Castilian
By which I know my 'Lusiads' and the 'Cid'.

Comradeship, though it's dated and antique,
Is all the Anthropology I know.
The Zulu and Swahili that I speak
I learned no more than water learned to flow.

Collective writers at my name grow raucous,
And pedants raise a loud indignant cry
Like the New Critics and the Kenyon caucus —
Or poultry, when a falcon cruises by!

I've had my share of solitudes and caverns.
What mountain-tops could teach I learned of old,
But got the true Provençal in the taverns
By which I sailed into then 'Isles of Gold'.

To sit with Mistral under the green laurels
From which his children gathered me my crown,
While the deep wine that is the end of quarrels
Glows through me like the sunset going down.

ROY CAMPBELL (1910-1983)

Many of Ezra Pound's Cantos refer to the Troubadours and their lyrics, often actually using Provençal language.

What you have done, Odysseus,
          We know what you have done .....
And that Guillaume sold out his ground rents
(Seventh of Poitiers, Ninth of Aquitain).
'Tant las fotei com auzirets
'Cen e quatre vingt et veit vetz ..... '
The stone is alive in my hand, the crops
          will be thick in my death-year .....
Till Louis is wed with Eleanor
And had (He, Guillaume) a son that had to wife
The Duchess of Normandia whose daughter
Was wife to King Henry e maire del rei jove ....
Went over sea till day's end (he, Louis, with Eleanor)
Coming at last to Acre.
'Ongla, oncle' saith Arnaut
     Her uncle commanded in Acre,
That had known her in girlhood
          (Theseus, son of Aegeus)
And he, Louis, was not at ease in that town,
And was not at ease by Jordan
As she rode out to the palm-grove
Her scarf in Saladin's cimier.
Divorced her in that year, he Louis,
          divorcing thus Aquitaine.
And that year Plantagenet married her
          (that had dodged past 17 suitors)
Et quand lo reis Lois lo entendit
          mout er fasché.
Nauphal, Vexis, Harry joven
In pledge for all his life and life of all his heirs
Shall have Gisors, and Vexis, Neufchastel
But if no issue Gisors shall revert .....
'Need not wed Alix .... in the name
Trinity holy indivisible ..... Richard our brother
Need not wed Alix once his father's ward and .....
But whomso he choose ..... for Alix, etc .....
Eleanor, domna jauzionda, mother of Richard,
Turning on thirty years (wd. have been years before this)

By river-marsh, by galleried church-porch,
Malemorte, Correze, to whom:
                'My Lady of Ventadour
'Is shut by Eblis in
'And will not hawk nor hunt
                nor get her free in the air
'Nor watch fish rise to bait
'Nor the glare-wing'd flies alight in the creek's edge
'Save in my absence, Madame.
                '"Que la lauzeta mover"
'Send word I ask you to Eblis
                you have seen that maker
'And finder of songs so far afield as this
'That he may free her,
                who sheds such light in the air.'

E lo Sordels si fo di Mantovana,
Son of a poor knight, Sier Escort,
And he delighted himself in chançons
And mixed with the men of the court
And went to the court of Richard Saint Boniface
And was there taken with love for his wife
                Cunizza, da Romano,
That freed her slaves on a Wednesday
Masnatas et servos, witness
Picus de Farinatis
and Don Elinus and Don Lipus
                sons of Farinato de' Farinati
'free of person, free of will
'free to buy, witness, sell, testate.'
A marito subtraxit ipsam .....
                dictum Sordellum concubuisse:
                'Winter and summer I sing of her grace,
                As the rose is fair, so fair is her face,
                Both Summer and Winter I sing of her,
                The snow makyth me to remember her.'

And Cairels was of Sarlat .....
                Theseus from Troezene
And they wd. have given him poison
But for the shape of his sword-hilt.
                EZRA POUND (1885-1972)

Paul Cézanne was born in Aix in 1839. For a while he lived in Paris where he worked briefly with the Impressionists, but he returned to his native town in 1870 preferring to work alone. This is how an English poet and painter visualises the scene.

Cézanne at Aix

And the mountain: each day
Immobile like fruit. Unlike, also
— Because irreducible, because
Neither a component of the delicious
And therefore questionable,
Nor distracted (as the sitter)
By his own pose and, therefore,
Doubly to be questioned: it is not
Posed. It is. Untaught
Unalterable, a stone bridgehead
To that which is tangible
Because unfelt before. There
In its weathered weight
Its silence silences, a presence
Which does not present itself.

CHARLES TOMLINSON (1927-)

Cézanne and the people of Aix were usually at loggerheads. They did not appreciate his work and he was constantly irritated by what he saw as their petty attitudes. Auguste-Henri Pontier, keeper of Aix Museum, particularly annoyed him. Here is a letter written to his son Paul in Paris.

My dear Paul,   Aix, 2nd September, 1906

It is nearly 4 o'clock, there is no air at all. The weather is still stifling. I am waiting for the moment when the carriage will take me to the river. I spend some pleasant hours there. There are some large trees, they form a vault over the water. I am going to a spot known as the *Gour de Martelly,* it is on the little *'chemin des Milles'* which leads to Montbriant. Towards the evening cows come which are being brought there to pasture. There is plenty of material to study and make masses of pictures. Sheep also came to drink, but they disappear rather quickly. Some workmen, painters, approached me and told me that they would willingly paint in the same way that I do, but that at the drawing school they are not taught that. I told them that Pontier was a dirty brute, they seemed to approve. You see that there is really not much news. It is still hot, it does not rain, and it does not seem as if it would rain for a long time. I do not really know what to tell you except that I met Demolins four or five days ago and that he seemed to me to be very artificial. Our judgement must be much influenced by our mental state.

I embrace you and mamma with all my heart.

Your father,   PAUL CÉZANNE (1839-1906) (translated by M Kaye)

Van Gogh wrote many letters from Arles to his brother Bernard explaining his developing ideas about art.

Arles, second half of June 1888

My dear comrade Bernard,

More and more it seems to me that the pictures which must be made so that painting should be wholly itself, and should raise itself to a height equivalent to the serene summits which the Greek sculptors, the German musicians, the writers of French novels reached, are beyond the power of an isolated individual; so they will probably be created by groups of men combining to execute an idea held in common.

One may have a superb orchestration of colors and lack ideas. Another one is cram-full of new concepts, tragically sad or charming, but does not know how to express them in a sufficiently sonorous manner because of the timidity of a limited palette. All the more reason to regret the lack of corporative spirit among the artists, who criticize and persecute each other, fortunately without succeeding in annihilating each other.

You will say that this whole line of reasoning is banal — so be it! However, the thing itself — the existence of a renaissance — this fact is certainly no banality.

Garden With Thistles : Vincent Van Gogh

A technical question. Just give me your opinion on it in your next letter. I am going to put the *black* and the *white,* just as the color merchant sells them to us, boldly on my palette and use them just as they are. When — and observe that I am speaking of the simplification of color in the Japanese manner — when in a green park with pink paths I see a gentleman dressed in black and a justice of the peace by trade (the Arab Jew in Daudet's *Tartarin* calls this honorable functionary zouge de paix) who is reading *L'Intransigeant* .....

Over him and the park a sky of a simple cobalt.

..... then why not paint the said zouge de paix with ordinary bone black and the *Intransigeant* with simple, quite raw white? For the Japanese artist ignores reflected colors, and puts the flat tones side by side, with characteristic lines marking off the movements and the forms.

In another category of ideas — when for instance one composes a motif of colors representing a yellow evening sky, then the fierce hard white of a white wall against this sky may be expressed if necessary — and this in a strange way — by raw white, softened by a neutral tone, for the sky itself colors it with a delicate lilac hue. Furthermore imagine in that landscape which is so naïve, and a good thing too, a cottage whitewashed all over (the roof too) standing in an orange field — certainly orange, for the southern sky and the blue Mediterranean provoke an orange tint that gets more intense as the scale of blue colors gets a more vigorous tone — then the black note of the door, the windows and the little cross on the ridge of the roof produce a simultaneous contrast of black and white just as pleasing to the eye as that of blue and orange.

Or let us take a more amusing motif: imagine a woman in a black-and-white checked dress in the same primitive landscape with a blue sky and an orange soil — that would be a rather funny sight, I think. In Arles they often do wear black-and-white checks.

Suffice it to say that black and white are also colors, for in many cases they can be looked upon as colors, for their simultaneous contrast is as striking as that of green and red, for instance.

The Japanese make use of it for that matter. They express the mat and pale complexion of a young girl and the piquant contrast of the black hair marvelously well by means of white paper and four strokes of the pen. Not to mention their black thornbushes starred all over with a thousand white flowers.

At last I have seen the Mediterranean, which you will probably cross sooner than I shall.

I spent a week at Saintes-Maries, and to get there I drove in a diligence across the Camargue with its vineyards, moors and flat fields like Holland. There, at Saintes-Maries, were girls who reminded one of Cimabue and Giotto — thin, straight, somewhat sad and mystic. On the perfectly flat, sandy beach little green, red, blue boats, so pretty in shape and color that they made one think of flowers. A single man is their whole crew, for these boats hardly venture on the high seas. They are off when there is no wind, and make for the shore when there is too much of it.

Gauguin, it seems, is still sick.

I am very eager to know what you have been working at lately — I myself am still doing nothing but landscapes — enclosed a sketch. I should also very much like to see Africa, but I

The Artist's Bedroom in Arles: Vincent Van Gogh

hardly make any definite plans for the future, it will all depend on circumstances.

What I should like to find out is the effect of an intenser blue in the sky. Fromentin and Gérôme see the soil of the South as colorless, and a lot of people see it like that. My God, yes, if you take some sand in your hand, if you look at it closely, and also water, and also air, they are all colorless, looked at in this way. *There is no blue without yellow and without orange,* and if you put in blue, then you must put in yellow, and orange too, mustn't you? Oh well, you will tell me that what I write to you are only banalities.

A handshake in thought,

Sincerely yours, Vincent

V I N C E N T   V A N   G O G H   (1 8 5 3 - 1 8 9 0) (translated by J Van Gogh-Bonger)

The creator of the G O R M E N G H A S T *novels pays tribute to a great painter.*

Van Gogh

Dead, the Dutch Icarus who plundered France
And left her fields the richer for our eyes.
Where writhes the cypress under burning skies,
Or where proud cornfields broke at his advance,
Now burns a beauty fiercer than the dance
Of primal blood that stamps at throat and thighs.
Pirate of sunlight! and the laden prize
Of coloured earth and fruit in summer trance

Where is your fever now? and your desire?
Withered beneath a sunflower's mockery,
A suicide you sleep with all forgotten.
And yet your voice has more than words for me
And shall cry on when I am dead and rotten
From quenchless canvases of twisted fire.

MERVYN PEAKE (1911-1968)

Picasso and Cocteau first met in 1915 and became friends. Although there were periods of coolness between them Cocteau's admiration for Picasso as an artist never wavered.

Ode to Picasso

I THE SEATED MAN

The mirror's gold
circles roundabout.

The tamer of muses, who ties
a saucepan
to the poodle in the troupe,
is punished in his turn
and contemplates
a dirty trick,
a spoke in the wheel, for,
having teased them, he was
caught in their fearsome dance,
and he's looking

for a way to get out.

II THE MUSES

The accident which could have happened
ends in flight.

CASTING OUT NINES;
he was playing alone
and his hand puts the muses out of place.

Four queens:
a hinge doubles the number;
eight of them now
    and the idler, Polyhymnia.

The
nine
new
muses,
all but one, for
the surplus Polyhymnia
(she lives with me)
takes me to the picador's place;
but the master's eye sends her
back at once
to number 9
and her thumb spreads out the group
like a fan.

Even in this cloister
little Erato is angry
through being lovely without any hair.
    A tonic sol-fa of thicknesses
    drapes Euterpe;

once they conducted orchestras
in the palace of the note factory,
whose motor beats
it's your heart.

Terpsichore, taking care
to support all these ladies
well balanced
on her hip,
with a costume of velvet and gold.

Listening to your magic guitar,
objects follow you Orpheus
until they acquire the shape you wish.

Bar-counter Clio, Calliope
telephones news items
and Urania lights the gas-lamps
which beautify the chestnut trees below.

Punch and Judy   the guillotine
        Thalia
         and
        Melpomene.
Then the drums of Santerre
make you silent, chattering queens.
              The solitary man
              eats the city.

His distributor delivers you
completely different.
     He shares out
   the sun   the shade
and since he's broken his guitar
over Clio's big head,
she sways and she forgets
the order of dates.

    He marries you. He sends you away.
    He walks along the asphalt pavement
    so soft at half past seven in September
    beside the great ink-anchor cafés
    where death wrote its letters
    beneath a Christmas chandelier.
    Where? Who? What? What? He frees you
    and consults obedience.

The bat opens a right-angled eye.

Dancer dressed in paint.

Maison close in every sense:
astonishing discovery.

A rope-soled silence
precedes the pimp

whom Mnemosyne pays nine times,
for she keeps precise accounts
concerning her daughters.

Nothing in his sleeves   Nothing in his pockets
      Would some gentleman
      lend his hat
to the harlequin from Port-Royal.

JEAN COCTEAU (1 8 8 9 - 1 9 6 3) (translated by Margaret Crosland)

Paul Éluard, the French lyric poet, wrote several poems about contemporary painters. This one is about Georges Braque who spent his last years painting at Le Cannet.

Georges Braque

A bird flies away,
It discards the clouds like a useless veil,
It has never feared the light,
Enclosed in its flight,
It has never owned a shadow.

Shells of harvests broken by the sun.
All the leaves in the woods say yes,
They know only how to say yes,
Every question, every reply
And the dew flows in the depths of this yes.

A man with roving eyes descries the sky of love.
He gathers its wonders
Like leaves in a wood,
Like birds in their wings
And men in their sleep.

PAUL ÉLUARD (1 8 9 5 - 1 9 5 2) (translated by D Gascoygne)

Matisse called his famous Chapel at Vence his 'masterpiece'. He designed and decorated it in four years between 1947 and 1951, when he was already an old man, and saw it as, 'the result of a lifetime devoted to the search for truth'. He presented the Chapel to the local Bishop with the following letter.

Your Excellency:

I present to you in all humility the Chapel of the Rosary of the Dominican Sisters of Vence. I beg you to excuse my inability to present this work to you in person since I am prevented by my state of health: the Reverend Father Couturier has been willing to do this for me.

This work has taken me four years of exclusive and assiduous work and it represents the result of my entire active life. I consider it, in spite of its imperfections, to be my masterpiece. May the future justify this judgment by an increasing interest over and above the high significance of this moment. I count, your Excellency, upon your long experience of men and your wisdom to judge an effort which issues from a life consecrated to the search for truth.

HENRI MATISSE (1869-1954)

Here is part of the Bishop's reply.

..... The human author of all that we see here is a man of genius who, all his life, worked, searched, strained himself, in a long and bitter struggle, to draw near the truth and the light .....

Remember the parable, 'it is not he who conceals the talents granted him by God, so as to guard them selfishly, who deserves to be rewarded, but he who at the price of much labour and suffering, having made the talents he received bear fruit, returns them to God on the day of accounting. Then truly he deserves to be called: good and loyal servant.'

(translated by A Barr)

The painter Marc Chagall spent many of his later years in Vence where he retained a strong commitment to Judaism. In June 1967 the Six Day War inspired this passionate letter from Vence.

I WOULD LIKE to be younger, leave my pictures and go to be together with you, bestow upon my last years the sweet pleasure of living amongst people loving as my colors. ..... I have steadfastly believed that without a manly and Biblical feeling in the heart, life has no value. If the Semitic folk have survived in the difficult struggle for a bit of bread ..... [it has been due to] ..... our burning national ideals on our national earth. They [the Jews] want to show that they are like other folk. The anti-Semites seek to attack us as once had done the Pharoahs. But we passed through the sea of the ghettos and our victory was eternalized in the Haggadah. We stand before the world as an example of manly soul. Will the wind carry away all our ideals, our courage, our culture of twelve thousand years? History again places the task into our hands — easy or difficult. Let the world tremble when they hear our call for righteousness. Thousands upon thousands of people everywhere are with you. Only those without a land are with our enemies.

Perhaps I am in my dotage. But I want to bless you instead of weeping and trembling. I would like to hope that the land of the great French Revolution, the land of Zola, Balzac, Watteau, Cézanne, Baudelaire, Claudel, Péguy will soon speak out to staunch this world shame. I hope that America with its democracy, [England] the land of Shakespeare and also [Russia] the land of Dostoevsky, Moussorsky, my native land, will begin to shout so that the world would have to put an end to this mania and give the people of Israel a possibility to live freely on their own land. ..... No one will any longer be able to breathe when people permit their awareness to fall asleep. The last token of talent will awaken and their words will be left without a resonance. To allow Israel and the Jews to be suffocated is to destroy the soul of the entire Biblical world. No new religion can survive without that precise drop of heart's blood and we will see if we are worthy to live any longer or to be disintegrated by the atomic bomb. My anguish is in my eyes which you cannot see and my hopes are locked in my windows of the twelve tribes which now lie hidden among you in Israel.

MARC CHAGALL (1887-1985) (translated by S Alexander)

This warm, light-hearted tribute to Chagall is from the pen of Louis Aragon, surrealist, poet and socialist.

A Very Small Chagall

A very small Chagall comprising the universe
With colour and perspective and everything provided
Painting all askew and the canvas in reverse
And far too many people all lop-sided
The guests look hungry and just a trifle silly
Nothing quite ready and the table needs setting
Send the horse to the grocer's to fetch some roses
A very small Chagall eyes larger than the belly
A very small Chagall like a wedding
A stray violinist from somewhere in the neighbourhood
A very small Chagall forgotten in a mirror
A very small Chagall looking rather good in a blue sunday suit
           with some orange near the ear
A very small Chagall with lovers on the roof
I've lost the ring and gloves whatever shall I do
For the key to the picture eludes me too
Besides the guests have left and they haven't seen the bride

Such a very small Chagall
        but I'm hanged if I know where to hang it

LOUIS ARAGON (1897-1982) (translated by W Alwyn)

Self Portrait with a Straw Hat : Henri Matisse

CHAPTER FIVE

Travellers

The Russian poet, novelist and critic Vladimir Nabokov lived in France and Germany as a young man between the wars. He wrote this poem while at Sollies-Pont near Toulon.

Provence

I wander aimlessly from lane to lane,
bending a careful ear to ancient times:
the same cicadas sang in Caesar's reign,
upon the walls the same sun clings and climbs.

The plane tree sings: with light its trunk is pied;
the little shop sings: delicately tings
the bead-stringed curtain that you push aside —
and, pulling on his thread, the tailor sings.

And at a fountain with a rounded rim,
rinsing blue linen, sings a village girl,
and mottle shadows of the plane tree swim
over the stone, the wickerwork, and her.

What bliss it is, in this world full of song,
to brush against the chalk of walls, what bliss
to be a Russian poet lost among
cicadas trilling with a Latin lisp!

VLADIMIR NABOKOV (1899-1977)

Robert Louis Stevenson, author of TREASURE ISLAND, *travelled widely throughout the world. It was while convalescing on a journey through France that he met his future wife.*

The Country of the Camisards

We travelled in the print of olden wars;
Yet all the land was green;
And love we found, and peace,
Where fire and war had been.

They pass and smile, the children of the sword —
No more the sword they wield;
And O, how deep the corn
Along the battlefield!

ROBERT LOUIS STEVENSON (1850-1894)

Here is the story of the founding of Marseilles by the Phoenicians.

BETWEEN THE 7TH and 6th Centuries BC, the Phoenicians ..... after consultation with the gods, made up an expedition of men and women, taking with them tools, plants and everything needed to found a colony. They set off under the command of Simos and Protis. The expedition landed at Ephesus, where the oracle had ordered it to halt, so that Diana could show them who was to lead them. There, a supernatural phenomenon occurred: a famous priestess called Aristarché saw the goddess in a dream. On her instructions she took one of the statues of Diana and a piece of the sacred fire and went aboard the Phoenicians' boat so that she could set up the worship of Diana in the new colony. Thus both spiritual and temporal needs were provided for and the boat set sail towards Gaul. They landed in the Bay of Lacydon. Impressed by the suitability of the place the immigrants wanted to settle there. To do so, they needed permission from the King of the Ségobriges who ruled the country. Protis was commissioned to negotiate a treaty of alliance with him. On that very day the old King, Mann, Nann or Cenomann was to give his daughter in marriage. Protis was invited to the banquet where the other suitors had gathered. At the end of the meal, tradition decreed that the young girl should offer a bowl of water to the young man of her choice. It so happened that Gyptis, struck by Protis' good looks (beauty) handed him the bowl. The old King Mann saw this as a divine command to give the strangers a favourable welcome. Accordingly he gave the land the Phoenicians requested to his daughter as her dowry. Thus Massala was founded.

JUSTIN: BOOK   43   (599 BC) (translated by J Selby-Watson)

The ancient Greek historian Polybius tells how Hannibal crossed the Rhône with thirty seven elephants.

MEANWHILE HANNIBAL HAD reached the river and was trying to get across it where the stream was single, at a distance of four days' march from the sea. He did all he could to make the natives living by the river friendly to him, and purchased from them all their canoes of hollow trunks, and wherries, of which there were a large number, owing to the extensive sea traffic of the inhabitants of the Rhône valley. He got from them also the timber suited to the construction of these canoes; and so in two days had an innumerable supply of transports, every soldier seeking to be independent of his neighbour, and to have the means of crossing in his own hands. But now a large multitude of barbarians collected on the other side of the stream to hinder the passage of the Carthaginians. When Hannibal saw them, he came to the conclusion that it would be impossible either to force a passage in the face of so large a body of the enemy, or to remain where he was, for fear of being attacked on all sides at once: and he accordingly, on the third night, sent forward a detachment of his army with native guides, under the command of Hanno, the son of the Suffete Bomilcar. This force marched up stream along the bank for two hundred stades, until they arrived at a certain spot where the stream is divided by an eyot, and there halted. They found enough wood close at hand to enable them, by nailing or tying it together, to construct within a short time a large number of rafts good enough for temporary use; and on these they crossed in safety, without any one trying to stop them. Then, seizing upon a strong position, they kept quiet for the rest of the day: partly to refresh themselves after their fatigues, and at the same time to complete their preparations for the service awaiting them; as they had been ordered to do. Hannibal was preparing to proceed much in the same way with the forces left behind with himself; but his chief difficulty was in getting the elephants across, of which he had thirty seven.

When the fifth night came, however, the division which had crossed first started before day-break to march down the opposite bank of the river and attack the barbarians; while Hannibal, having his men in readiness, began to attempt the passage of the river. He had filled the wher-ries with the heavy-armed cavalry, and the canoes with the most active of his foot; and he now arranged that the wherries should cross higher up the stream, and the canoes below them, that the violence of the current might be broken by the former, and the canoes cross more safely. The plan for the horses was that they should swim at the stern of the wherries, one man on each side of the stern guiding three or four with leading reins: so that a considerable number of horses were brought over at once with the first detachment. When they saw what the enemy meant to do, the barbarians, without forming their ranks, poured out of their entrenchments in scattered groups, feeling no doubt of being able to stop the crossing of the Carthaginians with ease. As soon as Hannibal saw by the smoke, which was the signal agreed upon, that the advanced detachment on the other side was approaching, he ordered all to go on board, and the men in charge of the transports to push out against the stream. This was promptly done: and then began a most anxious and exciting scene. Cheer after cheer rose from the men who were working the boats, as they struggled to outstrip each other, and exerted themselves to the utmost to overcome the force of the current. On the edge of either bank stood the two armies: the one sharing in the struggles of their comrades by sympathy, and shouting encour-agement to them as they went; while the barbarians in front of them yelled their war-cries and challenged them to battle. While this was going on the barbarians had abandoned their tents, which the Carthaginians on that side of the river suddenly and unexpectedly seized. Some of them proceeded to set fire to the camp, while the greater number went to attack the men who were standing ready to resist the passage. Surprised by this unlooked-for event, some of the barbarians rushed off to save their tents, while others prepared to resist the attack of the enemy, and were now actually engaged. Seeing that everything was going as he had intended, Hannibal at once formed the first division as it disembarked: and after addressing some encouraging words to it, closed with the barbarians, who, having no time to form their ranks, and being taken by surprise, were quickly repulsed and put to flight.

Being thus master of the passage of the river, and victorious over those who opposed him, the first care of the Carthaginian leader was to bring his whole army across. This being expeditiously accomplished, he pitched his camp for that night by the river-side, and on the morrow, when he was told that the Roman fleet was anchored off the mouths of the river, he detached five hundred Numidian horsemen to reconnoitre the enemy and find out their pos-ition, their numbers, and what they were going to do; and at the same time selected suitable men to manage the passage of the elephants. These arrangements made, he summoned a meeting of his army and introduced Magilus and the other chiefs who had come to him from the valley of the Padus, and caused them to declare to the whole army, by means of an interpreter, the resolutions passed by their tribes. The points which were the strongest encouragement to the army were, first, the actual appearance of convoys inviting them to come, and promising to take part in the war with Rome; secondly, the confidence inspired by their promise of guiding them by a route where they would be abundantly supplied with necessaries, and which would lead them with speed and safety into Italy; and, lastly, the fertility and vast extent of the country to which they were going, and the friendly feelings of the men with whose assistance they were about to fight the armies of Rome.

Such was the substance of the speeches of the Celts. When they had withdrawn, Hannibal himself rose, and after reminding the soldiers of what they had already achieved, and pointing out that, though they had under his counsel and advice engaged in many perilous and dangerous enterprises, they had never failed in one, he bade them not lose courage now that the most serious part of their undertaking was accomplished. The Rhône was crossed: they had seen with their own eyes the display of goodwill and zeal of their allies. Let this convince them that they should leave the rest to him with confidence; and while obeying his orders show themselves men of courage and worthy of their former deeds. These words being received with shouts of approval, and other manifestations of great enthusiasm, on the part of the soldiers, Hannibal dismissed the assembly with words of praise to the men and a prayer to the gods on their behalf; after giving out an order that they should refresh themselves, and make all their preparations with despatch, as the advance must begin on the morrow.

When the assembly had been dismissed, the reconnoitring party of Numidians returned in headlong flight, after losing more than half their numbers. Not far from the camp they had fallen in with a party of Roman horse, who had been sent out by Publius on the same errand; and an engagement took place with such fury on either side, that the Romans and Celts lost a hundred and forty men, and the Numidians more than two hundred. After this skirmish, the Romans pursued them up to the Carthaginian entrenchments; and having surveyed it, they hastened back to announce to the Consul the presence of the enemy. As soon as they arrived at the Roman camp with this intelligence, Publius put his baggage on board ship, and marched his men up the bank of the river, with the earnest desire of forcing the enemy to give him battle.

But at sunrise on the day after the assembly, Hannibal having stationed his whole cavalry on the rear, in the direction of the sea, so as to cover the advance, ordered his infantry to leave the entrenchment and begin their march; while he himself waited behind for the elephants, and the men who had not yet crossed the river.

The mode of getting the elephants across was as follows. They made a number of rafts strongly compacted, which they lashed firmly two and two together, so as to form combined a breadth of about fifty feet, and brought them close under the bank at the place of crossing. To the outer edge of these they lashed some others and made them join exactly; so that the whole raft thus constructed stretched out some way into the channel, while the edges towards the stream were made fast to the land with ropes tied to trees which grew along the brink, to secure the raft, keeping its place and not drifting down the river. These combined rafts stretching about two hundred feet across the stream, they joined two other very large ones to the outer edges, fastened very firmly together, but connected with the others by ropes which admitted of being easily cut. To these they fastened several towing lines, that the wherries might prevent the rafts drifting down stream, and might drag them forcibly against the current and so get the elephants across on them. Then they threw a great deal of earth upon all the rafts, until they had raised the surface to the level of the bank, and made it look like the path on the land leading down to the passage. The elephants were accustomed to obey their Indian riders until they came to water, but could never be induced to step into water: they therefore led them upon this earth, putting two females in front whom the others obediently followed. When they had set foot on the rafts that were farthest out in the stream, the ropes were cut which fastened these to the other rafts, the towing lines were pulled taut by the wherries, and the elephants, with the rafts on which they stood, were quickly towed away from the mound of earth. When this happened, the animals were terror-stricken; and at first turned round and round, and rushed first to one part of the raft and then to another, but finding themselves completely surrounded by the water, they were too frightened to do anything, and were obliged to stay where they were. And it was by repeating this contrivance of joining a pair of rafts to the others, that eventually the greater part of the elephants were got across. Some of them, however, in the middle of the crossing, threw themselves in their terror into the river: but though their Indian riders were drowned, the animals themselves got safe to land, saved by the strength and great length of their probosces; for by raising these above the water, they were enabled to breathe through them, and blow out any water that got into them, while for the most part they got through the river on their feet.

The elephants having been thus got across, Hannibal formed them and the cavalry into a rearguard, and marched up the river bank away from the sea in an easterly direction, as though making for the central district of Europe.

POLYBIUS (c 2 0 4 - 1 2 2 B C) (translated by Shuckburgh)

The troubadour Marcabru wrote between 1129 and 1150. An anonymous early biographer says, 'And he was famous throughout the world; people listened to him, and they feared him because of his tongue. And he said such evil things that finally he was killed by some chatelains of Guyenne of whom he had spoken ill'. Here however is one of his gentler lyrics.

By the orchard spring, where the grass
grows green near the bank,
beneath the shade of a fruit tree,
surrounded by white flowers,
amid the singing of the new season,
I found there all alone
one who did not want my solace.

She was a maiden, fair of body,
daughter of a castle's lord;
and when I thought the birds,
the verdure and the gentle
springtime would bring her joy
and that she would hear me out,
she suddenly became transformed.

There by the fountain, tears flowed from her eyes
and sighs came from deep within her breast.
'Jesus,' she said, 'King of the world,
it is You who bring me sorrow —
Your suffering has caused my grief,
for the world's finest men all leave
for Your service, according to Your wish.

With You goes my friend,
so handsome, gentle, valiant and noble;
and I am left with nothing but distress,
endless desire and tears.
Ah! curses on King Louis
with those pleas and commands of his
which have brought my heart such sorrow!'

When I heard her grieving so
by the clear stream, I drew near
and said, 'Fair lady, such tears
blemish your face and skin;
you have no reason to despair,
for He who filled the woods with leaves,
can yet bring you great joy.'

'My lord,' she said, 'I know
that forever in the world to come
God will show me mercy
as with other sinners;
but He has taken my only cause
for joy, of which so little's left
since he embarked for far-off lands.'

MARCABRU (c 1 1 3 0 - 1 1 5 0) (translated by A Bonner)

〰〰〰〰〰〰〰〰〰〰〰〰〰〰〰〰〰〰〰〰〰〰〰〰〰〰

Steven Runciman, who has worked extensively on the history of the Crusades, here relates the story of the Children's Crusade, a moving testimony to the devotion of the ordinary people to the cause of Christianity.

O N E   D A Y   I N May 1212 there appeared at Saint-Denis, where King Philip of France was holding his court, a shepherd-boy of about twelve years old called Stephen, from the small town of Cloyes in the Orleannais. He brought with him a letter for the King, which, he said, had been given to him by Christ in person, who had appeared to him as he was tending his sheep and who had bidden him go and preach the Crusade. King Philip was not impressed by the child and told him to go home. But Stephen, whose enthusiasm had been fired by his mysterious visitor, saw himself now as an inspired leader who would succeed where his elders had failed. For the past fifteen years preachers had been going round the country-side urging a Crusade against the Moslems of the East or of Spain or against the heretics of Languedoc. It was easy for an hysterical boy to be infected with the idea that he too could be a preacher and could emulate Peter the Hermit, whose prowess had during the past century reached a legendary grandeur. Undismayed by the King's indifference, he began to preach at the very entrance to the abbey of Saint-Denis and to announce that he would lead a band of children to the rescue of Christendom. The seas would dry up before them, and they would pass, like Moses through the Red Sea, safe to the Holy Land. He was gifted with an extraordinary eloquence. Older folk were impressed, and children came flocking to his call. After his first success he set out to journey round France summoning the children; and many of his converts went further afield to work on his behalf. They were all to meet together at Vendôme in about a month's time and start out from there to the East.

Towards the end of June the children massed at Vendôme. Awed contemporaries spoke of thirty thousand, not one over twelve years of age. There were certainly several thousand of them, collected from all parts of the country, some of them simple peasants, whose parents in many cases had willingly let them go on their great mission. But there were also boys of noble birth who had slipped away from home to join Stephen and his following of 'minor prophets' as the chroniclers called them. There were also girls amongst them, a few young priests, and a few older pilgrims, some drawn by piety, others, perhaps, from pity, and others, certainly, to share in the gifts that were showered upon them all. The bands came crowding into the town, each with a leader carrying a copy of the Oriflamme, which Stephen took as the device of the Crusade. The town could not contain them all, and they encamped in the fields outside.

When the blessing of friendly priests had been given, and when the last sorrowing parents had been pushed aside, the expedition started out southward. Nearly all of them went on foot. But Stephen, as befitted the leader, insisted on having a gaily decorated cart for himself, with a canopy to shade him from the sun. At his side rode boys of noble birth, each rich enough to possess a horse. No one resented the inspired prophet travelling in comfort. On the contrary, he was treated as a saint, and locks of his hair and pieces of his garments were collected as precious relics. They took the road past Tours and Lyons, making for Marseilles. It was a painful journey. The summer was unusually hot. They depended on charity for their food, and the drought left little to spare in the country, and water was scarce. Many of the children died by the wayside. Others dropped out and tried to wander home. But at last the little Crusade reached Marseilles.

The citizens of Marseilles greeted the children kindly. Many found houses in which to lodge. Others encamped in the streets. Next morning the whole expedition rushed down to the harbour to see the sea divide before them. When the miracle did not take place, there was bitter disappointment. Some of the children turned against Stephen, crying that he had betrayed them, and began to retrace their steps. But most of them stayed on by the sea-side, expecting each morning that God would relent. After a few days two merchants of Marseilles, called, according to tradition, Hugh the Iron and William the Pig, offered to put ships at their disposal and to carry them free of charge, for the glory of God, to Palestine. Stephen eagerly accepted the kindly offer. Seven vessels were hired by the merchants, and the children were taken aboard and set out to sea. Eighteen years passed before there was any further news of them.   STEVEN RUNCIMAN (1903-)

This famous legend is the reason behind the name of the little town of Stes-Maries-de-la-Mer.

AFTER THE DEATH of Christ the Jews still raged against those who had been His friends upon earth, and the high priests fanned the flames of their anger. Now they who had been His closest friends were these — Lazarus and his two sisters, Martha and Mary; Mazimin, the friend of Lazarus; Mary Salome, and Mary the mother of James; Parmenas, one of the seven deacons; St Trophimus, St Joseph of Arimathea, and some others. They were at Jaffa upon the

THE LEGEND OF LES SAINTES MARIES

M Nash

coast of Palestine.

Many of the Jews would willingly have slain them all, but fearing the effect of their courage and faith upon the people, they choose rather to put them to a more obscure, though not less certain, death.

They throw them all into a bark without sails, oars, pilot, rudder, or food; and deliver them thus to the mercy of the waves. When they are already some way from the shore, a cry comes to them over the water. 'Tis the cry of Sarah, the servant of Mary Salome, and of the Mother of James, who would fain share the blessed fate of her mistresses. Salome takes from her shoulders her cloak, throws it upon the water, and gently it glides to the shore. Upon that holy raft the young girl is borne to the side of the bark, and, no sooner is she safely on board, than the little vessel, piloted now by an angel hand, passes unharmed among the dangerous reefs, and, gliding into the open sea, turns its prow towards the west. And His voice who stilled the billows upon the Sea of Tiberias, stills the waves about its way.

Slowly, crest after crest, the hills of their sweet country vanish from their sight. 'Farewell, farewell, holy land! Farewell, Judaea, given over henceforth to sorrow, that hast driven away thy just ones and hast crucified thy God! Farewell, land of our birth, farewell!' Who shall tell the grief that fills them as they sail over alien seas, and range the coasts of unknown lands?

One morning, while the bark is moving, always westward, over a silent sea, what is this rumbling that, from the depths of the horizon, comes swelling and deepening into a mighty roar? The hurricane is upon them. Louder and louder it howls; higher and higher the waves rise, until great fear is upon all; and even the face of Lazarus, pale always with the mortal pallor of the tomb and the shroud, blanches to hear it. Long flashes of lightning pierce the gloom, and above them the thunder peals.

Then Lazarus cries out: 'My God who hast torn me once from the tomb, be now our pilot; help us, the vessel sinks.' From the high palace of His triumph, Jesus, with pitying eyes, looks down upon His friend; and, suddenly, a long ray of sunshine flashes across the tempest. The winds abate, the great waves are stilled, the clouds disperse; and across the gently heaving water appears a fringe of golden sand. There the bark softly touches, and there the travellers, falling prostrate, return thanks: 'Our lives, that Thou hast snatched from the tempest, we hold to proclaim Thy law, O Christ!' And at that name of joy the noble land of Provence is shaken; before that new cry the forest and the plain shudder through all their being.

The saints stay their hunger upon the shell-fish that the sea has thrown up, and, for their thirst, God opens, in the arid plain, a fresh and limpid stream, that still flows beneath the church where their holy bones now rest. There they build an altar, and perform the sacred rites; and then, bent upon the conquest of Provence for Christ, they part upon their several missions.

Lazarus goes to Marseilles, of which town he becomes the first bishop. St Mary Magdalene follows her brother thither, and, thence, after a sojourn at Aix, passes to Sainte Baume, there to expiate her sins by thirty long years of penitence and tears; until, in the grotto that is in the heart of the virgin forest, she passes away to God. St Maximin, too, goes to Aix; St Trophimus carries the gospel to the Roman paganism of Arles; St Martha triumphs over the dragon in the forest of Nerluc, and founds her Christian church at Avignon. Only the two Marys, because they are now already old, remain with their servant Sarah upon the shore.

There they build a little cell, close to the oratory, and there the simple fishermen of the Camargue come to them, to hear the new faith, to listen to the wonderful story of the journey across the sea, and to drink at the miraculous stream; and there many of them are converted. Sarah, their servant, was wont to make journeys into the Camargue to beg necessaries for the holy women, and that is why she became the particular friend, and is today the chosen saint, of the gipsies whom the French call the Bohémians. For more than thirty years Mary Salomé and Mary Jacobé laboured in Provence, before pious hands laid their bodies to rest, and built a little church over their bones.   P E R C Y   A L L E N   (1 8 6 9 - 1 9 3 3)

In 1645 a native of Tours visited Marseilles at the time of the Festival of St Lasarus and was horrified at what he saw.

T H E   T O W N   C E L E B R A T E S this feast by dances that have the appearance of theatrical representations, through the multitude and variety of the figures performed. All the inhabitants assemble, men and women alike, wear grotesque masks, and go through extravagant capers. One would think they were satyrs fooling with nymphs. They hold hands, and race through the town, preceded by flutes and violins. They form an unbroken chain, which winds and wriggles in and out among the streets, and this they call *le Grand Branle*. But why this should be done in honour of S Lazarus is a mystery to me, as indeed are a host of other extravagances of which Provence is full, and to which the people are so attached, that if any one refuses to take part in them, they will devastate his crops and his belongings.

A   T R A V E L L E R   F R O M   T O U R S   (1 6 4 5) (translated by S Baring Gould)

The ardent Catholic poet Francis Jammes, born and educated in the region of Pau and Bordeaux, writes of his wish for his last journey.

Prayer to go to Paradise with the Asses

O God, when You send for me, let it be
Upon some festal day of dusty roads.
I wish, as I did ever here-below
By any road that pleases me, to go
To Paradise, where stars shine all day long.
Taking my stick out on the great highway,
To my dear friends the asses I shall say:
I am Francis Jammes going to Paradise,
For there is no hell where the Lord God dwells.

Come with me, my sweet friends of azure skies,
You poor, dear beasts who whisk off with your ears
Mosquitoes, peevish blows, and buzzing bees ......

Let me appear before You with these beasts,
Whom I so love because they bow their head
Sweetly, and halting join their little feet
So gently that it makes you pity them.
Let me come followed by their million ears,
By those that carried paniers on their flanks,
And those that dragged the cars of acrobats,
Those that had battered cans upon their backs,
She-asses limping, full as leather-bottles,
And those too that they breech because of blue
And oozing wounds round which the stubborn flies
Gather in swarms. God, let me come to You
With all these asses into Paradise.
Let angels lead us where your rivers soothe
Their tufted banks, and cherries tremble, smooth
As is the laughing flesh of tender maids.
And let me, where Your perfect peace pervades,
Be like Your asses, bending down above
The heavenly waters through eternity,
To mirror their sweet, humble poverty
In the clear waters of eternal love.

FRANCIS JAMMES (1868-1938) (translated by J Bithell)

When Petrarch made his famous ascent of Mont Ventoux with his brother his thoughts turned to the spiritual .....

BUT, AS OFTEN happens, fatigue soon followed our strenuous effort. We sat down on a rock, and then went on more slowly, I especially keeping a more modest pace. My brother chose the shortest and steepest way, directly up the ridge. Softer than he, I kept turning along the slopes, and when he called to me and pointed to the shorter way, I kept answering that I would find an easier approach on another side, and I didn't mind a longer course which would not be so steep. But this was merely an excuse for laziness. While the others kept to the high ridge I wandered in the combes without finding any gentler upward path, and I just lengthened my journey and increased my useless labor. After this vain, perplexing wandering I decided to climb straight up. Exhausted and anxious, I found my brother seated, refreshed by his long wait for me. But hardly had we left that ridge than what do I do but forget my previous digression and again tend to take a downward course! And again, rounding the combes and looking for an easy way, I landed in much difficulty. Thus I kept putting off the trouble of climbing; but man's wit can't alter the nature of things, and there is no way for anybody to reach the heights by going down.

In short, to my brother's great amusement and to my fury, the same thing happened to me three or four times within a few hours. Being so befooled, I sat down in a combe. My thought quickly turned from the material to the spiritual, and I said to myself, in approximately these words: 'What you have experienced so often today in the ascent of this mountain certainly happens to you and to many who are striving for the blessed life. But the spiritual straying is not so easily to be perceived, for the movements of the body are in the open, while those of the soul are hidden and invisible. The life that we call blessed is situated on a high place; and narrow, we are told, is the way that leads to it; and many hills stand in the way, and we must advance from virtue to virtue up shining steps. The summit is the ultimate goal, the terminus of the road on which we journey .....

'What,' I said to myself, 'holds you back? Surely nothing but the level road that seems at first sight easier, amid base earthly pleasures. But after much wandering you will either have to climb upward eventually with your long-borne burden to the heights of the blessed life, or lie sluggishly in the valley of your sins. And if — I shudder at the thought! — the darkness and the shadows of death find you there, you will spend an eternal night in perpetual torture.'

These thoughts, remarkably enough, spurred my mind and body to accomplish what remained to be done. God grant that my soul may follow the road for which I long day and night, as today I journeyed with my corporeal feet, conquering all difficulties! .....

One hill dominates all the others; it is called by the mountaineers *Filiolus,* or Little Son; why, I don't know, unless by antiphrasis, for it seems the father of all the mountains round about. There is a small level space at the top. There, exhausted, we came to rest.

On reaching the top he experienced climber's euphoria which leads to one of his rare prose passages about his love for Laura.

AT FIRST, AFFECTED by the rare quality of the air and by the wide-spreading view, I stand as if stunned. I look about. Clouds lie far below. The tales of Athos and Olympus seem less incredible when what I read of them comes true on this less famous mountain. I look toward Italy, whither most my soul inclines. The noble snow-topped Alps seem close by, far away though they are. I admit that I sighed for the Italian skies, evident more to my thought than to my eyes, and unspeakable longing invaded me to see again my friend [Giacomo Colonna] and my native land, although I reproached myself for this somewhat unmanly weakness .....

Then a new thought came to me, rather of time than space. I said to myself: 'Today ten years have passed since you finished your youthful studies and left Bologna. Oh immortal God! Oh immutable Wisdom! What changes in your character have these years seen!' I suppress much, for I have not yet reached a safe harbor, from which to look back on the storms of the past. The time will perhaps come when I shall review all my past deeds in their order, prefacing them with the words of your St Augustine: 'I wish to recall the filth of my past and the carnal corruptions of my soul, not that I love them, but that I may love thee, O my God!' Indeed, an obscure and toilsome course lies before me. What I used to love, I love no longer. No, I am lying. I love it still, but more moderately. No, again I have lied. I love, but with more shame, more sadness; and now at last I have told the truth. This is the fact: I love, but I love what I long not to love, what I should like to hate. I love nonetheless, but unwillingly, under compulsion, with sadness and mourning. I feel in myself, wretchedly, the sense of Ovid's famous line: 'I shall hate if I can; otherwise I shall love in my own despite.'

FRANCESCO PETRARCH (1304-1374) (translated by Morris Bishop)

John Evelyn's fascinating diary of European travel was not published until 1818, about 170 years after he wrote this piece about his time in Avignon and Marseilles.

Avignon

HENCE LEAVING OUR barque, we tooke horse (se[e]ing but at some distance the Towne and Principality of Orange) and lodging one night on the Way ariv'd by noone at Avignon: This Citty has belong'd to the Popes ever since Clem: the 6ts tyme, being Anno 1352, alienated by Jeane Queene of Naples and Sicily. Entring the Gates of this towne the Souldiers at the Guard tooke our Pistols and Carbines from us, and examin'd us very strictly; after that having obtain'd the Governors leave, and Vice-Legat to tarry for 3 dayes, we were civily conducted to our lodging.

The City is plac'd on the Rhodanus, and divided from the newer part, or Towne (which is situate on the other side of the River) by a very faire bridge of stone, which has been broken, at one of whose extreames is a very high rock on which a strong Castle well furnish'd with Artillery. The Walls of the Citty (being all square huge free stone) are absolutely the most neate and best in repaire that in my life I ever saw: It is full of well built Palaces .....

We were in the Arsenale, Popes Palace, and in the Synagogue of the Jewes, who are in this towne distinguish'd by their red hats:

Vaucluse so much renound for the solitude of the learned Petrarch, we beheld from the Castle; but could not goe to visite it, for want of time; being now taking Mules, and a guide for Marcelles:

Sep: 30 we lay at Loumas, the next morning came to Aix; having pass'd that most dangerous and extreamely rapid rapid river of Durance: In this tract all the Heathes or Commons are cover'd with Rosemary, Lavander, Lentiscs and the like sweete shrubs for many miles together, which to me was then a very pleasant sight:

Aix is the chiefe Citty of Province, being a Parliament and Presidial towne, with other royal Courts and Metropolitan jurisdiction: It is well built, the houses exceeding high, and Streetes ample: The Cathedrall St Sauveurs is a noble pile, adornd with innumerable figures (especialy that of St Michael). The Baptistarie, the Palace, the Court, built in a most specious Piazza are very faire: The Duke of Guizes house is worth the seeing, being furnish'd with many

Antiquities in, and about it. The Jesuites have also here a royal Colledge, and the City is an University.

Marseilles

From hence Octob: 7 we had a most delicious journey to Marselles throug[h] a Country, sweetely declining to the South and Mediterranean Coasts, full of Vine-yards, and Olive-yards, Orange trees, Myrtils, Pomegranads and the like sweete Plantations, to which belong innumerable pleasantly situated Villas, to the number of above 15 hundred; built all of Free-stone, and most of them in prospect shewing as if they were so many heapes of snow dropp'd out of the clowds amongst those perennial greenes: It was almost at the shutting in of the Gates that we got in at

Marcelles: This Towne stands on the Sea-Coast upon a sweete rising; tis well wall'd, and has an excellent Port for Ships, and Gallys, secur'd by an huge Chayne of Yron which draw crosse the harbour at pleasure; and there is a well fortified tower: besides this, there are also three other Forts or small Castles, especialy that cald the If built on a rock: Ratonneau, and that of St John strongly garnison'd. But the Castle commanding the Citty, is that of Nostre dame de la Guard: In the Chapel hang up divers Crocodiles Skinns:

Galleys and Galley Slaves

We went then to Visite the Gallys being about 25 in number. The Captaine of the Gally royal gave us most courteous entertainment in his Cabine, the Slaves in the interim playing both on loud and soft musique very rarely: Then he shew'd us how he commanded their motions with a nod, and his Wistle, making them row out; which was to me the newest spectacle I could imagine, beholding so many hundreds of miserb[l]y naked Persons, having their heads shaven cloose, and onely red high bonnets, a payre of Course canvas drawers, their whole backs and leggs starke naked, doubly chayned about their middle, and leggs, in Cupples, and made fast to their seates: and all Commanded in a trise, by an Imperious and cruell sea-man: One Turke amongst them he much favour'd, who waited on him in his Cabine, but naked as he was, and in a Chayne lock'd about his leg; but not coupled.

Then this Gally, I never saw any thing more richly carv'd and Guilded (the Sovraigne excepted) and most of the rest were exceeding beautiful: Here, after we had bestow'd something amongst the Slaves, the Cap: sent a band of them to give us musique at dinner where we lodged. I was amaz'd to contemplate how these miserable Catyfs lye in their Gally, considering how they were crowded together; Yet was there hardly one but had some occupation or other: by which as leasure, in Calmes, and other times, permitts, they get some little monye; in so much as some have after many Yeares of cruel Servitude been able to purchase their liberty: Their rising forwards, and falling back at their Oare, is a miserable spectacle, and the noyse of their Chaines with the roaring of the beaten Waters has something of strange and fearfull in it to one unaccostom'd. They are ruld, and chastiz'd with a bulls-pizle dry'd upon their backs, and soles of their feete upon the least dissorder, and without the least humanity: Yet for all this they are Cherefull, and full of vile knavery: We went after dinner to see the church of St Victoire, where that Saints head is reserv'd in a shrine of silver which weighs 600 lbs: Thence to Nostre Dame, exceedingly well built: This is the Cathedrall: Then the Duke of Guizes Palace; The Palais of Justice; the Maison du Roy. But there is nothing more strange than the infinite numbers of slaves, working in the Streets, and carying burthens with their confus'd noises, and gingling of their huge Chaynes: The Chiefe negoce of the Town is silks and drougs out of Africa, Syria and Egypt: Also Barbara-horses which come hither in great numbers: The Towne is governd by 4 Captaines, and has 3 Consuls, and one Assessor: Three Judges royal; The Marchants have also a Judge for ordinary causes: Here we bought Umbrellos against the heate, and consulted of our jorney to Canes by Land, for feare of the Pickaron Turkes who make prize of many small Vessells about these parts, finding never a Gally bound for Genöa whither we were design'd .....

Oct: 10, as we proceeded on our way we passed by the ruines of a stately Aquae-duct; the soile about the Country being rocky; yet full of Pines, and rare simples:

JOHN EVELYN (1620-1706)

Aubin-Louis Millin, a northerner, had no great love for the Provençals. In particular he saw the Esterel as the home of all the crooks and rogues from Marseilles to the Var.

YOU CAN PUT no trust in the peasants of these parts. If you ask them the way, either they give no answer or they purposely misdirect you. Take good care that nothing is wrong with your carriage or harness, for they will not help you; if they see that you are in a difficulty they laugh at you, if you are in danger they go away. If a thirsty traveller plucks a bunch of grapes, he may think himself lucky if he is not beaten or stoned, or shot at by the owner. They yell like tigers, they behave like madmen if anything puts them out. They quarrel about a mere nothing, blackguard one another, and end the strife by a blow with a cudgel or a stone, or with a shot, which as often as not inflicts a mortal wound. The murderer in such a case does not stop to think of what he has done, or to see whether he can in any way help his victim; his only thought is how to make his escape, and sometimes he even kills the wounded man in order to prevent the evidence that might be given against him. He soon makes up his mind what to do; he takes to flight, and, hiding himself in the valley of Ollioules or in the fastnesses of the Estérel, starts his career as a robber, and soon completes it by becoming a murderer. From rascals such as these the highwaymen come who infest the roads of Provence.

AUBIN-LOUIS MILLIN (1759-1818) (translated by S Baring-Gould)

In 1787 the renowned Alpine writer Saussure was also travelling in the Esterel on a botanical expedition. He too felt threatened by the possibility of brigands.

THE MAIN ROAD is entirely exposed, and is dominated by salient rocks, on which the brigands plant their sentinels. They suffer travellers to advance to some open space between these points of vantage. Then, from their ambushes in the woods, they swoop down on them and plunder them, whilst the sentinels keep a good look-out, lest the guards should come and surprise them. In the event of any of these appearing, a whistle suffices to warn the robbers, and they dive out of sight into the forest. It is absolutely impossible to reach them. Not only is the undergrowth very dense, but it is encumbered with huge blocks of stone. There are neither by-roads nor paths; and unless one knows the intricacies of the woods as well as do the brigands themselves, no one can penetrate into them, except very slowly. The forest extends to the sea, and the whole district, entirely uncultivated, is a place of refuge for the convicts who have escaped from the galleys of Toulon, the nursery of all the robbers of the country.

FERDINAND DE SAUSSURE (1740-1799) (translated by S Baring Gould)

The composer Hector Berlioz went to Nice to recover from a disastrous love affair. His despair was fairly short lived .....

S O I L I V E D , and drank deep draughts of the balmy air of Nice. Life and happiness came flooding back to me, music sought me out: the future beckoned. I stayed in Nice for a month, wandering in the orange groves, immersing myself in the sea, dozing on the heather among the hills of Villefranche and watching from their splendid heights the silent traffic of ships coming and going across the shining water. I was entirely on my own. I wrote the overture to *King Lear*. I breathed, I sang, I believed in God. A convalescence indeed.

They were the three happiest weeks of my life. *O Nizza!*

The King of Sardinia's police, crossing my path for the second time, put an end to this idyllic existence.

I had taken to exchanging an occasional word with two officers of the Piedmontese garrison who frequented the same café. One day I went so far as to join them in a game of billiards. This was sufficient to arouse the darkest suspicions of the chief of police.

'Now clearly,' he reasoned, 'this young French musician has not come to Nice to see *Matilde de Shahran'* [an opera by Rossini, first heard in 1821 (conducted by Paganini) in Rome], 'since he never goes to the theatre. He spends whole days on the rocks at Villefranche; he must be waiting for a signal from some revolutionary vessel. He never dines at the table d'hôte. Of course — because he does not wish to be drawn into conversation by our agents. And now he is surreptitiously entering into relations with the officers of our regiments — undoubtedly in order to open negotiations with them — negotiations with which he has been entrusted by the leaders of Young Italy. A flagrant case of conspiracy.'

O man of great wisdom, sublime politician — thou ravest!

I was summoned to police headquarters and formally interrogated:

'What are you doing here?'

'Recovering from a painful illness. I compose, I dream, I thank God for the glorious sun, the blue sea and the great green hills.'

'You are not a painter?'

'No, sir.'

'Yet you are seen everywhere, sketch-book in hand, drawing. Are you by any chance making plans?'

'Yes, I am making plans for an overture on *King Lear:* in fact I have made them. The drafting and the instrumentation are complete. In fact I believe he will cause quite a stir when he appears.'

'Appears? Who is this King Lear?'

'Alas, a poor old English king.'

'English!'

'Yes. According to Shakespeare he lived some eighteen hundred years ago and was silly enough to divide his kingdom between two wicked daughters, who kicked him out when he had nothing more to give them. You will appreciate that few kings — '

'Never mind the king. This word instrumentation?'

'A musical term.'

'The same excuse again. Now, sir, I know perfectly well that's not the way people compose, without a piano, simply wandering about the beach with a sketch-book and pencil. Tell me where you wish to go, and your passport will be made out. You can't stay in Nice any longer.'

'Very well, I'll return to Rome, and by your leave continue to compose without a piano.'

And that was that. Next day I left Nice, very reluctantly but with a light heart and in the highest spirits. I was alive and cured. Thus was one more example provided of 'pistols that are loaded but do not go off.'

All the same, I think my little comedy had a certain interest. It really is a great pity it was not performed.   HECTOR BERLIOZ (1803-1869) (translated by David Cairns)

As Smollett started the English vogue for Nice, it was Lord Brougham, who was at one time Lord Chancellor, who really started the fashion for Cannes.

IN 1831 LORD Brougham, flying from the fogs and cold of England in winter, was on his way to Italy, the classic land of sunshine, when he was delayed on the French coast of the Mediterranean by the fussiness of the Sardinian police, which would not suffer him to pass the frontier without undergoing quarantine, lest he should be the means of introducing cholera into Piedmont. As he was obliged to remain for a considerable time on the coast, he spent it in rambling along the Gulf of Napoule. This was to him a veritable revelation. He found the sunshine, the climate, the flowers he was seeking at Naples where he then was, Napoule. He went no farther; he bought an estate at Cannes, and there built for himself a winter residence. He talked about his discovery. It was written about in the papers. Eventually it was heard of by the physicians, and they ceased to recommend their patients to go to Montpellier, but rather to try Cannes. When Lord Brougham settled there, it was but a fishing village; in thirty years it was transformed; and from Cannes stretches a veritable rosary of winter resorts to Hyères on one side to Alassio on the other; as white grains threaded on the line from Marseilles to Genoa. As this chain of villas, hotels, casinos, and shops has sprung up so recently, the whole looks

Bathers : Paul Cézanne

extremely modern, and devoid of historic interest. That it is not so, I hope to show. This modern fringe is but a fringe on an ancient garment; but a superficial sprinkling over beds of remote antiquity rich in story.   S BARING GOULD (1834-1924)

In 1848 Lord Brougham, who gave his name to a kind of horse-drawn carriage, mentioned Cannes in his treatise on Republican and Monarchical Government.

AT THIS INAUSPICIOUS period (1848), far removed from scenes of strife, we were calmly enjoying the delightful climate of Provence, its clear sky and refreshing breezes, while the deep blue waters of the Mediterranean lay stretched before us; the orange groves and cassia plantations perfumed the air around us, and the forests behind, crowned with pines and evergreen oaks, and ending in the Alps, protected us by their eternal granite, from the cold winds of the north, but tempered the heat which, for want of the sea-breeze, often becomes oppressive at this season of the year.   LORD BROUGHAM (1778-1868)

Here is another strange tale from Alphonse Daudet.

THE TWO INNS

IT WAS WHILE returning from Nîmes, one July afternoon. The weather was oppressively hot. As far as eye could see, clouds of dust hung over the burning white road between the gardens of olive trees and a few dwarf oak trees, under a huge sun of dullish silver which filled the whole sky. Not a patch of shade, not a breath of wind. Nothing but the quivering of the hot air and the strident cry of the cicadas, that crazy, deafening, urgent music whose loudness seemed the equivalent in sound of this immense quivering radiance ..... I had been walking for two hours without seeing a soul, when suddenly a cluster of white houses rose up in front of me through the dust of the road. They were what is called the posting station of Saint-Vincent: five or six small farm-houses, a few long, red-roofed barns, a drinking trough without water under a clump of lean fig-trees, and beyond them all, two large inns facing each other on either side of the road.

The proximity of these inns was somehow startling. On one side, a large new building, full of life and movement, all its doors open, the coach drawn up in front, the steaming horses being unharnessed, the passengers having a quick drink on the roadside in the narrow shade of the walls; its yard a jumble of mules and carts; carriers lying under the sheds, awaiting the cool of the evening. Inside, shouts, curses, banging of fists on tables, clatter of glasses, click of billiards, popping of lemonade corks, and, over-riding all this uproar, a voice singing, loudly, joyously, making all the windows shake:

> Margoton the lovely,
> Each morn rose up early,
> Her silver pitcher to fill
> With water from the well .....

..... The inn opposite was, in contrast, silent and apparently deserted. Grass in the gateway, shutters broken, on the door a mildewed holly bough hanging like a reminder of glory departed, the door steps wedged with stones from the road ..... Everything so poor, so pitiful, that it truly would be an act of charity to stop and have a drink there.

On entering, I found a long, drab, empty room which the dazzling light through the three large uncurtained windows made still more empty and drab. Even the furniture seemed asleep: some rickety tables on which stood a few dusty glasses, a billiard table holding out its torn pockets as if they were beggar's bowls, a yellow sofa, an old counter. And flies! Flies! I have never seen so many; on the ceiling, sticking to the window panes, on the glasses, whole clusters of them ..... When I opened the door, it caused a buzzing, a whirling of wings as if I had entered a hive.

At the back of the room, in the recess of a casement window there was a woman standing, completely absorbed in what she was looking at outside. I called to her twice:

'Hey, there! Mistress!'

She turned slowly, so that I was able to take in her poor peasant woman's face, lined, wrinkled, the colour of earth, encircled by long pinners of reddish-brown lace such as our old women wear. Yet this was not an old woman; rather she was one who had known sorrow too soon and too deeply.

'What is it you want?' she asked, wiping her eyes.

'To sit a moment and drink something.'

She gave me a look full of astonishment, without moving from the window, as if she did not understand.

'This isn't an inn, then?'

The woman sighed.

'Yes ..... you can call it an inn, if you like ..... But why don't you go over there like the others?

It's much more lively ..... '

'Too lively for me ..... I'd rather stay here.'

And without waiting for an answer, I seated myself at a table.

When she was quite sure I was speaking seriously, she began to move about with a very busy air, opening drawers, moving bottles, wiping glasses, disturbing the flies .... It made one feel that a customer was quite an event. Now and then the poor woman stopped and held her head as if she despaired of doing what she had to do.

Then she went off into the room at the back. I heard her rattling large keys, struggling with locks, rummaging in the bread bin, blowing, dusting, washing plates. From time to time there came a long-drawn-out sigh, a half-smothered sob .....

After a quarter of an hour of these goings on, I had before me a plate of raisins, an old Beaucaire loaf as hard as grit, and a bottle of inferior local wine.

'You are served,' said the strange creature, and returned quickly to her place at the window.

While I drank, I tried to make her talk.

'You don't often have people here, do you?'

'No, monsieur, never a soul! When we were on our own here it was different: then we had the posting station, meals during the duck-shooting season, carriages stopping all the year round ..... But since the people over the way came, we've lost everything ..... Everybody prefers to go there. It's too dull for them here ..... It's no use pretending it isn't. I've lost all my looks, I keep having feverish attacks since my two little girls died ..... Over there it's just the opposite. Everybody always laughing and joking. A woman from Arles runs it. A real beauty, with lace and gold round her neck. The coach driver's her lover, so he stops the coach there now. And all the chamber maids are the coaxing, come-hither sort. That helps to bring the money in as well! She gets all the young fellows from Bezonces, Redessan, and Jonquières. The carriers go out of their way just to call now she's there ..... And I, I'm stuck here all day without a soul, breaking my heart.'

She said all this in an apathetic voice, her forehead still pressed against the window pane. Obviously there was something about the inn opposite preying very much on her mind.

All at once, on the other side of the road, there was a great commotion. The coach was moving off in a cloud of dust. Whips could be heard cracking, a fanfare of the postilion's horn, girls shouting as they ran to the door: Good-bye! ..... Good-bye! ..... and above it all that same tremendous voice ringing out more beautifully than before:

> Her silver pitcher to fill
> With water from the well;
> She saw not on the hill
> Three knights all arm'd full well .....

At the sound of this voice my hostess shivered from head to foot and, turning to me, said in a low voice:

'D'you hear? That's my husband .... He does sing well, doesn't he?'

I looked at her dumbfounded.

'What? Your husband! ..... He goes over there also?'

Then, heartbrokenly, but with a great gentleness:

'What can you expect, monsieur? That is how men are. They don't like tears. And I am always weeping since my little ones died. And it's so sad, this big house, where there's never a soul ..... So when he gets too bored, my poor José goes and has a drink over there, and he's such a wonderful voice the woman from Arles makes him sing. Listen! ..... There ..... he's beginning again.'

And, trembling, with her hands raised and with huge tears making her still uglier, she stood there at the window as if in an ecstatic trance, listening to her José singing for the woman from Arles:

First of all he said to her:
'Good day, my pretty one,
My sweet one.'

ALPHONSE DAUDET (1 8 4 0 - 1 8 9 7) (translated by F Davies)

The Countess of Blessington paints a grim picture of the Riviera as a health resort in the early 1800s.

5 TH — THE SITUATION of this place justifies its reputation as a healthful residence; yet the climate is much less genial than I was led to expect; for though we have a cloudless sky and sunshine, a piercing wind meets one at the corner of every street, and reminds one that an extra pelisse or shawl is very requisite. I cannot think that Nice can be a suitable winter residence for consumptive people, unless they confine themselves to the house, or only venture out in a close carriage. The town is so built that those who traverse it are exposed to frequent and violent currents of air, which are fraught with danger to an invalid; nor are the houses well calculated to exclude cold. Yet, winter after winter, poor sufferers, who tremble at a breeze in their own comfortable homes, with all appliances to boot, to enable them to resist it, are sent from England by the mandate of physicians, who know little of Nice except its geographical position, to fade and die afar from the home they yearn to see again.

I am filled with pity when I meet some fair English girl with the bright hectic tinge on her delicate cheek, and the lustrous eyes, which betoken the presence of that most perfidious and fatal of all diseases, consumption, mounted on a pony, led by a father, a brother, or one who hoped to stand in a still more tender relation to her. I tremble when I see the warm cloak in which she is enveloped, swept by the rude wind from her shrinking shoulders, and hear that fearful cough which shakes her tortured chest. A few weeks, and such invalids (and alas! they are many), are seen no more; and the mourning parents retrace their route with the bitter knowledge that they left their home in vain, nay, that the change of climate which they fondly anticipated would have preserved their darling, had accelerated her death. Every turn here presents the sad view of some valetudinarian tottering along with feeble steps; and faces, on which death has set his seal, pale shadows, that alas! will soon disappear. Such sights make the heart sad; and who can turn with delight to the glowing landscapes around Nice, or the sparkling blue waters that lave its coast, when our paths are almost momentarily crossed by those who bear about with them the visible symptoms of approaching dissolution?

THE COUNTESS OF BLESSINGTON (1789-1849)

Here the novelist Virginia Woolf gives a glimpse of one of the happiest moments in her travels through France with her husband Leonard.

I AM WAITING to see what form of itself Cassis will finally cast up in my mind. There are the rocks. We used to go out after breakfast and sit on the rocks, with the sun on us. L used to sit without a hat, writing on his knee. One morning he found a sea urchin — they are red with spikes which quiver slightly. Then we would go and walk in the afternoon, right up over the hill, into the woods, where one day we heard the motor cars and discovered the road to La Ciotat just beneath. It was stony, steep and very hot. We heard a great chattering birdlike noise once and I bethought me of the frogs. The ragged red tulips were out in the fields; all the fields were little angular shelves cut out of the hill and ruled and ribbed with vines; and all red, and rosy and purple here and there with the spray of some fruit tree in bud. Here and there was an angular white or yellow or blue washed house, with all its shutters tightly closed,

A lithograph of the Papal Palace in Avignon

and flat paths round it, and once rows of stocks; an incomparable cleanness and definiteness everywhere. At La Ciotat great orange ships rose up out of the blue water of the little bay. All these bays are very circular and fringed with the pale coloured plaster houses, very tall, shuttered, patched and peeled, now with a pot and tufts of green on them, now with clothes, drying; now an old old woman looking. On the hill, which is stony as a desert, the nets were drying; and then in the streets children and girls gossiped and meandered all in pale bright shawls and cotton frocks, while the men picked up the earth of the main square to make a paved court of it. The Hotel Cendrillon is a white house with red tiled floors, capable of housing perhaps 8 people. And then the whole hotel atmosphere provided me with many ideas: oh so cold, indifferent, superficially polite, and exhibiting such odd relationships; as if human nature were now reduced to a kind of code, which it has devised to meet these emergencies, where people who do not know each other meet and claim their rights as members of the same tribe. As a matter of fact, we got into touch all round; but our depths were not invaded. But L and I were too too happy, as they say; if it were now to die etc. Nobody shall say of me that I have not known perfect happiness, but few could put their finger on the moment, or say what made it. Even I myself, stirring occasionally in the pool of content, could only say But this is all I want; could not think of anything better; and had only my half superstitious feeling at the Gods who must when they have created happiness, grudge it. Not if you get it in unexpected ways, though.   VIRGINIA WOOLF (1882-1941)

The theme of English people in France must have come easily to Robert Service, himself a native of England who spent much of his life in Canada and France.

Riviera Honeymoon

Beneath the trees I lounged at ease
And watched them speed the pace;
They swerved and swung, they clutched and clung,
They leapt in roaring chase;
The crowd was thrilled, a chap was killed:
It was a splendid race.

Two men, they say, went West that day,
But I knew only one;
Geranium-red his blood was spread
And blazoned in the sun;
A lightning crash .....Lo! in a flash
His racing days were done.

I did not see — such sights to me
Appallingly are grim;
But for a girl of sunny curl
I would not mention him,
That English lad with grin so glad,
And racing togs so trim.

His motor bike was painted like
A postal box of red.
'Twas gay to view ...... 'We bought it new,'
A voice beside me said.
'Our little bit we blew on it
The day that we were wed.

'We took a chance: through sunny France
We flashed with flaunting power.
With happy smiles a hundred miles
Or more we made an hour.
Like flame we hurled into a world
A-foam with fruit and flower.

'Our means were small; we risked them all
This famous race to win,
So we can take a shop and make
Our bread — one must begin.
We're not afraid; Jack has his trade:
He's bright as brassy pin.
'Hark! Here they come; uphill they hum;
My lad has second place;
They swing, they roar, they pass once more,
Now Jack sprints up the pace.
They're whizzing past ..... At last, at last
He leads — he'll *win* the race.

Another round ...... They leap, they bound,
But — where O where is he?'
And then the girl with sunny curl
Turned chalk-faced unto me,
Within her eyes a wild surmise
It was not good to see.

They say like thunder-bolt he crashed
Into a wall of stone;
To bloody muck his face was mashed,
He died without a moan;
In borrowed black the girl went back
To London Town alone.

Beneath the trees I lounged at ease
And saw them pep the pace;
They swerved and swung, they clutched and clung
And roaring was the chase:
Two men, they say, were croaked that day —
It was a glorious race.

ROBERT SERVICE (1874-1958)

Sailing Boats near Les-Saintes-Maries : Vincent Van Gogh

The Grocer : Raoul Dufy

An Evil Motherhood : Aubrey Beardsley

CHAPTER SIX

Riviera Towns

This gently comic song comes from THE BOYFRIEND, *most famous musical play of Sandy Wilson, British playwright.*

I'm often asked if I would like to travel
And visit other lands across the sea
But though it might be pleasant,
I think that for the present,
This is the place that I prefer to be.
Let others go to Sweden or Siam,
I think I'll stay exactly where I am.

They say it's lovely when a
Young lady's in Vienna,
But it's nicer, much nicer in Nice.
In Amsterdam or Brussels
The men have great big muscles,
But they're nicer, much nicer in Nice.
I've heard that the Italians
Are very fond of dalliance,
And they're also keen on it in Greece.
But whatever they may say,
This is where I want to stay,
For it's so much nicer in Nice.

She says it's nicer, much nicer in Nice
She says it's nicer, much nicer in Nice.

Some people's one desire is
To go to Buenos Aires,
But it's nicer, much nicer in Nice.
The laws are rather vague in
The town of Copenhagen,
But they're nicer, much nicer in Nice.
And some may like a flutter
In Bombay or Calcutta,
But they might have trouble with the police (Oh, la, la!)
Other places may be fun,
But when all is said and done,
It is so much nicer in Nice.

SANDY WILSON (1924-)

Augustus Hare's description of Nice, written in the 1890s, applies quite well today.

NICE, THE CAPITAL of the Département des Alpes-Maritimes, is much frequented as a sunny winter residence, but is ravaged in spring by violent mistral, which fills the air with a whirlwind of dust. It is a great, ugly, modern town, with Parisian shops and a glaring esplanade along the sea. A union of several towns compose it — the *'ville moderne,'* or foreign quarter, stretching along the shore as far as the bed of the Paillon torrent, and the *'ville centrale',* containing the principal shops and native residences, which is separated from the *'ville du port'* by the rock of the Château: besides these, the great suburbs of *Carabacel* and *S Étienne* are ever increasingly inland. AUGUSTUS HARE (1834-1903)

There was an Old Person of Nice, whose associates were usually Geese.
They walked out together, in all sorts of weather.
That affable Person of Nice!

Edward Lear, famous for his water-colours and his nonsense verse, also published accounts of his travels in Europe. Here, he is describing Nice in a letter to Chichester Fortesque in February 1865.

THIS PLACE IS so wonderfully dry that nothing can be kept moist. I never was in so dry a place in all my life. When the little children cry, they cry dust and not tears. There is some water in the sea, but not much: — all the wet-nurses cease to be so immediately on arriving: — Dryden is the only book read: — the neighbourhood abounds with Dryads and Hammer-dryads: and weterinary surgeons are quite unknown. It is a queer place, — Brighton and Belgravia and Baden by the Mediterranean: odious to me in all respects but its magnificent winter climate ..... EDWARD LEAR (1812-1888)

〜〜〜〜〜〜〜〜〜〜〜〜〜〜〜〜〜〜〜〜〜〜〜〜〜〜〜〜〜〜〜〜〜

Mrs Matilda Betham Edwards, novelist and writer on aspects of French life, also edited Arthur Young's T R A V E L S I N V E N I C E . *This is her opinion of Nice.*

N I C E I S A home for the millionaire and the working-man. The intermediate class is not wanted. Visitors are expected to have money, are welcomed on that account; and if they have to look to pounds, shillings, and pence, had much better remain at home.

M B E T H A M E D W A R D S (1 8 3 6 - 1 9 1 9)

Robert Louis Stevenson stayed in Nice in the winter of 1882-3.

I A M A L A N E myself, in Nice, they ca't, but damned, I think they micht as well ca't Nesty. The Pile-on, 's they ca't, 's aboot as big as the river Tay at Perth; and it's rainin' maist like Greenock. Dod, i've seen's had mair o' what they ca' the I-talian at Muttonhole. I-talian! I haenae seen the sun for eicht and forty hours.   R O B E R T L O U I S S T E V E N S O N (1 8 5 0 - 1 8 9 4)

Tobias Smollett, the English novelist, spent much time in Nice and was greatly responsible for its early rise to popularity with the British. His often irritable accounts of his travels earned him the nickname 'Smelfungus' from his contemporary Laurence Sterne.

W H E N I S T A N D upon the rampart, and look round me, I can scarce help thinking myself inchanted. The small extent of country which I see, is all cultivated like a garden. Indeed, the plain presents nothing but gardens, full of green trees, loaded with oranges, lemons, citrons, and bergamots, which make a delightful appearance. If you examine them more nearly, you will find plantations of green pease ready to gather; all sorts of sallading, and pot-herbs, in perfection; and plats of roses, carnations, ranunculas, anemonies, and daffodils, blowing in full glory, with such beauty, vigour, and perfume, as no flower in England ever exhibited.

Amidst the plantations in the neighbourhood of Nice, appear a vast number of white *bastides,* or country-houses, which make a dazzling shew. Some few of these are good villas, belonging to the noblesse of this country; and even some of the bourgeois are provided with pretty lodgeable *cassines;* but in general, they are the habitations of the peasants, and contain nothing but misery and vermin. They are all built square; and, being whitened with lime or plaister, contribute greatly to the richness of the view. The hills are shaded to the tops with olive-trees, which are always green; and those hills are overtopped by more distant mountains, covered with snow. When I turn myself towards the sea, the view is bounded by the horizon; yet, in a clear morning, one can perceive the high lands of Corsica. On the right hand, it is terminated by Antibes, and the mountain of Esterelles, which I described in my last. As for the weather, you will conclude, from what I have said of the oranges, flowers, etc. that it must be wonderfully mild and serene: but of the climate, I shall speak hereafter. Let me only observe, *en passant,* that the houses in general have no chimnies, but in their kitchens; and that many people, even of condition, at Nice, have no fire in their chambers, during the whole winter. When the weather happens to be a little more sharp than usual, they warm their apartments with a *brasiere* or pan of charcoal.

The shopkeepers of this place are generally poor, greedy, and over-reaching. Many of them are bankrupts of Marseilles, Genoa, and other countries, who have fled from their creditors to Nice; which, being a free port, affords an asylum to foreign cheats and sharpers of every denomination. Here is likewise a pretty considerable number of Jews, who live together in a street appropriated for their use, which is shut up every night. They act as brokers; but are generally poor, and deal in frippery, remnants, old cloaths, and old household furniture.

The lowest class of people consists of fishermen, day labourers, porters, and peasants: these last are distributed chiefly in the small cassines in the neighbourhood of the city, and are said to amount to twelve thousand. They are employed in labouring the ground, and have all the outward signs of extreme misery. They are all diminutive, meagre, withered, dirty, and half naked; in their complexions, not barely swarthy, but as black as Moors; and I believe many of them are descendants of that people. They are very hard favoured; and their women in general have the coarsest features I have ever seen: it must be owned, however, they have the finest teeth in the world. The nourishment of those poor creatures consists of the refuse of the garden, very coarse bread, a kind of meal called polenta, made of Indian corn, which is very nourishing and agreeable, and a little oil; but even in these particulars, they seem to be stinted to very scanty meals. I have known a peasant feed his family with the skins of boiled beans. Their hogs are much better fed than their children. 'Tis pity they have no cows, which would yield milk, butter, and cheese, for the sustenance of their families. With all this wretchedness, one of these peasants will not work in your garden for less than eighteen sols, about elevenpence sterling, *per diem;* and then he does not half the work of an English labourer. If there is fruit in it, or any thing he can convey, he will infallibly steal it, if you do not keep a very watchful eye over him. All the common people are thieves and beggars; and I believe this is always the case with people who are extremely indigent and miserable.

TOBIAS SMOLLETT (1721-1771)

John Evelyn sailed from Cannes to Genoa along the coast.

Cannes

ON THE 11TH we lay at Canes, which is a small port on the Mediterranean; here we agree'd with a Sea-man to transport us to Genöa, so having procurd a bill of Health (without which there is no admission at any Towne in Italy) we embarq'd on the 12 of Octob: touching at the Ilands of St Margaret, and St Honore, lately retaken from the Spanyards with so much bravery by Prince Harcourt: here, having payd some small duty, we bought divers trifles offerd us by the Souldiers but without going on Land: Thenc we Coasted within 2 leagues of Antibo which is the utmost towne of France: Thence by Nice a Citty in Savoy, built all of brick, which gives it a very pleasant aspect towards the sea, having a Castle built very high that commands it: Thus we also sail'd by Morgus now cald Monaco (having passd Villa Franca, heretofore Portus Herculis); where ariving after the Gates were Shut we were forc'd to abide in our Barque all night, which was put into the haven, the wind comming contrary; In the morning we were hastned away having no time permitted us (by our avaritious Master with whom we had made a bargaine) to goe up to see this strong and considerable Place: it now belongs to a Prince of the family of the Grimaldi of Genoa, who has put both it and himselfe under protection of the French: The situation (for that I could contemplat at pleasure) is on such a promontory of solid stone and rock, as I never beheld the like: The towne-Walls very fayre: Within it we were told was an ample Court, and a Palace furnish'd with the most princly and rich moveables imaginable, also collection of Statues, Pictures, and especially of Massie plate to an infinite value.

JOHN EVELYN (1620-1706)

'DECENT MEN DON'T go to Cannes with the — well with the kind of ladies you mean.' 'Don't they?' Strether asked with an interest in decent men that amused her. 'No; elsewhere, but not to Cannes. Cannes is different.' HENRY JAMES (1843-1916)

F Scott Fitzgerald, American novelist of the Jazz Age, for a time enjoyed his fame and popularity, living a high life with his wife Zelda.

THERE WAS NO one at Antibes this summer except me, Zelda, the Valentinos, the Murphys, Mistinguett, Rex Ingram, Dos Passos, Alice Terry, the MacLeishes, Charlie Brackett, Maude Kahn, Esther Murphy, Marguerite Namara, E Phillips Oppenheim, Mannes the violinist, Floyd Dell, Max and Crystal Eastman, ex-Premier Orlando, Etienne de Beaumont — just a real place to rough it, an escape from all the world.

F SCOTT FITZGERALD (1896-1940)

Oscar Wilde was in Cannes in time for the festival of the Battle of the Flowers and describes the event in a characteristic letter.

TODAY, FOR THE first time, rain — quite an Irish day. Yesterday was lovely. I went to Cannes to see the *Bataille des Fleurs*. The loveliest carriage — all yellow roses, the horses with traces and harness of violets — was occupied by an evil-looking old man, English: on the box, beside the coachman, sat his valet, a very handsome boy, all wreathed with flowers. I murmured 'Imperial, Neronian Rome'. OSCAR WILDE (1854-1900)

William Sansom gives a more modern view of Cannes in his book, BLUE SKIES, BROWN STUDIES.

CANNES FLIES FLAGS to welcome its many foreign visitors, and in symbol of its status as kingpin of this holiday coast. Once Nice held the blue riband of ritzy popularity; in the 'twenties it was Juan and Antibes; now the palm goes to relatively palmless Cannes. And the final proof of the gilded pudding is the weekly visit, unique on the French Mediterranean coast, of a liner direct from the USA. One almost listens, in the balmy *cannois* air, for the golden drip-drip-drip of coins, for the rustle of banknotes in the breeze. But despite such evident prosperity, most of it real, one may also hear the waiters whisper: 'Too many people ordering soda-water; too few champagne bottles about; and — believe it or not — there *is* a kind of visitor who books a room at the best hotel but cooks his own breakfast on a camping stove!' Taxes, prices are high: somebody must pay, or not pay, for it all.

The professional neatness of Cannes is contained in a precise crescent of a bay, edged with fine yellow sand, quilted with white hotels of which the celebrated Carlton raises its twin black cupolas most properly at the centre.

To the east, the crescent is tipped by a white building castellated like an Arab fort — the Summer Casino silhouetted against the wooded Isles des Lérins anchored out to sea. To the west lies the large yacht harbour, where orange masts gracefully sway and the yacht-owners eat huddled in the wells of their boats like bears in pits — with the populace unashamedly looking on. Beyond the yacht harbour rises the hummock of the Old Town, with its tall and ancient watch-tower repudiating the latterday glitter, and far out to sea behind rolls the protective range of the red-rocked Estérel mountains. So the sandy womb of Cannes is sheltered by mountains and islands — and with its flags and its calm, almost lake-like water and its water-level promenade there is nearly something Swiss in the air. A clean odour of placidity overcomes the promenade: though this is occasionally offset by a sudden floodlit parklet of palms, and, in from the sea, by all the usual condiments of a southern French town — sandy squares where the locals play their busily lazy game of *boules,* fishermen's nets laid out on the quay alongside the yachts, blue boats and purple flowers, roses round the cactus, fair-engines in a plane-flecked *place* and, among the fancy-dressed visitors, people of more everyday status: at random, a francless and un-merry widow in a black coat aged with green, and with white tennis-shoes on her black-stockinged feet, discussing with acumen and taste the fabulous window of an *haute couture boutique* well beyond her means but never her dreams; and the olive-skinned young Adonis, native to this flowered Provence with its near-paradisial weather, who had been to England and could only rave about wet Manchester — 'Ah, that's a place, now!' And the old man with the long Clemenceau moustaches who grunted, as he watched a group of young men jazzing off on their motor-scooters: *'Hommes? Omelettes* we call them today'. And the driver of a car with a very long bonnet gesticulating a peasant's lorry out of his way with a malicious: 'Back to the mountains with you!'

And ..... but come to think of it, these four vignettes are universal! The poor woman dreaming herself into a ball-gown, the young adventurer wishing to be anywhere else but home, the old man unable to come to terms with a younger generation, and a kind of rich man still somehow expecting the poor to give way. Yet — at the time it can all seem so typically French: precisely because it *looks* typical, and the language is French. Appearances, architectures and small habits are what mostly determine the character of a place and its people: human nature tends to run fairly constant beneath. The black-coated widow's 'riviera' concession to tennis-shoes coupled with the name of a Paris dress-maker, the young man's striped fisherman's jersey and the most un-Manchester snake-ripple of his walk, the old man's patrician air of pre-1914 France, the pink tie and gold teeth and many-ringed hand of the lordly Latin driver. And all happening in the sun, among smells of hot stucco and strange cigarette smoke, and with a thousand associations of language and sign in the corner of our minds — a *confiserie* window full of almond cakes, shutters to the windows of the houses, white pavement kerbs shining like alabaster, a traffic sign saying simply PRUDENCE, silk blinds and balconies, and the cafés everywhere with all their awnings marvellously advertising beer to what would seem a wine-drinking market.

Up and round the warm hills behind, away from the suave bustle of the Croisette — so-named from a cross that used to stand here — wind the gardens of the villas of the great. One could fill a column with the names: Maurice Chevalier, the Emperor Bao Dai, the Aga Khan, Picasso. Picasso's ex-villa, a fine square hunk of a small palace with ornate wavy windows, has a large walled garden which contained, among tropical leaves, a few of his sculptures: and just outside, almost hidden from view in an overgrowth of high hedge, it was a delight to discover an old iron street lamp-post through whose glassless lantern there now grew the real thick knobbled snake of an unreal-looking vine-branch — propitious reminder that Nature is still intent on imitating Art. The terrain here is called La Californie, and the villas are built in a hundred exotic styles: Indian, Norman manorial, mediaeval castellated, Spanish and whatever else anyone could think of (art now simply imitating Art). Their gardens are their pride: and each takes a leaf out of Tartarin's garden, where the native French vegetable was at a discount and all was a riot of 'gum-trees, gourds, cotton-woods, cocoa and cacao, mangoes, bananas, palms, a baobab, nopals, cacti, Barbary figs'. Such exotics flourish well in the sheltered air of Cannes, where previously the hills would have sported a maquis of rosemary, thyme and lavender — that wild lavender whose grazing makes the local lamb a gourmet's pleasure. Lord Brougham would have seen the hills thus when in 1834 he stayed one fateful night at the small yellow *Hôtel des Postes* in what was then a small fishing town. Milord was frustrated at the Italian border (then a few miles this side of Nice, at the Var river) by news of a cholera epidemic in Italy. So he stayed at Cannes, liked it, and returned in following winters. So began the long story of the town's growth and popularity. Reading the annals, it is plain to see how fortuitous was this choice of a night's rest. Anything could happen in the wild Provence of those days. If not cholera, then bandits. There was, for instance, the memorable case of an English milady travelling in those parts whose coach was taken by bandits: but the bandits also took the interesting little bottle that contained the lady's chloral, drank it, and, moustaches and ear-rings and all, beatifically succumbed to the power of that most efficient of tranquillisers, allowing the lady to take her leave for a better night's rest elsewhere.

WILLIAM SANSOM (1912-1976)

John Ruskin, the influential theorist and historian of art, gained a love of travel from early tours in Europe with his parents. From his autobiography PRAETERITA, *here is his view of the Riviera.*

I HAD MY father's love of solidity and soundness, — of unveneered, unrouged, and well-finished things; and here on the Riviera there were lemons and palms, yes, — but the lemons pale, and mostly skin; the palms not much larger than parasols; the sea — blue, yes, but its beach nasty; the buildings pompous, luxurious, painted like Grimaldi, — usually broken down at the ends and in the middle, having sham architraves daubed over windows with no glass in them; the rocks shaly and ragged, the people filthy; and over everything, a coat of plaster dust.   JOHN RUSKIN (1819-1900)

By 1960, the Riviera had palled even on the dramatist Noel Coward, who had once found it sophisticated.

THE WHOLE OF the Côte d'Azur has become one vast honky-tonk. Millions of cars, millions of people, thousands of 'motels' and camping sites. The coast, viewed from the sea, is still romantic and beautiful, but once ashore it is hell.

The whole place was filled with ghastly tourists augmented by hordes of gormless American sailors with vast Adam's apples and rimless glasses. Except for Felix au Port at Antibes, the South of France, as far as I am concerned, has had it.

                                                       NOEL COWARD (1899-1973)

William Sansom describes 'The Old Blue Strip':

DROP DOWN INTO Villefranche, and its long deep-water gulf-cut that can take a fleet of warships. From the small quay the town climbs straight up the hill, infested with steps and thin streets and bright sailors' dives. One street is no more than a long dark tunnel under tall Italian houses — truly a tunnel, a good place for a knifing, and nicely called the Rue Obscure. Villefranche's weather is naval, and queerly changeable: one week American ships will be there, in the next weeks Greek, French, Argentinian, British — and the streets will for the period take on the clothes and songs and customs of the crews ashore. Villefranche is so small that the effect becomes fantastic — like a house changing its whole furniture once a week. Meanwhile, Cocteau has decorated the church and, on fleetless days, such arresting craft as Niarchos's black three-master *Créole* may stand for you at anchor against the sloping gardens of Cap Ferrat.

On Cap Ferrat, a bushy promontory wilder than the lateral coast, lie embedded some of the seats of the mighty, Somerset Maugham, Lady Kenmare; Leopold II's palace and the fine villa left by an Ephrussi-Rothschild as the *Musée Ile de France,* a rich collection of mixed valuables in a precious setting of moorish halls and cypresses. A lot of Boucher here; and among much other detail, a painting of a particularly splendid and wicked Korean elephant, an alcoholic's dream canvas. As so often and charmingly happens with these provincial French collections, the attendant who takes you round has a deeper reverence for the *objets* than the best of his guests; his voice is low with love and awe, he does truly plead with you to share his joy in each date and provenance, his eyes shine, and though there must be bad times when he consigns the whole lot and all visitors to the devil, this would only be further proof of an emotional pride close to ownership.

Before we get to Monte Carlo there is Beaulieu, the hottest and most sheltered spot on the coast, sporting its soubriquet 'Little Africa' and a lusty banana-growth. (Menton is the other quiet hotspot.) Beaulieu has a little port, a couple of hotels on the sea and off the road, but suffers too heavily from rail and road traffic. Alas for the petrol engine among these haunts of bougainvillaea and morning glory, roses and palms! Not only does little Beaulieu suffer — the whole coast, like every other coast equipped for pleasure, must submit to an overdose of this painful comfort. It is no longer possible to write, as Scott Fitzgerald did, of the Cap d'Antibes in 1925: ' ..... below the balustrade a faded Buick cooked on the hotel drive.' Now there would never be one — more likely a score: and a rattling line of lorries and scooters and *motos* and anything else you can think of passing in a cloud of gas to poison your café-side aperitif and deafen all good conversation. Nowadays the prime importance of having some money is to afford some kind of sanctuary from transport.   W I L L I A M S A N S O M   (1 9 1 2 - 1 9 7 6)

I N E V E R S A W any scenery that could surpass that which presents itself to the eye on crossing the mountains that lead to Antibes; and the eye is not the only organ of sense that is gratified; for the most grateful odours are inhaled at every step. The arbutus, myrtle, and jessamine grow in wild profusion at each side of the road; and the turf is bedded with wild thyme and innumerable other odoriferous plants and heaths, that exhale their perfumes. Orange trees are seen in greater abundance as Antibes is approached; and the dark green of their foliage relieves the sombre hue of the olive. Antibes has nothing to recommend it except its situation, and the port, which is of a circular form, with an extensive quay, and a range of arcades whose whiteness and good proportions have a light and elegant effect. Viewed from the distance, these arcades appear isolated; and look like fairy palaces rising from the sea. Two Roman towers must also be noticed, an examination of which cannot fail to gratify an antiquarian.

The prospect from the height above Antibes, is one of the finest I have ever seen. Hills covered with wood, whence a spire, village, or chateau, is seen to peep forth — the blue waters of the Mediterranean spread out in front, and the snow-crowned mountains of the maritime Alps rearing their heads to the clouds, form a magnificent picture.

COUNTESS OF BLESSINGTON   (1 7 8 9 - 1 8 4 9)

For the last ten years of his life, the short story writer Guy de Maupassant (1850-1893) was served by the valet François Tassart, who wrote a biography recalling his master's failing health and reason. This episode describes their stay at Antibes when disaster struck .....

WE WERE NEARING the anniversary of Sainte Colette, always celebrated in the family. The winter hardly exists on this coast, it had already vanished before the advent of spring, which had beautified the garden. This sunny region, said to be the loveliest in the world, desired apparently to maintain its reputation.

This morning, at half-past five, all the bells in the house rang furiously, all the wood-work of the northern part of the châlet began to twist itself with a frightful noise, as if the house was coming down.

I sprang out of bed, and reached the staircase without understanding what was happening. Then I heard my master shouting with the whole strength of his lungs: 'Hurry! hurry out! it's an earthquake!' But the first shock was already over.

'Let us make haste to dress,' said my master, 'and go down into the garden, for the counter-stroke is sure to come in a few minutes.' We reached the garden, M de Maupassant stamped impatiently on the ground, because neither Madame nor her maid had run downstairs. Then came the second strike, and at last Madame appeared.

'No, my dear boy,' said she, 'when this kind of thing happens, think of yourself, but not of me, I pray you, for I can't hurry, and you know any earthquake leaves me perfectly indifferent.'

We then went into the gardener's dwelling, which only consists of a ground-floor. My master thought it more prudent, expecting other shocks. I kindled the fire, and prepared breakfast. When our milkmaid appeared, she was still frightened to death, and sobbed out:

'Yes, I was climbing the Badine hill, when suddenly I lost my balance and was about to fall backwards; instinctively I threw myself forward. But my milk-pans, which I carried on my head, had been thrown down, quite a long way off.' Here she wiped the tears from her eyes. 'I can't give you any milk this morning,' added she, 'on account of that horrid earthquake.'

After drinking the tea we returned courageously to the châlet, though large cracks were visible everywhere. We decided on leaving all the doors open, so as to be ready to go out the instant we felt the slightest movement under our feet.

About eight my master was ready to take his shower-bath. There was another violent shock, but we were not disturbed, being already accustomed to that sort of surprise. On the whole, we had not suffered, and few things were broken in the house. It was not so in the neighbouring villa; the ceilings had fallen down, and caused a good deal of damage. Happily, no one was hurt.

My master went in the afternoon to the telegraph office, and heard about the awful disaster at Nice. A good deal of harm had been done at Antibes, particularly in the old streets, but only one person had been killed, and few were wounded.

My master told us in the evening that, according to the indications given by the Nice observatory, one might expect more shocks, but not such violent ones. This was not a great inducement to go to bed! Madame declared that she was on no account to be disturbed, as she certainly would not come downstairs for any earthquakes!

A week went by, during which we heard about all the misfortunes that had happened in Italy; one day, when my master was at Nice, he called at the Meteorological Office, where they had registered seventeen shocks since the first day of the earthquake, and he was told there would be more.

When he came home he sent for M Mary, who was a master-builder at Antibes. This man examined the house, and said it would be the height of imprudence to continue living in the two-storied part, as there were long cracks extending from the cellars to the garrets, the floors were now separated from the walls, and felt like spring-boards as you walked on them.

My master was thus obliged to leave his study; he established himself in a gallery covered with glass, just above the hall where he used to fence. I slept for six weeks on a mattress placed on the floor of this lobby, which was about fifteen yards long; the door remained open night and day all this time, I had only hung up a blind so as the night air should not strike my eyes .....

Custom is everything; we had no fear; my master, who generally bolted even his room door, now slept as it were in the open air, none of the outlets of the house were closed, they all gave on to the high road, pervaded night and day by all the rascals sent out of Italy towards the coast, and marching on to Toulon and Marseilles. I must confess that not one of them was even rude to us; it is true that when the same tramp came begging four times in the same day, I made as if I did not know him again, and bestowed another mite on him, without making any remark.

Sometimes in the evening my master and I would walk to the end of the garden, whence one could see Nice and the long row of gas lamps on the Promenade des Anglais; the conversation always returned to the earthquake; my master described it so as to make me shudder, and frightened me to death for the whole night.

One evening we remarked that on the Antibes fortifications the watch-fires were much more numerous than before; about two hundred families camped out there, having had to quit their dwellings which were tumbling down after all these shocks. My master went one evening to see them; he was most generous towards those who were really in want. It was a melancholy and miserable sight; here a mother and her four children slept on two straw mattresses joined together. Next to them lay a whole family, from the grandmother to the babies; here and there, stoves, night lights, Jewish lamps hung on wooden posts. It was a lugubrious sight, but luckily the weather was not cold.

I am surprised my master did not write an article on all this wretchedness, his pen would have described it so graphically. He would only have had to transcribe the account he gave his mother the next day.

The End of March. — Our house is still standing; but the cracks get broader and broader, particularly above the door and windows.

To forget our trials, I sometimes go and pick violets in the field with the neighbours. We are often fifteen and it is great fun; everyone cracks jokes; but we do not linger by the way, as there is no time to lose. Each of us has his basket and his two rows, and his pride is in being the first to finish the job. My master often passes by, and looks as if he would like to imitate us .....

Everything is blossoming in the garden, a small arbutus is already covered with its ripe fruit, red as any strawberry.

〰️〰️〰️〰️〰️〰️〰️〰️〰️〰️〰️〰️〰️〰️

At the end of April we left the châlet, where we had stood seventy-two shocks. My master has given his orders; the masons will succeed us.

FRANÇOIS TASSART (1912) (translated by M Round)

I WENT TO Hyères and St Tropez, both of which were bosh.

EDWARD LEAR (1812-1888)

St Tropez is situated on one of the most beautiful bays of the South coast. It apparently got its name when Tropez, a Pisan centurion, was beheaded by Nero in his native town. He was then put, with his head, in a boat with a dog and a cock who were supposed to devour it. The boat landed where St Tropez now stands with the body intact. Until the beginning of this century the little port was still fairly unknown to tourists, but now all that has changed and its recent history is crowded with celebrities and sunseekers.

ST TROPEZ IS for the birds — in every sense of the word. There is one exception, Les Mouscardins, a restaurant awarded two stars by the *Guide Michelin* and owned by Pierre Brasseur, the leading French actor. Its specialities include grilled langouste and chapon farci. Anyone who insists on staying in the neighbourhood should try the Residence de la Pinède. It has only twenty-two rooms and not all of them have bathrooms attached.

In the good old days, when the Duke of Windsor discovered it before World War II, St Tropez was a delightful place. Then Brigitte Bardot appeared and for a time it was as gay as a lark. But the word went round and today it is full of French larrikins. The Café Sénéquier and the Restaurant des Artistes are the best places from which to watch them. Possibly the stern police action in 1965 may improve things for the future. [Any teenagers unable to produce a legally witnessed letter from their parents permitting them to be on their own in St Tropez were frog-marched out of the place.] Madame Vachon had a huge success with her 'marine' clothes for some years. In 1965, however, she sold out. As for the Pampelonne beach where the nudes congregated, its sand dunes have now been leveled by bulldozers.

CHARLES GRAVES (1966)

Menton claims to be the warmest, most temperate place on the Riviera. Backed with pleasant slopes covered with olive and citrus trees it has been popular both as a winter and summer resort.

OF ALL THE beasts of countries I ever see, I reckon this about caps them. I also strongly notion that there ain't a hole in St Giles's which isn't a paradise to this. How any professing Christian as has been in France and England can look at it, passes me. It is more like the landscape in Browning's *Childe Roland* than anything I ever heard tell on. A calcined, scalped, rasped, scraped, flayed, broiled, powdered, leprous, blotched, mangy, grimy, parboiled, country, *without* trees, water, grass, fields — *with* blank, beastly, senseless olives and orange-trees like a mad cabbage gone indigestible; it is infinitely liker hell than earth, and one looks for tails among the people. And such females, with hunched bodies and crooked necks carrying tons on their heads, and looking like Death taken seasick. Ar-r-r-r-r! Gr-r-r-rn!

ALGERNON CHARLES SWINBURNE (1837-1909)

19th-century engraving of The Verandah, Monte Carlo

On a trip to the continent Tennyson pressed a daisy in the book he was reading. On seeing the flower two years later, he wrote down his memories of various towns, including La Turbie and Monaco.

What Roman strength Turbia showed
In ruin, by the mountain road;
How like a gem, beneath, the city
Of little Monaco basking glowed.

ALFRED, LORD TENNYSON (1809-1892)

The present reigning family in Monaco, the Grimaldi, first rose to power there in 1297. Apart from a brief spell during the Revolution, the Principality has remained in their hands constantly since 1363.

A F I N E , C A L M January day by the Mediterranean was drawing to a close. Inside the castle of Monaco — a fortress with four towers and a thirty-seven-sided circumference of wall built eighty years earlier by Foulques de Castello — no ruffle of uneasiness disturbed the drowsy garrison of Genoese soldiers. Yet not long since, at the end of 1295, fighting had again broken out in Genoa between the Guelphs and the Ghibellines — the former, the party for the Pope, the other for the Holy Roman Emperor — and the defeated Guelphs had fled to take refuge in Provence. Charles II of Anjou, King of Naples and Count of Provence, although a supporter of the Guelphs because he owed allegiance to the Pope, favoured the Ghibellines when they were in the ascendancy. He had unavailingly ordered his Seneschal in Provence to disarm the Genoese Guelphs taking refuge there, among whom were the turbulent and astute Grimaldis. But these had found help and support at Nice and at La Turbie, just inland from Monaco, and had started to attack their enemies again by sea and by land too .....

Twilight had fallen and the dusk was now thickening around the fortress; the fires had burned out. Only a few men, half asleep, were on guard when someone knocked on the postern gate. It was a friar, a Franciscan, asking hospitality for the night. The soldiers let him in, paying no attention to the fact that his shod feet were in contradiction with his garb. Once inside, the man drew a sword from under his gown, killed the heavy-eyed soldiers and called to his waiting companions pressed silently along the castle wall.

And so, on January 8th, 1297, François Grimaldi, nicknamed the Spiteful, captured Monaco.

Although François the Spiteful is the first Grimaldi to be associated with Monaco, the head of the clan at that time was a certain Rainier, his uncle after a fashion. These *Albergo dei Grimaldi* were an eminent family. Made wealthy by sea-trading, its members were often called upon to fill the highest posts in the Genoese Republic. In times of peace from internal strife, Grimaldis were Consuls or Ambassadors of the Republic; but they were always, first and foremost, sailors.

Their first known ancestor, Otto Canella, was a Consul of Genoa in 1133. When he died ten years later he left several sons; the youngest, Grimaldo, who on three occasions between 1162 and 1184 was entrusted with consular missions, to the German Emperor, Frederick I, to the Sultan of Morocco, and to the Emperor of Constantinople, gave his name to the family. His son Oberto also became prominent in the affairs of the Genoese Republic, and Oberto's four sons were the founders of the chief branches of the Grimaldis. It was the eldest of these, another Grimaldo, who was Rainier's grandfather and the great-grandfather of François the Spiteful.

The Grimaldis and the Genoese Guelphs were unable to hold Monaco for long, after François the Spiteful's seizure of the fortress in 1297. By 1301 they were forced to abandon it to the Seneschal of Provence, who restored it to Genoa where the Ghibellines were still in power. One hundred and twenty years were to pass, the space of three generations, before the Grimaldis definitely recovered possession of the Rock, through the great-grandsons of Rainier. F R A N Ç O I S E   D E   B E R N A R D Y (1 9 6 1) (translated by L Ortzen)

Osbert, brother of Edith and Sacheverell Sitwell, recalled their notorious and iconoclastic literary activities in his autobiography, from which this open-eyed description of Monte Carlo is taken.

I HAD NOT seen Monte Carlo since the visit I had paid it for the day when I was eleven, and it was so long since I had been in a Mediterranean country — for four years at twenty is a long time — that I had forgotten, in those fifty months of darkness, the sumptuous plenitude of Italian light — the spears and beams, and banners illuminated even on apparently sunless days, the golden-spangled afternoons, the glowing of hillside and mountain in the evening sun — which clothes it with eagle wings; still more, the marvel of its flawless days, when the great azure dome is only flecked occasionally with a golden ripple, or a huge, flat, white cloud sails like a swan across the calm immensity, and when there are minute beauties as well as majestic, and every small rock-cactus or tiny plant can be seen radiating light, drawing in the heat, basking like an emerald lizard; and then the beauty of the hackneyed sunset hour, when the sea has a pallor as though the moon were already shining on the blue transparency of its water, and the vast circular sun sinks into it, and as it goes, piles and rains rose petals on to the mountains before the acronychal grape-bloom of sky and sea enfolds them. I had forgotten the bombastic, contaminated beauty of this particular place, the cliffs of bright painted houses, row after row of cube and rectangle lying on the rock shelves, the lines and garlands of lights at night, the iron stations, light as Chinoiserie pavilions, throughout the year wreathed carelessly with clumps and clusters and bouquets of flowers in pastel shades, the flights of steps, steep or shallow, the bulbous, preposterous hotels, the citadel of the whole Principality, the Casino, contorted, heavy, over-rich, but the very Temple of Chance, situated in a sacred grove, the statue by the hand of Sarah Bernhardt that graces the side of the enormous building, the miniature quays down below, the tunnels, with their sudden blare of daylight, loud as a great sound, the small yachts and sailing vessels in the harbour, the bars and cafés, the Italian smell of coffee in the back streets, the shapes of octopus, sun-fish and mollusc in the Marine Museum, repeated in fleshy but more stilted green forms by the succulent vegetation outside.

Now, in March 1919, the little pleasure-city was balanced between two worlds, past and present. The Russian influence was already dead or dying: but its symptoms remained, the great villas, to be pulled down later or split up. People still talked of the luxury in which the Grand Dukes had lived here, of how, when they went back to Russia, they would send their linen from St Petersburg right across Europe, to be washed at Charvet's, the famous shirt-maker in the Place Vendôme in Paris, and of how, when they could not come to Monte Carlo in the winter, special trains from the Principality and its neighbourhood would bring them carnations and roses for their Muscovite banquets. But today the members of the Imperial family who had frequented Monte Carlo were scattered, many of them in prison or murdered. Only the Grand Duchess Anastasia, whose behaviour had not long ago shaken whole countries — notably Germany, where her daughter had married the Crown Prince — was still to be seen, wearing a flaxen wig, sitting on a stool at the bar of the Hôtel de Paris or in the old Sporting Club. The Grand Duke Dmitri, on the other hand, subsequently for many years to be met in these surroundings, was still near to the horror of Rasputin's death, which he had helped to plot and carry out, and had not yet arrived here. Harry Melville, that stylised cosmopolitan, the singular product of the genteel 'eighties and epigrammatic 'nineties, was staying at the Hôtel de Paris, and in the intervals of telling those interminable stories that won him a certain social renown, was working excessively hard at introducing his many acquaintances to one another, especially, I thought, — he being perhaps actuated in this by the genuine spice of wit and grain of malice in his nature — those least equipped by disposition and circumstances to make friends. But, if this were so, the great conversationalist, as many had for long deemed him, defeated his own purpose, for, when present, he prevented all others from making their views heard, stifling them under the lightweight *longeurs* of his tortuous and trivial monologues: nevertheless, he was by habit gay, and by conviction he wanted others to enjoy themselves. Among the persons to whom he ceremoniously presented me were the mistresses of several Grand Dukes now lost, captive or massacred in the country which for so long had cherished them. These placid Frenchwomen, of middle age, so well conducted, so quietly if fashionably dressed, who still liked to dance a little, had pastured for almost a generation on meadows of malachite, where the field flowers to be plucked were composed of diamonds, rubies and sapphires: yet now they could hear nothing of the fate of their masters. One must make the best of things, they would sigh to themselves: they were not badly provided for, with enough to leave to their relatives, to give their nephews and nieces a start in life (they were full of family feeling and domestic virtues, and did not wish their young people to know the same privations they had been through). Their little musical laughs trilled out as coyly as ever, and their jewels shone under the winking electric light of the Principality.

OSBERT SITWELL (1892-1969)

In his book THE MONEY SPINNER *Xan Fielding describes Monte Carlo in its hey-day.*

MONTE CARLO WAS beginning its golden age, the period in its history which more or less coincided with the Edwardian Era in England and the Belle Epoque in France. Gambling had become accepted as a fashionable but legitimate pastime, an allowable recreation even for ladies of most exalted station. 'Sooner or later all the world is to be seen in the gaming rooms,' a young English debutante wrote home enthusiastically. 'At Monte Carlo I saw Lady Randolph Churchill in the height of her dark Southern beauty, lovely Miss Muriel Wilson, Mrs Langtry ..... .

She might have added the king of Sweden to her list and the king of Württemberg, the prince and princess of Braganza, the prince of Saxe-Meiningen, the prince of Serbia, Prince Mirza Riza Khan of Persia, the Aga Khan, the rajah of Pudukota, the prince of Denmark, the princess of Pless, Prince Hohenlohe, Prince Kotchoubey, Prince Radziwill, Grand Duke Serge of Russia, the grand duke of Luxembourg, Grand Duke Nicholas, Grand Duke Boris, the duchess of Roxburgh, the duke and duchess of Marlborough, the duke of Norfolk, the duke of Montrose, the duchess of Sutherland, Lord Victor Paget, Sir Hugo de Bathe, Sir Walter Ingram, Lord Wolverton, Lord Farquhar, Lord Cecil Manners ..... She could have ended with a handful of the American millionaires — Charles M Schwab, Pierpont Morgan, W K Vanderbilt and James Gordon Bennett. The catalogue was interminable.

Special trains carried all these fashionable visitors to the Riviera. They ran from the principal capitals of Europe, and the most luxurious was the St Petersburg-Vienna-Cannes express, which had card-rooms and writing-saloons in addition to a dining-car where the cooking was equal to that of the best restaurants in Paris. Passengers made a point of dressing for dinner.

Evening dress too — not merely a dinner-jacket, but tails and a white tie — was always worn at the Monte Carlo Sporting Club, but these sartorial standards did not apply in the casino itself. Once, poorly-dressed people had been kept out in the hopes of raising the tone of the rooms: Lord Salisbury, when he was actually Foreign Secretary, was refused admission for looking too shabby, and he was not at first believed when he said who he was. But now fashion experts set on record the most extraordinary mixture of clothes. Everything but knickerbockers was admitted ..... and the people were equally mixed: respectable English matrons, harridans with systems, harlots from Paris. The presence there of so many rich and extravagant visitors drew *filles de joie* to Monte Carlo in convoys. During the season the famous Paris cocottes, who were usually seen at Maxim's, thronged the casinos. Their beauty roused the wonder of the newly wed young duchess of Marlborough, who asked her husband who they were. 'I was surprised,' she later wrote, 'by his evasive answers and still more startled when informed that I must not look at the women whose beauty I admired. It was only after repeated questioning that I learned that they were ladies of easy virtue ..... '

The most spectacular were Liane de Pougy and La Belle Otero, both at the height of their beauty and glory. Liane, born Anne de Chassaigne, the daughter of a French army officer, was deferentially known as *'notre courtisane nationale'*. It was said that Caroline Otero, an Andalusian gypsy dancer, had slept in more royal beds than any other woman in Europe. They both gambled heavily and their rivalry was the subject of countless anecdotes.

One evening La Belle Otero decided to outdazzle her rival by entering the casino in an evening gown as low-cut as the law allowed and wearing her entire collection of jewellery, which included two pearl necklaces that had once belonged to the Empress Eugénie and the empress of Austria respectively, and a diamond bolero made for her by Cartier and valued at nearly three million francs. A few mintues later Liane, who had been forewarned of La Belle Otero's decision, made her own appearance wearing a white dress of classic simplicity and a single diamond drop at her throat, but followed by her maid carrying all her other jewels on a velvet cushion. This, like all anecdotes about Monte Carlo, must not be taken quite literally. According to a second version, the maid was not carrying the jewels but wearing them. In a third version they were worn not by Otero's maid but by her dog — either a fox-terrier or a poodle; even on this point the version disagrees. Dogs were not allowed in the casino ..... But then a fourth version claims that the incident did not happen in Monte Carlo at all but at Maxim's; while a fifth depicts Otero, in a *black* dress, turning the tables on Liane de Pougy.

It was Monte Carlo that had originally launched La Belle Otero. The child bride of an Italian nobleman who had gambled away his fortune, she is said to have restored it by staking two louis — all the money she had — on red at trente-et-quarante. She knew nothing of the game, and thinking she had lost, moved away. A few minutes later, she records, 'I happened to pass by the table where I had staked my two louis. I noticed an imposing pile of money ..... Red had come up twenty-eight times running and my two louis had become fifty thousand francs.' (This story, too, must be taken with a grain of salt. Another version states that although she had never set eyes on a roulette wheel, she played four single winning numbers in turn and placed all the winnings back on the table each'time and all but broke the bank.)

It was Monte Carlo that broke her, too. She retired in 1922 at the age of forty-five with capital reckoned at fifty million francs, but in a few years she had gambled it all away. Penniless, she moved into a one-room apartment in Nice, where she lived on a small allowance paid by the casino. She died there more than forty years later.　　XAN　FIELDING　(1918-)

Writer of short stories, wife of John Middleton Murry, friend of D H Lawrence, Katherine Mansfield spent many months in the South of France in an effort to combat the effects of tuberculosis.

Monday 23 February

Monte is *real hell* .....

The villas are huge and they have strange malignant towers. Immense poppies sprout out of the walls and roses and geraniums hang down like carpets. All the shops are magasins de luxe, lingerie, perfumes, fat unguents and pawnbrokers and patisserie. The Rooms are the devil's headquarters. The blinds are down, there's a whitish glare from the electric light inside — carpet on the outside steps — up and down which pass a continual procession of *whores,* pimps, governesses in thread gloves — Jews — old, old hags, ancient men stiff and greyish, panting as they climb, rich great fat capitalists, little girls tricked out to look like babies — and below the Room a huge outside café — the famous Café de Paris with *real* devils with tails under their aprons cursing each other as they hand the drinks. There at those tables sit the damned. The gardens, darling — if you could see them — the gardens in Hell. Light, bright delicate grass grown in half a night, trembling little pansies grown in tiny beds that are nourished on the flesh of babies — little fountains that spray up into the air all diamonds .....

I've never heard of Monte before — never dreamed there was such a place. Now I want to go to the Rooms and see it all. It's *dreadful,* but it's *fascinating* to me. I thought of the Heron and *our* life — and I thought how strange it was that at the Heron I should no doubt write a story about that woman over there, that ancient long-nosed whore with a bag made of ostrich feathers ..... I wonder if you'd like to see such a thing, would you? I don't in the least know. Cruelty is there — and vultures hover — and the devil-waiters wear queer peaked caps to hide their horns.　　KATHERINE　MANSFIELD　(1888-1923)

Memories of the Ballets Russes – Self Portrait : Jean Cocteau

CHAPTER SEVEN

Riviera
Lifestyles

As early as Roman times (and very probably earlier), villas started springing up along the Riviera.

HERE AND THERE in fertile parts of the countryside, that is to say in the wide corridor from the Rhône to the Var, including Aix, St Maximin, Brignoles, Draguignan and Grasse; or taking in Marseilles, Aubagne, Cuges, Toulon, Cuevs, Gonfaron Le Luc, Cannes and Cagnes, sumptuous villas started appearing on the most picturesque sites and in the shadiest valleys, after the battle of Pourrières. Every year their number grew, every political upheaval heralded new buildings.

Naturally these villas had a considerable influence on Provence. Their owners, rich or at least comfortably off, put up buildings which were often luxurious and always bigger and more comfortable than the dwellings of the country folk. Romans taking up residence in Provence brought furniture, wall coverings, materials etc. from Marseilles and neighbouring towns which greatly stimulated commerce and industry.

Under these circumstances, masons, carpenters, furniture makers, locksmiths, iron workers, painters, etc.; in a word, building workers flocked to this area .....

Finally, as neither military nor civilian Romans (citizens) were manual workers they employed slaves taken from the Ambro Tentous, the Cimbres, Asia Minor and Africa; or better still, hired Ligurian Celts selling the sweat of their brow to till fields they previously owned.

L J B   B E R E N G E R   F E R A U D   (1 9 0 0 -) (translated by J Karslake)

A typical day at La Mauresque with Somerset Maugham (1874-1965), as described by Ted Morgan .....

THERE WERE OFTEN five or six staying at the same time. There were regulars who came each year, sedate ones, such as Kenneth Clark and his wife, in March, more lively ones, such as Cyril Connolly and Noel Coward, in the summer. But sedate or lively, they were not allowed to interfere with the master's inflexible schedule. He had his breakfast tray — porridge and cream and tea and milk — brought with the papers at 8am. Then he took his bath, in which he would repeat lines of dialogue to see how they sounded. He shaved in his bath, thanks to a fixture called the Gentleman's Helper, which fitted across the tub, with a mirror and space for a razor and a shaving brush.

After breakfast he conferred about the day's menus with his cook, Annette Chiaramello, an Italian woman whom he had promoted from kitchen maid. Annette came to him with the menu book and stood behind his chair, and Maugham put on his spectacles and the consultation began. *'Alors, pour commencer, une vichyssoise. Et ensuite, des escalopes de veau au madère. Et pour terminer, une crème brûlée.' 'Bien, monsieur,'* Annette would say. *'Merci, monsieur.' 'Merci, Annette.'* Among Annette's specialities were *brie en gelée,* with the crust removed, and avocado ice cream, a Riviera exclusive, laced with Barbados rum. Maugham enjoyed asking his guests if they could guess what it was. Annette would leave to do the shopping with Jean Larregle, the chauffeur. Maugham was resigned to the practice of the cook's getting kickbacks from the stores where she shopped. 'In France,' he wrote, 'your cook has a tacit right to charge you five per cent more for everything she buys in the market than she has paid for it, and if she does no more than double that you must consider yourself the happy employer of an honest woman.'

There came a time when Annette protested that she was overworked. 'I cannot bring myself to be very sorry for you,' Maugham said, 'because you work for three months and then we go away for three months and all the time you are paid full wages.' 'But, monsieur,' said Annette, 'for the months while you are away I lose my commission on everything I buy.'

Maugham then went to his study to write until 12.45. He said he worked mornings, because 'my brain's dead by one o'clock'. He felt that if Darwin could work no more than three hours a day and still develop the theory of evolution, that was enough desk time for him. He wrote with a specially designed fountain pen, with a thick collar for a better grasp, on San Remo pads purchased from *The Times* bookshop, each page of which held about two hundred and fifty words of his handwriting. He thought of himself as the last professional writer to write everything with his own hand. 'I wish some learned professor of English would think it worth his while to write a brief treatise on the possible difference this may make in the production of literature now that every author uses a machine on which to express himself.' He cannot have known that Mark Twain used a typewriter and that Tolstoi's niece took dictation on a typewriter. He sat with his back to the view because the seascape was distracting. He preferred to look at the bookshelves; the view of his collected works spurred him on.

At 12.45 cocktails were served. Maugham never had more than one — a very cold dry martini. He would sometimes scowl at a guest who ordered seconds and say, 'Mr So-and-so seems to want another martini,' his voice shivering with irritation. Lunch was informal. Maugham generally wore white ducks, espadrilles, and a blazer with a folded scarf. He had good English silver from Phillips in Bond Street, and silver *sous-plats* with large ducal crests. He would apologize for the lightness of the lunch and then serve an egg dish, followed by a joint which he liked to carve, salad, fruit and cheese. When there was chicken, he liked to say that he had not been able to afford white meat until he was thirty.

In good weather lunch was served on the patio. The service was brisk, and if you were caught up in the conversation, the servants removed your plate before you had finished. On the other hand, Maugham wanted the food to be appreciated. He told a young man at lunch one day, 'You may think you're eating gruel, but it is in fact zabaglione — and very expensive to make.' He had a sweet tooth and would say while eating one of Annette's deserts, 'I like Gide, I like Claudel, but I prefer caramel.' Coffee was taken in the garden. If there were guests of note, he liked to do autopsies on them after they had left. When Jean Cocteau, his Riviera neighbor, came to lunch and held the floor, Maugham said, 'He talks for the benefit of the servants.' (But he would have approved of Cocteau's definition of fiction: 'Literature is a force of memory that we have not yet understood.') At 2.30 Maugham took a nap, and then went for a walk or did his correspondence with Gerald. He also liked to play golf and tennis. In golf, said George Doran, 'he disdains the beaten path of the fairway, adventuring to the right and to the left and to the slightly discovered bramble or gorse. As he emerges his sentences are scarcely printable, but on the putting-green his acccuracy restores his score to approximate par.'

Dinner at eight was a more formal affair. Maugham wore a velvet jacket, a black tie, and initialed velvet slippers from Peels, a gift from Churchill. The meal was served by a butler and a footman, who wore white jackets with silver buttons bought in Italy. There was always champagne, and more courses on the menu than for lunch. Guests were expected to leave early unless a game of bridge had been arranged.

One of the few who turned down an invitation to the Mauresque was Max Beerbohm, who objected to being summoned by telegram, whch led to the following response from Maugham in February 1928, written in a parody of Beerbohm's style:

Cher Monsieur de Max

I should have considered it MOST PRESUMPTUOUS to write to ask to stay with me

(i) a master of English style

(ii) a distinguished hermit

(iii) the only caricaturist in the world who has never been able to do a caricature of me by means of a vulgar telegram.

Anyone of those persons, should I ever have found in myself the temerity to communicate with him on such a matter, I should have thought worthy of a special envoy. I should have sent a Chevalier de la Rose in white satin who would have caroled my invitation in a pure contralto. How much less then would I have made use of a piece of wire attached to a post when these three are one, and that one, by Heaven (have not newspapers drummed it into my envious ears for five and forty years?) none other than   THE INCOMPARABLE MAX

And did you really think that modest wire could be meant for you? Truly the modesty of the great is admirable. I will not conceal from you that a little while ago I asked Reggie [Turner] whether he thought you would like to come here and his reply was as follows:

Yes, I think he'd like it very much. I don't think he'll come. He never goes anywhere. Perhaps you'd better not ask him. He might like to be asked, of course. He's in very bad health. I'm quite sure he won't come. On the whole I wouldn't ask him if I were you. I'm quite sure he won't come. Perhaps you'd better ask him. I don't see why he shouldn't come. I don't think you'd better ask him. It'll bother him to be asked. There's no reason why you shouldn't ask him. Yes, ask him. But perhaps you'd better not.

So what can I do? What indeed can I not do? But this I will say, I have a very good cook and a very nice garden, and if you and Madame *were* passing this way — there now, I was just going to say you would be very welcome; and in your letter you say that nothing will induce you to accept any invitation from me. I will not expose myself to the mortification of another refusal.

TED   MORGAN   (1 9 3 2 -)

In a letter to Bernhard and Elizabeth Förster, the German philosopher Nietzsche describes a Christmas he spent alone in Nice in 1885.

Nice, after Christmas 1885

MY DEAR ONES: — The weather is magnificent, and so your animal must once again put on a glad countenance despite the fact that he has experienced quite melancholy days and nights. Nevertheless, Christmas turned out to be a feast day. Your letter reached me at noon. Quickly the chain was put round the neck and the cute little calendar went in hiding into the vest pocket. But in the process, unfortunately, the 'money' dropped out, provided — as our dear mother wrote — there was money in the letter. Forgive your blind animal for opening his mail on the street. It could well have been that something slipped out, for I was looking very anxiously for the letter. Let's hope a poor little old woman was around and thus found her 'little Christ Child' in the street.

Later I went to my peninsula St Jean, walked a long way around the coast, and finally sat down among a group of young soldiers who were bowling. In the hedges fresh roses and geraniums, and everything was verdant and warm, not at all Nordic. Then your animal drank three glasses, quite large, of a sweet country wine and was nearly a li'le tipsy. At least I began to address the waves when they came rushing on too boisterously as you say to the chickens 'shoo! shoo!' After that I rode back to Nice and supped royally at my boarding house. A large Christmas tree also was lit. Just imagine, I discovered a *boulanger de luxe* who knows what a cheese pie is. He told me that the King of Württemberg had ordered one for his birthday. This came to my mind as I was writing the word 'royally.' —

      F R E D E R I C H   W   N I E T Z S C H E   (1 8 4 4 - 1 9 0 0) (translated by K F Leidecker)

In her novel T H E T H I N K I N G R E E D , *Rebecca West shows all the glamour and tedium of a Riviera honeymoon in the twenties and thirties.*

M A R C A N D I S A B E L L E found themselves constantly attacked by this world, and they fell under its total domination the day they spent with Gustave Bourges and his American wife at their villa on Cap Ferrat. They went over before lunch, taking their evening clothes, because they had all been invited to a party in Monte Carlo. The day began well, with a walk along a cypress avenue that ran its dark cool vista to a round swimming-pool lined with blue tiles, where they bathed in fresh water and looked as they swam at the salty blue glint of the sea a hundred feet below, and the far range, vague now with distance but still sharply fantastic, of the Esterel mountains. Afterwards they lay on mattresses on a marble bench, a little Capuchin monkey skipping backwards and forwards over their bodies. They patted it tenderly, feeling pity for its animal folly. But it began to seem a very long time until lunch, and after they had discussed for some time whether Gordon Lloyd had had a right to do what he did on Ferdy Monck's yacht at Saint-Tropez last week, and were unable to follow through by discussing whether Laura had said what Annette said she did at Super-Cannes, because Laura herself was present, the backgammon boards were brought out. Then the menservants came up with cocktails, which recalled a children's party by their light and creamy appearance and sweetish taste, but which acted like a powerful brake on all discontented and aggressive movements of the mind. The party moved with calmer spirits through a vaguer world down to the house, where they dressed again and sat down to lunch, and ate and drank as happy as if they were in Eden.

But the afternoon was endless. Marc and Isabelle played bridge and backgammon until their eyes ached, and then they revolted, though Laura grew waspish, since she could gamble for ever. Then they went out to the tennis-courts but there they had to choose their partners from Madame Bourges, who was unalterably a rabbit, and the professional, whose play with his employer's guests was panderish, and young Dan Creed, who was six foot six, and Mrs Postleham, whose game was said, by those who ought to have known, to represent the excess of an insatiable temperament. Later they went to the sea and tried surf-riding with the Bourges' new motor boat. But Marc and Isabelle had long mastered that art, which is exciting only so long as one is a novice and uncertain of one's balance; once it becomes a matter of standing upright on a board till muscular fatigue makes one drop off, it ceases to be a sport and resolves into its component parts, of which the last two, the impact with the sea at a high speed and immersion until people in a boat choose to pick one up, are not in themselves attractive. Later they went back to the swimming-pool and drank more cocktails, the Capuchin monkey skipping backwards and forwards over their bodies. They patted it tenderly, envying its animal wisdom. Then they went back to the house to dress. Isabelle flung herself down on the bed, and Marc came and lay beside her, nuzzling his face against the curve of her waist and grumbling, 'I'm bored! I'm bored!' To him boredom was a tragedy, for he had no more realization than if he had been an animal that any state he was in would ever come to an end. She murmured comfort to him and stroked his hair, which was strong and wiry like a dog's coat, and presently rose and began to put on her evening garments. She walked up and down the room, brushing her hair, in a white satin slip that made astonishing the gold of her sunburned arms and legs. Marc rolled over on the bed and grunted wistfully, 'Ah, if we hadn't had this dreary day, I could have done soemthing about that!'

It was difficult to get him up and make him dress, because he had gone back to being a little boy, and his starched shirt affected him as if he were five instead of thirty-two. But downstairs, when they were all gathered together, their sunburn glistening like grease paint and giving their evening clothes a look of theatrical costume, and had drunk some more cocktails, the feeling that at some point during this expedition they were going to have a good time regained the ground it had lost during the day. They found further exhilaration in the speed of the great automobiles, and the brilliance of their swoops round the darkening curves of the Corniche, and they dismounted laughing at the Duchess's villa. They cried out with admiration when they passed through the house and were greeted by her and the other guests beside the lily pool, for by some device of lamps set on the ground the whole air was flooded with gentle, diffused beams, and the terraced gardens marched down the hill to the sea like a staircase of starlight. Men and women alike turned to each other faces shining with magic, romantically hawklike with deep shadows, and distant groups either floated in silver or were silhouetted black and leaner than they were, like gay and fluid skeletons. Presently they all sat down at a long table, the length of the terrace, and shadows filled their glasses with the muted sharpness of champagne and covered their plates with food that was either burning hot or icy cold. A flower of good cheer ought to have burst into bloom, were it not that there is a special foe of dedicated persons known as accidie. It descends on them suddenly and is not to be repelled by argument. They are living their customary life, they are performing the exercises they have found most suitable for the promotion of their faith, but the wells of the spirit run dry. The purpose to which they have vowed their souls stares at them like a senseless monster, not worth nursing. The support of grace is withdrawn from them, melancholy flows in their veins. This disorder has most often been noticed in monasteries and convents, but no votaries are exempt from it, whatever their vows.

It was here in the villa gardens, triumphant as the plague, before the dinner was eaten. As the diners sat over their coffee, the window of the music-room above them was thrown open, and the voice of a famous Polish tenor strode out and was suspended in the night. But it would not serve; the auditors sat glum. When there was silence again, they scattered miserably among the flowers and fountains, murmuring that they had never known a lousier party. Later the gardens suddenly became dark around them, and there was a moment's hush, when only the sea spoke on the rocks below. Then there began the hissing, tearing, knocking sounds of fireworks, which touch and lacerate because we remember them from our earliest childhood, and the soft curtain of night was riven by showers of golden rain, by burning Catherine-wheels, by emerald flowers wider than a constellation, and a peacock that for a minute blotted out half the universe with its more brilliant fires. Those who sat and watched in the darkness did not find the darkness in their souls dispersed by these simple but supreme achievements of light. Even as anchorites in their cells are at times tormented by voluptuous visions, so these people, who had come together with the intention of breaking down their experience to elementary sensations of pleasure, were distraught by a momentary disability to find anything whatsoever agreeable. When the peacock had furled its tail and was itself furled into the night, and the blackness closed in on them again, they turned to each other, muttering plans for immediate flight, and when the lamps were switched on again, the white beams disclosed most of them already on their feet, in fugitive attitudes. It seemed to Isabelle as they went out that the Duchess was near to tears; she was growing old. But Isabelle could do nothing, she and Marc had been brought by the Bourges, who were now murmuring frenetically that they would feel better at the Sporting Club. In the great automobiles the whole party sat huddled up, saying over and over again, 'Say wasn't that terrible? Wasn't it perfectly terrible?'

The Sporting Club was shut, because it was summer. They had to go to the Casino, at which some of them exclaimed in distress, though they did not abandon their intention of gambling, just as good Church people will grumble if they have to attend a place of worship higher or lower than their habit, but will not contemplate missing a service. When Marc and Isabelle were sitting on opposite sides of the roulette table in the Casino, they exchanged sickly smiles, and she perceived from a shadow of concern in his eyes that she was looking ghastly. She was indeed aching with that depression, which oddly takes the form of a sense of guilt, that comes to those who find themselves alone in sobriety among the alcoholized; but he was looking ghastly too. Through boredom he had accepted most of the drinks that had been offered him during the last twelve hours, and though he was not drunk, since the resilient composition of which his nerves were made was almost impermeable to alcohol, he was suffering from indigestion, just as if he had stuffed himself with a like quantity of cakes or fruit. His pallor was blue in the shadows, and he kept on yawning, to his own great distress, for he had had perfect manners drilled into him in his children's party days, and he felt he was being rude to the two women on each side of him. When he yawned, it filled her with panic lest she should go to sleep, and she began to talk with a drowning grip on animation to the man next to her. The only subject she could think of was the mural decorations, feeble and yet robust in their presentation of their feebleness, decadent and yet strong as any pioneer in their confident assault on their audience, the pictorial equivalent of the ballet *Coppélia*. When they were finished laughing at a panel depicting some girls in that kind of peasant costume which involves wearing their corsets outside instead of inside their clothes, she looked across the table and saw that Marc had left his place. She thought that he must have gone out because he was ill, and she was much relieved when he came back with a handful of chips.

'Ah!' she said to her neighbour, 'I'm so glad. I thought my husband had gone out because he was ill, but he only went to change some money.' 'Ah, did he now!' answered her neighbour, in such a peculiar tone, amused and cynical, and something even more malicious than this, that she stared first at him and then at Marc. But she could see no reason for the amusement or the malice. Marc had bought chips for ten thousand francs or so, and he was putting them out in fairly substantial piles; the amount was no larger than what was being risked by at least two others of their party, and his procedure differed not at all from anybody else's at the table. It was true that his expression was sulky and desperate, and fitted grotesquely on a face that had been designed for good humour, and she suspected that perhaps her neighbour had been misled by this into thinking him a little drunk. But then, had that been so, there would have been nothing specially noteworthy about it, for both Gustave Bourges and Prince Ostrogin were in a state of being moonishly amused at anything that passed before their glassy eyes. She passed her hand over her forehead, and was about to dismiss the matter as a fantasy born from the toxins of her fatigue and the hot stagnant air, when she looked across the table and recognized on Sarah Bourges's face an envenomed version of the expression she had suspected in her neighbour. It was impossible to mistake its meaning. It betrayed the glee felt by the mean-spirited when they see people who do not deserve humiliation forced to suffer it through some accidental contact, of which they themselves are unaware. So do they look when a wife finds herself in the presence of a woman who is or has been her husband's most beloved mistress, but, knowing nothing of it, sits unperturbed. It suddenly seemed to Isabelle that there was something ashamed and voluptuous about the heavy mask Marc was bending over his counters, and she had to exercise the sternest self-control to prevent herself staring round the room to see if it contained any specially desirable woman. It was a great relief that Marc lost his money in a very few turns of the wheel, shrugged his shoulders, and rose in an almost churlish insistence on departure.   REBECCA WEST (1892-1983)

Another letter from Katherine Mansfield to John Middleton Murry.

Tuesday 6 April

WE ARE MOTORING to Nice this afternoon. Early lunch in hats and then down come the maids with cushions and rugs for the car — the baby dog is captured: 'Coming for nice tatas with Missie,' and he growls with joy. 'Has little Murry got her fur?' 'Where's Connie?' You know that kind of *upheaval.* It reminds me of my early days. May is going to look after me. The others want to shop, and I can't rush even if I would, so May, carrying the baby dog, trips along. 'Oh *Ma*-dam! Isn't the little pot ever so sweet — and on a *blue* tray, Madam, with just a *little* cloth, not too big and a Mappin and Webb tea-service!' I can hear her already. She's such a little gem, carries the parcels and looks after one beautifully, and the Peke sits on her arm. 'No, Chinnie, be a good girl, my ducksie-pet!'

Does that all sound very strange to you? I love it. I *bathe* in it. And it's all gay, and there are flowers and music and sparkling sea, and we go and have tea in a queer place and eat ice-cream, and little Murry has no choice but must drink chocolate.

'L'auto est là, Madame.'   KATHERINE MANSFIELD (1888-1923)

The Riviera society inevitably had its problems with people rubbing each other up the wrong way. Garson Kanin, American biographer and writer on the cinema, describes the pressures of being a Society host.

July 1953. Les Rochers, St Jean-Cap Ferrat

SPENCER TRACY IS here with us and what a joy it is to have him. He is one of the few original thinkers I know. He says what he thinks, not what he has read or heard someone else say. He makes up his own mind, and he has a mind to make up.

He arrived on the *Constitution,* and we drove to Cannes to meet him. The ship was to dock at 7.30 am. We thought we had better be there in plenty of time, so we set out at 6, which meant getting up at 5. But the drive was pleasant and the look of the country absolutely new at that hour. We reached Cannes far ahead of schedule, had coffee in a bar, and proceeded to the dock. Right on time we saw the ship come in and, soon after, the small tender carrying the passengers who were disembarking at Cannes. As it came into sight, we saw that great American head, with its white thatch, in the bow of the tender looking something like a classic figurehead. It was grand to see him, and he seemed happy to be here after all the indecision about should he come or not and several changes in plans and arrangements.

We drive home, stopping on the way at Cap d'Antibes because Spencer wants to. Having heard about it and read about it, he wants to see it. We stop at Eden Roc, more coffee. He creates a sensation around the hotel and its grounds, with practically everyone greeting him, saying, 'Bonjour, M'sieu Spen-*saire!*'

We reach Les Rochers. By this time we are all over-heated and go immediately to the water and dive in. We are swimming about happily. Spencer turns out to be an accomplished and powerful swimmer. At one moment, floating on his back, looking up at the lovely towers of Les Rochers, the incomparable sky, and luxuriating in the celebrated Mediterranean, Spencer spouts a whale-like stream of water.

Ruth shouts, 'Isn't this great?'

Spencer replies quietly, 'Well, it's no more than what we deserve.'

Since that morning everything has been going beautifully, until last night. I do not understand it, but the sequence of events is as follows: We told Maugham that Spencer had come to spend some time with us here. A few days later he invited us all up to dinner. Without consulting anyone, I accepted. At lunch I announced that we were going up to Maugham's to dinner the following evening. I was certain that Spencer would be interested in seeing Maugham and the Villa Mauresque and especially the paintings, since that is something Spencer knows about. In fact, he has been doing some painting himself. I was therefore startled to hear Spencer say casually as he wolfed his salade Niçoise, 'Not me'.

I did not fuss about it too much at the time, since I know that Spencer is not devoted to the social ramble. After lunch, while we were doing the long walk around the peninsula, I brought the subject up again, and Spencer said, without further explanation, 'Thank you very much, but I don't want to go.'

It is always difficult for me to know when Spencer is joking. He is such a consummate actor that even after all these years of friendship he can fool me easily with pretended anger or joy. Sometimes he will recite a long account of an adventure and, when I have been properly bowled over by it, will reveal that the whole thing was an invention.

I put his refusal down as one of his elaborate jokes and said no more about it. The following day as we began to make definite plans to go up the hill, it became increasingly clear that Spencer had no intention of joining us. I phoned the Villa Mauresque late in the afternoon and said that Mr Tracy was not feeling well. Maugham was sympathetic and solicitous, asked if there was anything he could do, would we want him to send his doctor down? I said we were sure Spencer would be all right, but perhaps we should cancel dinner. Maugham said no, we were to come along. I did not think his invitation had full enthusiasm, but he is a routined man and clearly did not want to have his evening upset.

I kept thinking that at the last minute Spencer would come along, but he did not, and we went up alone.

After breakfast this morning we were telling Spencer about our visit and about the fascinating things which had occurred. He seemed eager to hear it all.

(Ruth interposed a story about being here in the South of France in 1928, staying with Woollcott and Harpo and living the Riviera life. Charlie Brackett had the villa next door. Woollcott and Ruth and Harpo would go to dinner parties and events and the next day describe them to Charlie. Charlie plunked for being invited to some of these affairs, eventually was. Now the four of them went off, and the next morning Charlie said, 'I liked it *much* better when you went without me and described it all in the morning.')

Breakfast is over and we sit about.

I say, 'Now that it's done, Spence, will you *please* tell me why you wouldn't go?'

'I don't like him,' said Spencer.

'Why not, for Heaven's sake?'

'I just don't.'

'You mean you don't like his writing?'

'Did I say that? I love his books and his stories. I've read them all.'

'Well, then, why wouldn't you be interested in meeting him?'

'I've met him,' said Spencer grimly.

'Oh?'

'Oh.'

Ruth asks, 'And you didn't hit it off?'

'Well,' said Spencer, 'I'll tell you. A few years ago I was making *Dr Jekyll and Mr Hyde* with Ingrid Bergman. Vic Fleming was the director. That damned part was something that had haunted me for years. They used to play the play a lot when I was a kid in stock, and it always bothered me that the transformation was so overdone and unreal, so corny. I'd read the book and it seemed to me to be a marvellous study in schizophrenia. The idea of two personalities was fascinating to me — of course it would be to any actor — but blowing it out to the point of big false teeth and putty noses and scraggly hair ..... God, there used to be guys got themselves up looking like orang-outangs for the Mr Hyde part. And I thought for years about the possibility of doing it with acting only and not with the laying on of hands of all the Westmore brothers. I'd seen some remarkable feats of acting by now — small actors become tall and tall actors, by the force of their talent, seem insignificant. I'd seen people become almost invisible on the stage — and pretty common fellows become convincing kings and noblemen — gents become bums — and it wasn't only costumes and make-up, it was *acting*. And for a long time I'd had this idea that *Dr Jekyll and Mr Hyde* could be done realistically, believably. That the portrayal should be that of a *personality* change, not so much a *physical* change. Well, I used to talk about it around and nobody was much interested, but by this time I'd gotten to be well set at Metro and a few of the pictures had done okay and I was in a position to do pretty much what I wanted. So I talked it over with Fleming and he was nuts about the idea, and we decided it was worth doing. The studio agreed and then damned if we didn't get Ingrid Bergman, who was the hottest thing going at the time, and it was on. We studied the book and Johnny Lee Mahin did a hell of a good screenplay, and pretty soon we started shooting. Well, one day George sent a message that Somerset Maugham was visiting him and was going to be coming over to the studio that day, and could he bring him on to the set. We had a strictly enforced 'no visitors' rule because of the rugged work, but hell, if Cukor asks can he bring Maugham, you don't say no, do you? So we didn't. That day it happened to be one of the wild Mr Hyde scenes, where he has the girl locked up and she's trying to get away. Now, visitors on the set make me nervous enough, but *Maugham,* you can imagine. Anyway, believe me when I tell you that we played the hell out of that scene, and I could see, back of the camera, George standing with this little guy and one or two others. When it was over, I sort of expected some applause. Instead, there was a little laugh. It was a print and we knocked off while they changed the set-up. George introduced me to Maugham, and we talked for a minute. Pretty soon they left, or started to leave. I took George aside and said, 'What was so funny?' George said, 'Funny?' And I said, 'That laugh.' And George said, 'Well, while we were watching the rehearsal, Maugham asked me what you were shooting, and I told him it was *Dr Jekyll and Mr Hyde*. And then while you were doing the scene, he looked at me and asked, 'Which one is he now?''

Spencer took a swig of coffee, put it down, and said, 'And that's why I didn't go up there last night.'

Genius is difficult. I still do not know if this is really the reason, used as a reason, or simply a joke. Probably I shall never know.

Spencer did not seem to mind when we all laughed at the punch line. If fact, he laughed himself. But then there is always the fact that he did not go up to the Villa Mauresque last night to have dinner with Somerset Maugham.   G A R S O N   K A N I N   (1 9 1 2 -)

The Cannes Film Festival was inaugurated in 1939 and for the next forty-six years brought a mass of stars to the Riviera. The writer Laurie Lee attended the festival in the year of Jules Verne's smash hit 'Around the World in Eighty Days' and describes the intoxicating chaos of the event.

I N T H E A F T E R N O O N I collected my press card, together with publicity material weighing one and a half kilos. It was to be, it seemed, a very Olympiad of Films, with entries from thirty countries. The major powers had booths in the Festival Hall; the minor ones worked from the bars. Most of the iron-screened countries were represented, as were the obvious free States, and such unknown starters as Tunisia, Ceylon, and the Lebanon. There would be four films a day for the next two weeks. Meanwhile the curtain had not yet risen, and there was little to be witnessed save the pasting of posters that were going up all over the town.

These posters, bright as heraldic shields, seemed part of a private battle. Those of Britain, it's true, were remote and exclusive. They showed white waves breaking on rocky cliffs, or over the bows of destroyers, or against the stern British chin of Mr Richard Todd. They properly told our rough island story and seemed to claim to have invented the sea. But the other big countries mixed the battle more closely. Hollywood led with a girl in black tights. Italy countered with a girl in brown tights; even younger, and with a doll. Japan from Italy reclaimed her rice-fields with a young girl knee-deep in a bog. And Russia, astonishingly, moved right in on Hollywood with two lovers embracing in water.

With a book of free tickets stuffed into my pocket, and no films to be seen till the morrow, I walked up the sunlit, windy front, thinking how lucky I was. A mile of white poles were set out like standards, each bearing its propaganda. And my country was not at all backward here, for every fourth pole bore a well-known likeness, each done in that malted-milk tradition so suggestive of homely night-caps. The cosy pantheon of Pinewood stars — brother, sister, scout-leader, and nurse — they gazed reassuringly down upon me alone in that sinful crowd.

Further up was the Carlton, sugar-white and beflagged, holding the Festival's flesh and blood. In the street outside a crowd of witnesses had gathered. Butter-faced schoolgirls with autograph books were waving at a porter in an attic window. The porter waved back — it was Eddie Constantine. I continued my walk and came back an hour later. The girls had all gone, but Eddie C was still there, drumming his fingers on the window sill. The crowd had moved to stare at the beach, where a large gas-balloon was swelling. As the balloon inflated, so Eddie wilted, but bravely he stuck to his post. The air-bag was one of Mike Todd's devices and a squad of police were on guard. I approached one of these and showed him my card. *'A quelle heure partir le ballon?'* I asked. The official turned crimson and could not speak. But an older, more

Two Girls : Henri Matisse

sober comrade answered, 'It departs, Monsieur, at eight o'clock — but only to fifteen metres.'

I sat down at a beach-bar and ordered a drink. It was that lambent half-hour, before the setting of the sun, when the light of this coast works miracles with one's self-esteem. The wind had dropped and the world seemed transfigured. Never had mankind looked so well. A coral glow embossed the crowds with a rich and magnificent carnality. Old women passing by looked flushed as flowers, old men as noble as Aztec gods; lovers went wrapped in immortal hues; and little pink girls ran over the sands with bare feet trailing pink powdery clouds. There were smells in the air of wine and pine, scorched leaves and sun-festering lilies. For a long, slow instant this minor Babylon hung up gardens of seven wonders. Then the sun sank at last, the cold wind rose, our cheeks turned grey; and the neon lights took over .....

That opening night was America-Night, thanks to Todd and his Jules Verne Colossus. With a series of exclamation marks, nicely chosen, he dominated the town. First came the balloon, a corking stunt: precisely at eight, as the policeman said, it rose floodlit over the sea. And there it swung, at fifteen metres, like a tethered planet or lantern. Two gum-chewing boys, in Victorian dress, hung precarious in its basket. From time to time they doffed their toppers, released more sand, snatched wildly at ropes, looked sick, and cried out through their megaphones. An attempt by ruffians to cut them adrift was beaten off by the police.

Next came the showing of the film — a mink and tiara job. A magnificent squadron of mobile police — the Household Cavalry of Dough — in rampant uniform, with motor-bikes couchant, had been hired to line the approaches. A hundred more, armed with sticks and revolvers, hid in side-streets behind the Hall. Fish-finned cars slid up to the entrance dispensing blonde girls like eggs. Mr Todd and his wife arrived at last — he biting his lips like a worried schoolboy, she moist as a bunch of violets. Up the carpeted steps he shielded her, scowling most stern and proud. Then the Hall of Festival shut firmly down for the three and a half hours of the film.

Later, at midnight, came the Casino Party, with champagne and caged lions and lobsters. The invitation list of course was limited; but such was Mike Todd's popularity that we all wished to do him honour. Two hundred cards, stolen beforehand, were sold in the streets and bars. Then as the guests arrived, their cards were collared and whipped back to the streets again. The whole of Cannes was at the party; it was the greatest party of all. Mr Todd, with his missile in the sky; and Todd A-O, the ultimate detergent, had together captured the Festival.

I didn't see Todd's film that night; instead I went to a cinema in the town where an unofficial film was showing — *L'Empire du Soleil,* a blazing trail of the Andes, made by the makers of *The Lost Continent.* How contrived it is I cannot say, but I watched it with drunken pleasure. It is a visual bombardment by a world unknown: a vast cinescope of thunderous mountains; there are Peruvian Indians dressed like straw dolls of harvest; dances, festivals, work, and love. There is a woman in labour hanging from a tree; a vulture riding a fighting bull; clouds of black cormorants bombing the sea; surprise, amazement, and poetry .....

Dazed by, and dreaming of, this film, I went next morning to see Mike Todd's — which was being shown again for the peasantry. Vigorously conceived, superbly made, and acted with immaculate polish, it sets a girdle round the earth in eighty clichés. (I know where I'm going, and I know what they'll show me .....) France? — there was Paris and a postcard chateau. Spain had its bullfight and gypsy dance. ('For the bulls get the best, what's-his-name? Dominguin; for the gypsy dancer that guy José Greco.') Then India, yes, a pretty big place. We'll have rope-tricks and elephants and sacred cows, suttee, a Princess, and Colonel Blimp. Siam is easy; it's King and I. For the old USA, the old-time works: democratic elections, saloon-bar molls, a free-lunch counter, a Kentucky crook, the railroad spanning the Middle West, a Red Indian raid, and some buffaloes. England, of course, is club-life and cabs, a hint of Royalty, and incipient decline ..... It was jolly, bounding fun all round; but as globe-circling Fogg neared the shores of Britain (sailing mysteriously into a westering sun) I felt the merriment pale a little. It was like being dragged, at once, through a Baedeker dream-book and an international casting-directory (starred pages only). Nothing was spared to us except surprise.

From *Around the World* I came out to the sun, blinded as by a sea of milk. When my sight returned I looked about me. A noonday party was in full swing on the beach, watched by a solemn crowd. I flashed my card and joined the revellers and a drink was thrust into my hand. It was one of those gilded anonymous gatherings which seemed to spring up instantly whenever there was a patch of sun. Fat, busy film-men, their backs to the wind, sold projectors one to another. Long-haired girls languored here and there in stately Borzoi silences. Cameramen clicked and crawled and hunted, selecting and rejecting the girls. They posed a red-head with a rubber horse; she flashed frantic smiles, they flashed their bulbs, and the glaring old sun was ignored. A tasty morsel in a raffia skirt watched glumly for a while. Presently the cameras turned upon her. She dilated, and stripped in the gritty wind, and took up a hundred postures. She writhed on the sands, nubile and shiny, knotting and unknotting her limbs. The cameras sought her, circling slowly. Their long phallic lenses pried and prodded; and she opened generously to them all, fondling with every gesture her idea of the knowledge they had of her.

LAURIE LEE (1914-)

Scott and Zelda Fitzgerald spent the summer of 1925 in a rented villa next to the Casino at Antibes. They had spent the previous summer on the Riviera where they had been immensely popular and sociable.

IN CONTRAST TO the previous summer, he and Zelda were behaving their worst. When they exploded into the casino, people would groan, 'Here come the Fitzgeralds!' If things were dull at Scott's table, he would pick up an ashtray and flip it quoit-like to the table adjoining. It didn't matter whether it had ashes in it or not; the whole idea was to get a reaction. He threw furniture about and heaved salt cellars at the windows, for a little breakage was part of the evening's entertainment. Once he crawled under the coconut matting in front of the main door, making a huge lump that resembled some monstrous turtle and emitting strange sounds.

When introduced, he would say in his nicest Princeton manner, 'I'm very glad to meet you, sir — you know I'm an alcoholic.' His drinking was much on his mind; he inscribed a book for a friend, 'You can drink some of the cocktails all of the time and all of the cocktails some of the time but — (Think this over, Judah).' Once he deliberately kicked over an old woman's tray of nuts and candies all prettily laid out for sale, and by way of recompense emptied his pockets of the soggy roll of bills he usually had with him. On a visit to Monte Carlo, when the doorman refused to let him gamble without his American passport, Fitgerald said, *Très bien,* you son-of-a-bitch,' and passed out at the doorman's feet.

Egged on by Charlie MacArthur, who had a Scotch elfin quality and a touch of the hoodlum in him, Fitzgerald did things which might have led to serious consequences. Late one evening he and MacArthur were alone in a bar disputing the possibility of sawing a man in half. Fitzgerald said it couldn't be done, MacArthur said it could. 'There's one way of finding out,' MacArthur said at length. They persuaded the barman to lie down on a couple of chairs to which they tied him with ropes, and while MacArthur was out getting a two-man saw, the barman made such a commotion that the police arrived. The incident was embroidered in *Tender is the Night,* where Abe North plans to saw the waiter in half with a *musical* saw, to eliminate any sordidness.

Zelda, too, was acting strangely. With her angry sidelong glances and barbed remarks there was something crouching and inimical in her posture. She was a wily antagonist who lay in wait for you conversationally and gave compliments that turned out to be brickbats. 'Did you ever see a woman's face with so many fine, large teeth in it?' she might say of some one she didn't like — after which she would retreat into herself. But the Murphys remained fond of her and she of them.

'She was very beautiful in an unusual way,' Gerald recalled. 'She had a rather powerful, hawk-like expression, very beautiful features, not classic, and extremely penetrating eyes, and a very beautiful figure, and she moved beautifully. She had a beautiful voice as some — I suppose most — Southern women do have. She had a slight Southern accent. She had a great sense of her own appearance and wore dresses that were very full and very graceful and her sense of the color that she should wear was very keen. [Murphy particularly remembered certain dusty pinks and reds.] She had a great head of tousled hair which was extremely beautiful, neither blonde nor brown, and I always thought it was remarkable that her favourite flower was a peony. They happened to grow in our garden and whenever she came to see us she would take a great bunch of them and do something with them and pin them on her bodice and they somehow were very expressive of her.'

When you knew Zelda as well as the Murphys did, you discovered that in her way she was just as rare a person as Scott. She had a sweet, lasting quality that inspired affection despite her erratic, sometimes terrifying, behaviour. Driving along the Grande Corniche one evening, she said to her companion, 'I think I'll turn off here,' and had to be physically restrained from veering over a cliff. Another time she lay down in front of a parked car and said, 'Scott, drive over me.' Fitzgerald started the engine and had actually released the brake when someone slammed it on again. Zelda was bold — bolder than Scott — though the cool madness with which she performed her outrages seldom offended good taste. Late one evening at the Casino, when everyone had gone home except the Murphys and a scattering of Frenchmen, Zelda emerged from the dressing room onto the dance floor with her skirts held so high one could see her bare midriff. The Frenchmen's faces went cold with surprise, then warmed with interest and delight as she pirouetted about the hall, completely dignified and self-absorbed. The orchestra got into the swing of it and when she sat down at the end of three or four minutes, she was in such a trance that she scarcely heard the Murphys' congratulations.

'Why do you do it?' friends would ask the Fitzgeralds mornings after on the beach. 'How do you stand these awful hangovers? Besides, you're so much more attractive when you're sober.'

The Fitzgeralds agreed, but every night was the same, and you went out with them at your own risk. In September the Murphys gave a dinner at which Scott went further than even their leniency would permit. Dessert consisted of figs with pineapple sherbet, and he picked up a fig and threw it at the bare back of a French countess. The countess stiffened as the icy fruit slid down her décolletage, but she never said a word, thinking no doubt that a waiter had been careless.

After dinner, when the guests had gotten up to stroll about the garden, Fitzgerald was drifting among the tables with a dream in his eye. Suddenly, without calling attention to it, he picked up one of the Venetian glasses with white and gold spinning which the Murphys were specially fond of and tossed it over the high wall that surrounded the garden, listening to it break on the bricks outside. The gesture had an eighteenth-century extravagance and impromptu reminiscent of gentlemen dashing their glasses on the hearth after a single drink. Fitzgerald wasn't trying to be ugly; it was as if he thought this a fitting death for such exquisite goblets. He had sent two more into the night before the Murphys stopped him and forbade him to enter their house for three weeks. His mouth was a line of resentment as the sentence was passed, and exactly three weeks later he appeared at their door, without, however, alluding to the reason for his absence.

The Fitzgeralds stayed at Antibes through the autumn. 'Now all the gay decorative people have left,' Zelda wrote Perkins the end of September, 'taking with them the sense of carnival & impending disaster that colored this summer. Scott is working and still brooding about the war. Ernest Hemingway was here for a while — seeming sort of a materialistic mystic. ..... It's heavenly here when its burnt & dusty and the water crackles in the fall. Scott's novel is going to be excellent.' But before they sailed for America December 10th, Fitzgerald wrote Perkins that the novel was 'not nearly finished.'

On shipboard with them was Ludlow Fowler, who had been best man at their wedding. He sat with the Fitzgeralds at a large uproarious table, and after the meals Scott would lead discussion in the lounge. 'You stay out of this because you're on your honeymoon,' he would tell Ludlow. Then turning to the others he would ask, 'Is there any man present who can honestly say that he has never hit his wife in anger?' In the ensuing attempt to define the word 'Anger,' Fitzgerald was the moderator. He loved to be the cynosure of a group.

Meanwhile Zelda was telling Fowler, 'Now Ludlow, take it from an old souse like me — don't let drinking get you in the position it's gotten Scott if you want your marriage to be any good.'   A N D R E W   T U R N B U L L   (1 9 6 2)

To Maurice Goudeket   Saint-Tropez, August 1933
..... M Y   D I N N E R   L A S T night was magnificent. L'Escale made me a stuffed bass and a dish of partridges with cabbage, bacon, and sausages that overwhelmed the Vanders. By way of drink, we had an awfully good, light Alsatian wine. (Oh, you oaf, not to have been here!) It was a lovely Saturday. Lots of people out, and a warm evening. The *Almanach de Gotha* in overalls. A much-titled fairy in a khaki cotton blouse with a workman's belt. 'Fashionable' ladies in bargain-basement men's shirts. Fernande C in an evening gown, with jewels, lacquered hair, and a butcher's mug tending to fat. She wore enormous jade beads on her arms and around her neck, and was accompanied by a décolleté gigolo in a yellow and maroon sweater, a tall, skinny marmoset with shaved eyebrows painted on again, and a head of hair like a Mary Stuart cap. Astonishing.

From a table of women dressed as boys and men with long scarves arose a tall, bony harridan dressed in cheap blue jeans and a striped-cotton sailor's shirt. Overly made-up face of a kitchen maid out of work, with a tiny beret perched on her dyed hair. This spectacle came up to me and said, 'I'm delighted to see you again!' As you can guess, I didn't utter a word. 'We haven't seen each other since that evening at Madame de _____ ' she went on, and then confronting my look of a stunted hedgehog, she told me her name ..... You'd have howled. Afterwards, the ladies danced together, cigarettes dangling from their lips ..... They danced as no one would dare dance at the rue Blomet. The Negro girls there do show a little restraint.

So I watched the passing parade. At eleven I even beheld the arrival, with male escort, of a poor, flattened-out, diminished creature wearing an ambitious panama hat and a face that was so ravaged I was frightened and pained at the same time ..... She was looking for a table. She had changed radically but I was sure it was Madame de _____. Then she saw me, said something to her husband, and they pretended to be unable to find a place and left. It was very curious. That woman was never any more than a piece of scenery, and now nothing remains. It's logical, but surprising still .....   C O L E T T E   (1 8 7 3 - 1 9 5 4) (translated by R Phelps)

YES, THE WEATHER, the sun, the light are lovely. Man is everywhere vile. They are just beginning to mess this coast up — but the messing seems to proceed rapidly, once it starts. Little villas 'tout comfort' — yes my word ..... .

When the morning comes, and the sea runs silvery and the distant islands are delicate and clear, then I feel again, only man is vile. But man, at the moment, is very vile.

D   H   L A W R E N C E   (1 8 8 5 - 1 9 3 0)

This disturbing anecdotal poem is by Louis MacNeice, Irish poet and friend of Auden and Spender.

Provence

It is a decade now since he and she
Spent September in Provence: the vineyard
Was close about the house; mosquitoes and cicadas
Garrulous day and night; and by the sea
Thighs and shoulders tanning themselves and one
Gay old man in particular who never
Missed a day, a glutton for the sun,
But did not bathe. He and she with swimming
Every noon were wild for food; a Basque
Woman cooked on charcoal — aubergine with garlic,
And there were long green grapes exploding on the palate
And smelling of eau de Cologne. They had nothing to ask
Except that it should go on. Watching the vintage —
A file of bullock carts and the muzzle of each
Animal munching purple — he suddenly said

'We must get married soon.' Down on the beach,
His wife and three of his three children dead,
An old man lay in the sun, perfectly happy.

LOUIS MACNEICE (1907-1963)

Noel Coward paints an interesting picture of Winston Churchill at Biot at the age of eighty-three.

THIS PLACE IS enchanting. We are lodged temporarily in a sixteenth-century farmhouse looking out over terraces of carnations to the Mediterranean.

We have gambled a little, unsuccessfully, lain in the sun, eaten some delicious meals and enjoyed ourselves. On Thursday ..... Edward and I drove to Rocquebrune to lunch with Emery Reves, Wendy Russell, the most fascinating lady, Winston Churchill, Sarah, and Winston's secretary. The lunch was a great success, particularly from my point of view, for it seems, from later reports, that I was charming, witty, brilliant, etc. What I really was was profoundly interested. There was this great man, historically one of the greatest our country has produced, domestically one of the silliest, absolutely obsessed with a senile passion for Wendy Russell. He followed her about the room with his brimming eyes and wobbled after her across the terrace, staggering like a vast baby of two who is just learning to walk. He was extremely affable to me and, standing back to allow me to go into a room before him, he pointed to a Toulouse-Lautrec painting of a shabby prostitute exposing cruelly and cynically a naked bottom, flaccid and creased, and said in a voice dripping with senile prurience, 'Very appetizing!'.

This really startled me. To begin with I doubt if Lautrec had ever for an instant intended it to be alluring, and the idea of the saviour of our country calling it appetizing once more demonstrated his extraordinary flair for choosing the right word. I am convinced that 'appetizing' was what he really thought it. I reflected, on the way home, how dangerous an enemy repressed sex can be. I doubt if, during the whole of his married life, Winston Churchill has ever been physically unfaithful to Lady Churchill, but, oh, what has gone on inside that dynamic mind? This impotent passion for Wendy Russell is, I suppose, the pay-off. Sex heading its ugly rear at the age of eighty-three, waiting so long, so long too long. It was disturbing, laughable, pitiable and, to me, most definitely shocking. I forgave the old man his resolute enmity of years, then and there. He, the most triumphant man alive, after all has lived much less than I.

NOEL COWARD (1899-1973)

Henri Matisse spent much of the war in Nice. He wrote to Pierre Matisse in New York describing his life in September 1940.

I AM TRYING hard to settle down to my work. Before arriving here I had intended to paint flowers and fruits — I have set up several arrangements in my studio — but this kind of uncertainty in which we are living here makes it impossible; consequently I am afraid to start work-

Self Portrait : Henri Matisse

ing face-to-face with objects which I have to animate myself with my own feelings — Therefore I have arranged with some motion picture agents to send me their prettiest girls — if I don't keep them I give them ten francs. And thus I have three or four young and pretty models whom I have pose separately for drawing, three hours in the morning, three hours in the afternoon. This keeps me in the midst of my flowers and my fruits with which I can get in touch gradually without being aware of it. Sometimes I stop in front of a motif, a corner of my studio which I find expressive, yet quite beyond myself and my strength and I await the thunderbolt which cannot fail to come. This saps all my vitality.

I have seen Bussy very little; he had guests, Gide, etc, literary people, that is, quite a strange crowd to me, so I stay at home. Nevertheless, if I had not written I would have gone to have a cup of tea with them — but I cannot chat and be intimate in their circle in which one does not understand painting. They are absorbed by the war and politics and that tires me and interests me very little.

I shall take a look around Cannes or St Raphaël with a view to moving there in case of need. I am expecting a bird dealer who will, I hope, relieve me of a part [of my collection]. It is not the necessity of doing these things which preoccupies me, but the uncertainty in which we are living and the shame of having undergone a catastrophe for which one is not responsible. As Picasso told me: 'It's the Ecole des Beaux-Arts!' If everybody had minded his own business as Picasso and I did ours, this would not have happened.

I hope I shall start painting again soon, but that overwhelms me so — I have to invent and that takes great effort for which I must have something in reserve. Perhaps I would be better off somewhere else, freer, less weighed down. When I was at the other frontier and saw the endless march of those escaping I did not feel the slightest inclination to leave. Yet I had a passport with a visa in my pocket for Brazil. I was to leave on June 8th via Modane and Genoa, to stay a month in Rio de Janeiro. When I saw everything in such a mess I had them reimburse my ticket. It seemed to me as if I would be deserting. If everyone who has any value leaves France, what remains of France?

HENRI MATISSE (1869-1954) (translated by A Barr)

Monte Carlo's Casino was designed in 1878 by Charles Garnier, architect of the Paris Opera House. But there are those who, like the creator of suave James Bond, find its ostentatious grandeur rather hard to take.

I AM NOT by any means a passionate gambler nor a very audacious one, but I greatly enjoy the smoke-filled drama of the casino and the momentary fever of the game. The casino at Monte Carlo is not my favourite. For me the casino at Beaulieu has the greatest charm, followed by Le Touquet, with, at the bottom of the list, Enghien les Bains outside Paris, which has the unenviable distinction, for a gambler, of making the highest annual profit of any casino on the Continent. The Monte Carlo casino is rather too much of a show-place and there is a railway-station atmosphere about the vast gaming rooms that, despite the glorious vulgarity of the decor (note, in the inner *salon vert,* the naiads on the ceiling; they are smoking cigars), is slightly chilling. The intimate surroundings of the Sporting Club, decorated, as the casino hand-out charmingly puts it, *'par les peintres Waring et Gillows,'* are far preferable, but this select enclave has strict winter and summer seasons and was closed at the end of May.

Part of the trouble with the Monte Carlo rooms is that they were built in an age of elegance for elegant people, and the gambling nowadays has the drabness of a Strauss operetta played in modern dress. The Italians, Greeks and South Americans, who are by far the richest post-war gamblers, are almost totally without glamour and, if they support beautiful cocottes in the true casino tradition, they leave them at home so as not to be distracted from what used to be a pastime but has now become a rather deadly business of amassing tax-free capital gains. Monte Carlo and its casino were designed for flamboyants — for Russian Grand Dukes, English Milords, French actresses and an occasional maharajah, but now the beautiful stage is occupied only by the scene-shifters who have inherited it from a race of actors that is bankrupt or dispossessed.

IAN FLEMING (1908-1964)

In 1911 the impresario of the Ballets Russes Diaghilev signed a major agreement with Monte Carlo and from then on the Principality became an important centre for his company, which at one time included the celebrated Nijinsky.

THE YEAR 1911 was a decisive one for Diaghilev; it saw the establishment of his own permanent company, the signing of the important contract with Monte Carlo and the company's London début.

The Monte Carlo contract arrived in time to give him some welcome security. There were only three performances a week; the programme served as a *répétition générale* for Paris and gave the artists time in which to rest. Monte Carlo was also the resort of the rich and influential from all countries, a perfect centre for the personal word-of-mouth propaganda of which Diaghilev was a master, sounding out on occasions the barber or the *maître d'hôtel*. In addition Monte Carlo came to fulfil a far more important function; it was essential to Diaghilev's method of creation from 1911 to his death.

Diaghilev created through others. He prided himself on being 'a collector of geniuses'. He would visit art exhibitions and concerts, meet poets and musicians, contacting those whom he thought useful to his work. He relied on his flair in the first place, but a ballet could not be produced by snap decisions. The various artists must meet together in a relaxed atmosphere, they must talk, produce ideas, tear them to pieces and think again. His painters were easel-artists and they had to get to know the nature of ballet; the composer and the choreographer, with the aid of a piano, had to learn to speak the same language. Monte Carlo was the ideal centre for such work. Every season artists flocked there, often as his guests, and many a ballet was conceived in the Hôtel de Paris, at a supper table presided over by Diaghilev. It was his Versailles. On one occasion at a première in the Monte Carlo Opera House, he told the present writer, 'If the theatre burned down tonight, a large part of the world's creative artists would be wiped out.' And it was true.   ARNOLD   HASKELL   (1903-1981)

George Santayana, poet, philosopher and critic, was a Spaniard brought up in Boston. He came to Europe in 1912, living in France and England and later in Italy, where he died. Here he describes Monte Carlo.

I F L E D T O the comparative innocence and moral simplicity of Monte Carlo. I took a small room flooded with sunshine and overlooking the toy port of Monaco, and I established a routine of life, going always for the same walks and to the same restaurants, which enabled me to rest thoroughly, and to do some little work. The gilded hall of the Casino did not swallow me up; I went there only once, on the first day of my sojourn in the place, and never returned, as I found it crowded and dingy, full of uninteresting middle-aged people, not even fascinatingly ugly or obviously gnawed by all the vices. They were for the most part fat greedy Germans, millionaire sausage-makers in appearance and in smell. I went sometimes to the theatre, and I saw several amusing ultra-Parisian things, to make up for the Teutonic real life about me. Above all, I delighted in the climate and in the old town of Monaco, to which I walked up every day, and where I sometimes read or wrote in the gardens. The only friend I came upon in all that time was X, who was living just beyond Nice, with a lady variously described as his wife, his *bonne*, his mistress, his model, his cook, and his mother. She might be any of these, as far as appearances went, and several at once, most probably; at any rate, she was very amiable, and the pair seemed quite happy.

GEORGE   SANTAYANA   (1863-1952)

〰〰〰〰〰〰〰〰〰〰〰〰〰〰〰〰〰〰〰〰〰〰〰〰〰〰〰〰〰〰〰〰〰〰

Early in 1904 the writer Arnold Bennett stayed at Menton with friends. He visited the casino at Monte Carlo to 'study human nature and find material' for his novels .....

M O N T E   C A R L O — T H E initiated call it merely 'Monte' — has often been described, in fiction and out of it, but the frank confession of a ruined gambler is a rare thing; partly because the ruined gambler can't often write well enough to express himself accurately, partly because he isn't in the mood for literary composition, and partly because he is sometimes dead. So, since I am not dead, and since it is only by means of literary composition that I can hope to restore my shattered fortunes, I will give you the frank confession of a ruined gambler. Before I went to Monte Carlo I had all the usual ideas of the average sensible man about gambling in general, and about Monte Carlo in particular. 'Where does all the exterior brilliance of Monte Carlo come from?' I asked sagely. And I said further: 'The Casino administration does not disguise the fact that it makes a profit of about 50,000 francs a day. Where does that profit come from?' And I answered my own question with wonderful wisdom: 'Out of the pockets of the foolish gamblers.' I specially despised the gambler who gambles 'on a system'; I despised him as a creature of superstition. For the 'system' gambler will argue that if I toss a penny up six times and it falls 'tail' every time, there is a strong probability that it will fall 'head' the seventh time. 'Now,' I said, 'can any rational creature be so foolish as to suppose that the six previous and done-with spins can possibly affect the seventh spin? What connection is there between them?' And I replied: 'No rational creature can be so foolish. And there is no connection.' In this spirit, superior, omniscient, I went to Monte Carlo.

Of course, I went to study human nature and find material. The sole advantage of being a novelist is that when you are discovered in a place where, as a serious person, you would prefer not to be discovered, you can always aver that you are studying human nature and seeking material. I was much impressed by the fact of my being in Monte Carlo. I said to myself: 'I am actually in Monte Carlo!' I was proud. And when I got into the gorgeous gaming saloons, amid that throng at once glittering and shabby, I said: 'I am actually in the gaming saloons!' And the thought at the back of my mind was: 'Henceforth I shall be able to say that I have been in the gaming saloons at Monte Carlo.' After studying human nature at large, I began to study it at a roulette table. I had gambled before — notably with impassive Arab chiefs in that singular oasis of the Sahara desert, Biskra — but only a little, and always at *petits chevaux*. But I understood roulette, and I knew several 'systems'. I found the human nature very interesting; also the roulette. The sight of real gold, silver and notes flung about in heaps warmed my imagination. At this point I felt a solitary five-franc piece in my pocket. And then the red turned up three times running, and I remembered a simple 'system' that began after a sequence of three.

I don't know how it was, but long before I had formally decided to gamble I knew by instinct that I should stake that five-franc piece. I fought against the idea, but I couldn't take my hand empty out of my pocket. Then at last (the whole experience occupying perhaps ten seconds) I drew forth the five-franc piece and bashfully put it on black. I thought that all the fifty or sixty persons crowded round the table were staring at me and thinking to themselves: 'There's a beginner!' However, black won, and the croupier pushed another five-franc piece alongside of mine, and I picked them both up very smartly, remembering all the tales I had ever heard of thieves leaning over you at Monte Carlo and snatching your ill-gotten gains. I then thought: 'This is a bit of all right. Just for fun I'll continue the system.' I did so. In an hour I had made fifty francs, without breaking into gold. Once a croupier made a slip and was raking in red stakes when red had won, and people hesitated (because croupiers never make mistakes, you know, and you have to be careful how you quarrel with the table at Monte Carlo), and I was the first to give vent to a protest, and the croupier looked at me and smiled and apologised, and the winners looked at me gratefully, and I began to think myself the deuce and all of a Monte Carlo *habitué*.

Having made fifty francs, I decided that I would prove my self-control by ceasing to play. So I did prove it, and went to have tea in the Casino café. In those moments fifty francs seemed to me to be a really enormous sum. I was as happy as though I had shot a reviewer without being found out. I gradually began to perceive, too, that though no rational creature could suppose that a spin could be affected by previous spins, nevertheless, it undoubtedly was so affected. I began to scorn a little the average sensible man who scorned the gambler. 'There is more in roulette than is dreamt of in your philosophy, my conceited friend,' I murmured. I was like a woman — I couldn't argue, but I knew infallibly. Then it suddenly occurred to me that if I had gambled with louis instead of five-franc pieces I should have made 200 francs — 200 francs in rather over an hour! Oh, luxury! Oh, being-in-the-swim! Oh, smartness! Oh, gilded and delicious sin!

Five days afterwards I went to Monte Carlo again, to lunch with some brother authors. In the meantime, though I had been chained to my desk by unalterable engagements, I had thought constantly upon the art and craft of gambling. One of these authors knew Monte Carlo, and all that therein is, as I know Fleet Street. And to my equal astonishment and pleasure he said, when I explained my system to him: 'Couldn't have a better!' And he proceeded to remark positively that the man who had a decent system and the nerve to stick to it through all crises, would infallibly win from the tables — not a lot, but an average of several louis per sitting of two hours. 'Gambling,' he said, 'is a matter of character. You have the right character,' he added. You may guess whether I did not glow with joyous pride. 'The tables make their money from the plunging fools,' I said privately, 'and I am not a fool.' A man was pointed out to me who extracted a regular income from the tables. 'But why don't the authorities forbid him the rooms?' I demanded. 'Because he's such a good advertisement. Can't you see?' I saw.

We went to the Casino late after lunch. I cut myself adrift from the rest of the party and began instantly to play. In forty-five minutes, with my 'system', I had made forty-five francs. And then the rest of the party reappeared and talked about tea, and trains, and dinner. 'Tea!' I murmured disgusted (yet I have a profound passion for tea), 'when I am netting a franc a minute!' However, I yielded, and we went and had tea at the Restaurant de Paris across the way. And over the white-and-silver of the tea-table, in the falling twilight, with the incomparable mountain landscape in front of us, and the most *chic* and decadent Parisianism around us, we talked roulette. Then the Russian Grand Duke who had won several thousand pounds in a few minutes a week or two before, came veritably and ducally in, and sat at the next table. There was no mistaking his likeness to the Tsar. It is most extraordinary how the propinquity of a Grand Duke, experienced for the first time, affects even the phlegm of a British novelist. I seemed to be moving in a perfect atmosphere of Grand Dukes! And I, too, had won! The art of literature seemed a very little thing.   A R N O L D   B E N N E T T   (1 8 6 7 - 1 9 3 1)

The British novelist Peter de Polnay lost both his money and his fiancée, Purity, in Monaco.

I   W A S   F O R   two glorious months the favourite of Fortune, feared by the Furies, admired even by my rather stolid Nymph. Now all that had gone. Those who continued to like me shook their heads and felt sorry for me; for all the others I became a dim figure, and which is worse a fool. It wouldn't have occurred to anybody to say any more that I was a clever player. Only the lucky ones know how to play cleverly. The knight was incredibly clever.

I refused to admit I was beat. I saw myself engaged in war. To step aside would have meant defeat which my pride couldn't acknowledge. Money acquired even less importance than it had while I was winning. It was purely a desire to win again, to prove thereby I was the better man. My vanity didn't pursue me outside the casino, and if somehow I could have been kept out of it, I would have seen the whole silly thing in its true dimensions, and my vanity would have become interested in other matters. But inside the casino I was a general fighting a rear-guard action, his divisions badly mauled but still fighting on, never surrendering. Surrender would come only after the last man fell, which in plain English means having no money left to play in the casino.

The entire set-up of that elegant gambling den helped to exasperate my vanity. The croupiers and inspectors watched me anxiously, and when, as they had expected, I lost I could see in their eyes they felt sorry for the idiotic young man who didn't know when to stop. Those eyes spurred me on to further effort.

The other gamblers treated me like a leper, which was reasonable since nobody cares for the reflection of defeat, and those who had envied me could now despise me to their heart's content. They must have found me irritating too because I pretended it didn't matter to lose. To smile and say perfectly good when another goodish slice of my inheritance was taken away by cards, belonged to sham heroism and false panache in which I believed implicitly. Nothing gave me greater pleasure than to overhear them say he knows how to lose.

Gone were the days when I was asked to share banks because with my luck the other person was bound to win. Nobody turned to me to say let us say banco the two of us. They rather flocked to say banco to my banks.

'Why don't you,' one of the inspectors advised me, 'play at the other tables for smaller stakes? You are out of luck, so limit your losses.'

'My luck will come back,' I said.

The knight left for London. His holiday was up, and he had to attend to his affairs again. On his last night he stood in the bar with his stooge, both sunburned and fit. An acquaintance hailed them, and as I wasn't far from them at the bar, I overheard the knight telling him he was leaving on the following day.

'Did you have a flutter?' asked the acquaintance.

'Yes, a little flutter.'

'Did you lose or win?'

'As a matter of fact I think I won a bit.' He smiled broadly. 'I think my winnings paid for my stay here.'

I couldn't help reflecting that I had contributed about ten thousand pounds to his stay. Serves me right.

Purity was angry because I went on playing, and furious because I lost. I had ceased to be a success, and she held like so many others that an unsuccessful gambler is a pitiful fool, something that drops on the wayside while you march on. She told me she wouldn't speak to me in the gaming room if she saw me gambling, and one evening she sailed in accompanied by the elder of her old suitors whom she eventually married, and gave me a cold distant smile, after which they went into the bar. All I said to myself was: you'll be different when I start winning again.

My casino girl-friends took a poor view of Purity's behaviour to me. Paula, Mabel and a Canadian called Josey who looked like nothing on earth, all said so. I told them to shut up, but that wasn't meant for Paula whom I liked, though it was annoying that I couldn't pity her any more.

Purity wasn't to be blamed. She had liked to see me win since to win is hilarious and has its aura. To watch, however, a fool strenuously seeking his ruin was a different matter. She knew that I was telegraphing almost daily to the lawyer who looked after my waning interests, to sell securities at any price as long as money was transferred to me. She tried to dissuade me, whereupon I blackmailed her.

'If you marry me at once,' I said, 'I'll never touch a card again.'

'You have no right to speak like that,' was her answer.

She gave me that answer only on the next day, for she wanted to think it over. She had to work out whether it was or wasn't the right thing. It wasn't. I met her for a drink at the Malmaison where she embroidered on her no. I was weak: no girl respected a man who hadn't the moral strength to stand on his own: without respect she couldn't marry him. She suggested I had time to mend. That was my interpretation of her words. If I gave up gambling and decided to lead a serious life she might reconsider it. So I asked her to lunch with me, she accepted, and we spent the afternoon together too. We had, that is I had, a drink at the Malmaison again, she had tea, her elderly suitor came, and they went off to play bridge. I was left to meditate.

Though nobody on the face of it could profess more conservative sentiments than I, rebellion is the power behind my decisions. In my oppressed childhood and early youth I had but one desire, namely to break away from it all, which I did when I escaped to South America. That failed miserably, and now I was in the middle of another failure. I never was good at cutting my losses; moreover, Purity had asked me to conform like anybody else. Instead of exploring the possibilities of conforming, I looked at the shining road that could lead only to doom.

In fact doom had already settled down on it. I refused to accept that. If I started to win again then I would be in the right again; for I had been in the right while I was winning. I handled the same cards, said banco in the same voice, yet then I was great, whereas now I was a poor noodle that should mend its ways. Was I a serious young man just because I was winning? Apparently I was, therefore worthy of her. I reached the conclusion that winning alone could bring about a change of heart in her. And how glorious it would be to go up to her and be able to say: 'Look, who was right?' And having said that to scatter ten-thousand-franc counters all over the room. The vision beckoned, and I went to the casino to lose again.

I wrote a life of the Young Pretender twenty years later, and my enemies said it was too carefully documented. I spent a year or so in the Royal Archives in Windsor Castle, and because the Prince was an assiduous letter-writer and received ten times as many as he wrote, I could follow his life almost from day to day. While I sat with that mass of letters I often asked myself when exactly did he turn from Bonny Prince Charlie into the poor fellow who did everything wrong. Not only everything went wrong but one felt that the impetus that had carried him to Scotland and to the glorious campaign of the Forty-Five, had completely left him. I reached the conclusion that it was his arrest in Paris in 1748 that brought an end to the impetus. I saw him like one who is running fast, then falls, slides forward and still believes he is gaining ground. Though it is a far cry from him or from Napoleon after the retreat from Moscow, there comes a moment too in the gambler's career when unbeknown to him the impetus ceases.

I am now quite certain that while I lost so heavily there were moments when I could have grasped my luck again; but because the impetus had deserted me I didn't get hold of my luck; for with open palms you can grasp nothing. Of course I was unaware of that.

Looking back I believe that I lost my grasp on the day of my first skirmish with the knight, thus my subconscious had from that day onward no confidence left in my gambling. From then on it was but a mechanism, a reflex.

One could say that applies to most things in life. That may be so, though there are such things as belief in the justice of one's cause, confidence in one's talent and ability to work which suffice to lift you up again: but all the gambler has at his disposal is self-confidence, and for self one should substitute luck. Once that is gone he has nothing left to fall back on.

After twenty-eight years I still clearly remember the glorious days while I won. I can trace in my mind practically every banco, every bank, and every face I saw at that time in the casino remains as clear as if I had seen it only this morning. The six or seven weeks during which I lost are covered in pea-soup fog, which is understandable since my real self was already looking for something else. Having suffered defeat it was preparing for a new attack — but very much elsewhere.   PETER   DE   POLNAY   (1906-)

Ce qu'on ne nous prend pas
nous reste,
C'est le meilleur de
nous-
même

Whatever is not taken from us remains with us. It is the best part of ourselves : Georges Braque

CHAPTER EIGHT

Love Songs

Petrarch first saw the girl he called Laura when he was twenty-three.

Era il giorno ch' al sol si scoloraro

It was the day when the sun darkened, as God
Himself vanished into death, when I was taken.
I took myself in, Madam, bound by your looking at me.

It did not seem to me a fit time to take shelter
Against the stroke of love; therefore I walked on,
Without suspicion, vulnerable — whence woe to me
Begins in our common sorrow.

Love found me altogether unarmed,
My eyes, my heart's gates, opened by tears
To give free passage toward the heart.

It was dishonourable of him to take me
Unawares in my pity;
Not to have tried his weapon on your armor.

FRANCESCO PETRARCH (1 3 0 4 - 1 3 7 4) (translated by N Kilmer)

This extract from the Will of John Deydict of Ollioules dated 1447 shows the two most important items in a young girl's trousseau.

I ALSO LEAVE to my darling daughter Marguerite: a headdress of pearls to the value of five pounds, a girdle of silver lined with red silk.

The French historian Ribbe mentions the significance of these items.

FIRSTLY THE HEADDRESS — a sort of diadem decorated with garlands and ribbons and almost always containing some precious stones, was in such general use that the humblest labourer's or peasant's daughter, would have felt she had lost status if she had not received one in her dowry worthy of the match *ad honorem partium* as they say in marriage contracts .....

The girdle of the young bride was even more important. It was both a symbol of investiture through the keys which were hung from it, and one of the main items of adornment, if not the foremost; it too seems to wipe out all distinction of class. The only difference lay in its costliness. Among the great families the costliness was revealed in the clasps, masterpieces of the goldsmith's art and in exquisite enamels surrounded by numerous gold studs. Middle class women often had theirs of silver gilt and the common people simply of silver.

CHARLES DE RIBBE (1 8 9 8 -) (translated by J Karslake)

Ford Madox Ford introduces his translation of this lovesong by Cabestanh thus .....

AND ACROSS THE projection of the dark garden that my memory gives me there seems to depend, in letters of light, that poem and the translation of it that I made. I cannot have been more than eleven at that date — certainly I was not more than twelve, because by that time my father was dead, and I have never looked at his book or the poem of Cabestanh again. But the poem remains fresh in my mind and innumerable times in wakeful nights or walking amongst sun-baked rocks, quite unexpectedly, I find myself going in memory over and over again through my translation.

Li dous cossire and *That pleasant fever,* they began — though *cossire* does not mean 'fever' ..... and that bothers me a good deal at night ..... But rhymes that are so frequent in Provence are so scarce in the Northern World that is ours!

Li dous cossire	That pleasant fever
Quem don amors soven	That love doth often bring
Domnam fan dire	Lady, doth ever
De vos mas vers plaszen	Attune the songs I sing
Pessan remire	Where I endeavour
Vostre cors car é gen	To catch again your chaste
Cui eu desire	Sweet body's savour
E cui non fasz perven	I crave but may not taste

FORD MADOX FORD (Hueffer) (1873-1939)

There were several female troubadours about whom little is known. The Countess of Die probably came from north of Montelimar and was said to have been in love with the troubadour Raimbaut d'Orange to whom she wrote her songs.

For a while now a certain knight
has caused me great distress,
and I want it known, once and for all,
how excessively I have loved him;
    yet I've been betrayed
on pretext of not giving him my love,
and ever since, in bed or dressed,
    my life's been one of grief.

How I would like to hold him
one night in my naked arms
and see him joyfully use my body
as a pillow, for I am more
    in love with him
than Flore with Blanchefleur,

and offer him my heart, my love,
my mind, my eyes and my life.

My handsome friend, gracious and charming,
when will I hold you in my power?
Oh that I might lie with you
one night and kiss you lovingly!
Know how great is my desire
to treat you as a husband;
but you must promise me to do
whatever I may wish.

COUNTESS OF DIE (c 1 1 8 0) (translated by A Bonner)

The story of Aucassin and Nicolette is one of the most widely known love ballads of the South. It was probably first heard in the castles of Provence in the 13th Century. Percy Allen recounts the story with poetry translations from the version by F Bourdillon.

THE COUNT GARIN of Beaucaire was old and feeble; and he had no children, save only his one dear son Aucassin, who was young and fair and well-fashioned, but so overcome by love that he would not be knight nor take arms. When his father reproached him because he would not help to defend his land against Count Bougars of Valence, by whom it was beset, Aucassin replied that he would never go to onset nor to battle again 'except you give me Nicolette, my sweet friend whom I love so much.'

But his father refused, in anger, because Nicolette was but a slave-girl from Carthage; and he went to the rich viscount who had adopted Nicolette and told him what had happened. Then the viscount shut up Nicolette in a high storey of his palace, in a chamber with a window over against the garden, and put only an old woman to keep her company. And when Aucassin heard of it he went to the viscount and threatened him, but all in vain; and so he returned sorrowfully to his palace chamber, and there broke out weeping for 'his sweet sister friend'.

Nicolette is prisoner,
In a vaulted bed-chamber,
Strange of pattern and design,
Richly painted, rarely fine.
At the window-sill of stone
Leaned the maiden sad and lone.
Yellow was her shining hair,
And her eyebrow pencilled rare,
Face fine-curved and colour fair!
Gazed she o'er the garden-ground,
Saw the opening roses round,

Heard the birds sing merrily;
Then she made her orphan cry:
    'Woe's me! what a wretch am I!
Caged and captive, why, ah why?
Aucassin, young lord, prithee,
Your sweetheart, am I not she?
Ay, methinks you hate not me.
For your sake I'm prisoner,
In this vaulted bed-chamber,
Where my life's a weary one.
But by God, sweet Mary's son,
Long herein I will not stay,
    Can I find way!'

But Count Bougars had not forgotten his war; and when the assault was great and furious, Count Garin came to his son and begged of him to take arms in defence of the town. And Aucassin said, 'I will take arms and go to the onset by such covenants that, if God bring me again safe and sound, you will let me see Nicolette, my sweet friend so long, till that I have spoken two words or three to her and that I have kissed her one single time.' 'I grant it,' said the father, and Aucassin was glad, and armed himself, and rode into the battle.

And he was tall, and fair, and slim. But Aucassin thought so much upon Nicolette, his sweet friend, that he forgot what he ought to do; and his horse led him into the thick of his foes, who took him prisoner. But when he heard his enemies discussing by what death they should cause him to die, he knew that, if he would see Nicolette again, he must bestir himself; so he seized his sword and fought his way out from among his enemies, and wounded the Count Bougars, whom he brought a prisoner to his father. But when Aucassin asked for the fulfillment of his covenant, the father would not grant it. 'Certes,' said Aucassin, 'I am very sorry when a man of your age lies,' and he set his prisoner free; and Count Bougars rode back to his own people again.

But Count Garin was very angry with Aucassin his son, and put him into a deep dungeon. It was in the summer time, in the month of May, when the days are warm and long and bright, and the nights still and clear. Nicolette lay one night in her bed, and saw the moon shine bright through a window, and heard the nightingale sing in the garden; and she bethought her of Aucassin her friend, whom she loved so much. She perceived that the old woman who was with her was asleep. She got up and put on a gown of cloth of silk she had, that was very good; and she took bedclothes and towels and tied one to the other, and made a rope as long as she could, and tied it to the pier of the window, and alighted down into the garden; and she took her dress in one hand before and the other behind, and kilted her, for the dew which she saw great in the grass; and went away down the garden.

Her hair was yellow and instep small; and her eyes grey and laughing; and her face shapely; and her nose high and well cut; and her lips warmed, more than cherry or rose in summer time; and her teeth white and small; and her breasts were firm and heaved her dress as it had been two walnuts; and she was slender between the flanks that in your two hands you could have clasped her; and the blossoms of the daisies which she broke off with the toes of her feet, which lay on the narrow of her foot above, were right black against her feet and her legs, so very white was the maiden.

She came to the postern and unfastened it, and went out through the streets of Beaucaire, over against the shadow, for the moon shone very bright; and she went on till she came to the tower where her friend was. The tower was cracked here and there, and she crouched down beside one of the pillars, and wrapped herself in her mantle, and thrust her head through a chink in the tower, which was old and ancient, and heard Aucassin within weeping and making very great sorrow, and lamenting for the sweet friend whom he loved so much. And when she had listened awhile she spoke her thought to Aucassin that for his sake she would pass to some far country, and she cut tresses from her hair and gave them to him; and he took them and kissed them and put them in his breast.

But he dissuaded her from fleeing to another land, and Nicolette went her way into the forest to hide herself, lest Count Garin should take her and harm her; and the very herd-boys were bewildered by her beauty. In the forest she built herself a lodge of leaves and flowers, and there dwelt; and the cry went through all the land that Nicolette was lost.

To cheer Aucassin his father gave a great feast, but the youth was all sorrowful and downcast. Then a knight said to him, 'Aucassin, of such sickness as you have, I too have been sick. Mount on a horse and go along yon forest-side to divert you; and you will see the flowers and the herbs and hear the birds sing. Peradventure you shall hear such a bird for which you shall be better.' 'Sir,' said Aucassin, 'Grammercy! So will I do;' and he rode into the forest.

Presently he met the herd-boys, who told him how they had seen a fair maiden pass that way; and he rode on, never heeding the briars and thorns that tore him so that the blood flowed from him in forty places or thirty; and at last he came to the lodge which Nicolette had made, so pretty that prettier it could not be. The light of the moon shone within it. While he lit from his horse he thought so much of Nicolette that he fell upon a stone and put his shoulder out of its place; but he crept on his back into the lodge, and then he began to sing; and Nicolette, who was not far, heard him and came to him.

They kissed and caressed each other, and their joy was beautiful. Then she placed his shoulder into its place again, and with the lappet of her smock bound it with flowers and fresh leaves; and he mounted his horse, and taking his love in front of him they set out into the open fields.

So they rode on until they came to the sea and descried merchants sailing near the shore. And he dealt with them so that they took both into their ship. And when they were on the high sea a great storm arose and took them to the land of Torelore; and Aucassin took service with the King of Torelore, but Nicolette remained in the queen's chamber. Strange adventures befell Aucassin there, and he had with him Nicolette his sweet friend whom he loved so much. But while he was in such content, a fleet of Saracens came by sea and took the castle by storm; and Aucassin and Nicolette were made prisoners and were put into different ships. And a great storm arose and Aucassin's ship drifted to the castle of Beaucaire, and so after three years Aucassin came home again and was received by the people with great joy, for his father and mother were dead. And he ruled his land in peace; but he mourned the while for Nicolette.

Now the ship in which was Nicolette was that of the King of Carthage; and when Nicolette came to the castle and saw the land about her, she recognised that she had been brought up there, and had been daughter to the King of Carthage. When the king and the people heard that, they were filled with joy and treated her royally; but Nicolette thought only by what device she might return to Aucassin.

Then she procured a viol and learned to play on it, and then she stole away by night, and darkened her face, and so, disguised as a minstrel, took ship for Provence, and came to the castle of Beaucaire, where Aucassin, with his barons around him, was sitting upon a terrace. She sang him a song of Nicolette, and Aucassin was rejoiced to hear her, and bade her, if she knew where Nicolette was, to go and bring her to him. This the minstrel promised, and away she hied to the house of the viscountess where she had lived before, and to her confessed the truth. Then she anointed herself with a plant which was called Esdain, and all her beauty returned to her. And after eight days she clad herself in rich silk stuffs and bade the lady go for Aucassin her friend. And she did so. And when the lady came to the palace she found Aucassin weeping and lamenting for Nicolette his love, because she had delayed so long. And the lady accosted him and said —

'Aucassin, now make no more lament, but come away with me, and I will show you the thing in the world you love most, for it is Nicolette your sweet friend, who from far lands is come to seek you.'

And Aucassin was glad.   PERCY ALLEN (1869-1933)

Mythological drawing : Pablo Picasso

Aucassin was of Beaucaire;
His was the fine castle there;
But on slender Nicolette
Past man's moving is he set,
Whom his father doth refuse;
Menace did his mother use:
    'Out upon thee, foolish boy!
Nicolette is but a toy,
Castaway from Carthagen,
Bought a slave of heathen men.
If for marrying thou be,
Take a wife of high degree!'
    'Mother, I will none but her.
Hath she not the gentle air,
Grace of limb, and beauty bright?
I am snared in her delight.
If I love her 'tis but meet,
    So passing sweet!'

TRADITIONAL (translated by F W Bourdillon)

Following the example of another troubadour Peire Vidal, Bertrand of Marseilles stole a kiss from a sleeping lady. She, however awoke in a fury and was probably not particularly soothed by the song he then wrote.

Like a peasant who thinks he has lit on a casket
    O'erflowing with silver and gold —
To find he has only dug up a basket
    That nothing but rubbish doth hold —

So was my delight when I thought I had found in you
    A heart full of sweetness and truth
Changed to grief when instructed that nothing was sound in you
    Except just your outside and youth.

Away, then, I'll wander a lady to seek out
    In whom truth and constancy meet,
Instead of yourself, who, the plain fact to speak out,
    Are only a heap of deceit.

BERTRAND OF MARSEILLES (c 1180) (translated by J Rutherford)

The 14th Century rogue Jean-l'ont-pris describes his parents' courtship in the Pays d'Oc.

MARGOT, A TRULY buxom wench, as I said, did not lack for lovers. There was not a mother's son in Solorgues or in the whole district who did not spend his Sundays and feast-days in her company. The whole throng devoured her with their eyes, pinched her, chased her, jostled her here and there, through fields, meadows, vineyards, hedges or ditches, taking no more account of other girls than nightingales do of bats. In the end, Truquette joined the company and, for his deserts or good fortune, was preferred above all the others. What favoured him exceedingly was that his work kept him at her side. He saw Margot the whole blessed day and every day of the week, while the others, obliged to earn their miserable liveli-hoods travelling the countryside, had to make shift as best they could.

You have to admit, my lord, that, providing he does what's expected of a man, a sharp fellow like my father, who spends six days of the seven alone with a girl, will make light work of his courtship. Margot's mother made matches, and she did not stay at home the whole day. Margot took the matches to Truquette's shop; there she cut them to the right size, tipped them with sulphur and bound them into bundles; and as she worked, she was not behindhand in doing whatever she could to arouse my father's good humour, humming the latest song from Paris, poking him between the ribs with an awl or gently rubbing his chops with a ball of wax. My father, who did not take any of this seriously, stopped cobbling his shoes and, flinging his stir-rup delicately round her neck, rode off with her. Thereupon, they frolicked about, legged it, rolled around, fell and got up again when they could, suddenly bursting into fits of laughter. All this, not to mention the fact that Truquette mended her shoes for nothing, put Margot so much in mind to love him that, on the Sundays following, all the other young men of the dis-trict found her prouder and more unyielding than the housekeeper of the *curé* of Bezouces. However, this did not stop them from singing their lovelorn nonsense at her door for a long time yet; but, whatever they did, it was to her harsher music than that of tom-cats in February, when the females have had their fill.

Truquette found them one evening, and just to enrage them further, he whistled as usual, pretending that he had not seen them, and bang!, there was Margo at the window. You can imagine how sheepish they all looked!

Another evening, as they were bawling their heads off to no avail whatsoever, Truquette walked by, sneezed, and bang!, there was Margot at the window.

Finally, another evening, when they had expended all their skills and were no further advanced in their suit, Truquette arrived, farted, and, this time, Margot appeared at the window so inflamed with desire that it was all she could do not to leap upon him. It is said that lovers recognize each other from afar; but, you have to admit, my lord, that one has to love someone pretty strongly to recognize him by a password of that sort!

The young greenhorns saw the success of this gallantry as an absolute discharge; they made off without a word, kept quiet night and day, and left my parents the peace that they so desired. They did feel a certain resentment, however, for in front of the other girls, they could not help saying: 'Heavens! What a pity that Margot should go and lose her head with Truquette first!' The girls, their curiosity aroused by my father's deserts, contradicted them: 'Oh yes, of course! It's an even greater pity that this Truquette should have chosen Margot.' 'Margot has taken Truquette, Truquette has taken Margot. Margot and Truquette, Truquette and Margot': for a month or more there was no other subject of conversation throughout that Babylon of a Solorgues.

But at last, when enough had been said, people fell silent; my parents still loved each other despite all the what-will-they-says, and the marriage stilled the tongues of the envious.

A B B É   J - B   C A S T O R   F A B R E   (1 4 t h   c e n t u r y)   (translated by A Sheridan)

Paul Cézanne and Émile Zola spent their early childhood together near Aix with another friend Baptistin Baille. But in the late 1850s Zola moved away.

To Émile Zola   Aix, 9th April, 1858

Good morning my dear Zola.

I have just seen Baille, this evening I am going to his country house (it is Baille senior that I am talking about), therefore I am writing to you.

> The weather is foggy
> Gloomy and rainy,
> And the pale sun in the skies
> No longer dazzles our eyes
> With its opal and ruby flames.

Since you left Aix, my dear fellow, dull sorrow has oppressed me; I am not lying, on my word. I can no longer recognize myself, I am heavy, stupid and slow. By the way, Baille told me that in a fortnight he would have the pleasure of permitting a sheet of paper to reach the hands of your most eminent Greatness in which he will express his sorrows and his griefs at being far from you. Really I should love to see you and I think that I shall see you, I and Baille (of course) for the holidays, and then we shall carry out, we shall do what we have planned, but in the meantime I am bemoaning your absence.

Do you remember the pine-tree which, planted on the banks of the Arc, bowed its hairy head above the precipice stretched out at its feet? With its foliage it protected our bodies from the ardour of the sun, ah! may the gods preserve it from the dread stroke of the woodcutter's axe.

We thought that you would come to Aix for the holidays and that then, by Jove, then joy would reign! We had planned hunting on as vast and unusual a scale as our fishing. Soon dear friend we shall start to hunt for fish again if the weather continues; it is magnificent today, for I am finishing my letter on the 13th.

> Phoebus pursuing its brilliant course
> Bathes all Aix in its waves of light.

Salve, carissime Zola.   P A U L   C É Z A N N E   (1 8 3 9 - 1 9 0 6)   (translated by M Kaye)

The Medieval chronicles describe the life and loves of Raimbaut d'Orange in these words .....

RAIMBAUT D'ORANGE WAS lord of Orange and Courthézon and of a great many other castles. And he was clever and well educated, and a good knight-at-arms and gracious in his conversation. He had a great liking for honorable ladies and honorable gallantry. He wrote good *vers* and *chansons;* but he preferred to write in difficult, subtle rhymes.

And for a long time he loved a woman of Provence whose name was Maria de Vertfuoil, and he called her 'Jongleur' in his songs. For a long time he loved her and she him. And for her he wrote many fine songs and did many other good deeds.

And then he fell in love with the good Countess of Urgell, who was from Lombardy, daughter of the Marquis of Busca. She was honored and esteemed over all the other noble ladies of Urgell, and Raimbaut, without having seen her but simply because of the good things he heard tell of her, fell in love with her and she with him. And he then wrote his songs for her, and he sent them to her by means of a jongleur called Nightingale, as he states in one song:

> My Nightingale, though
> you are full of grief,
> rejoice through my love
> in a little song you shall take
> for me without delay
> as a present for the worthy
> countess who lives in Urgell.

For a long time he courted this countess, without ever having the opportunity of going to see her. But I heard her say, after she had become a nun, that if he had come she would have granted him his pleasure and permitted him to touch her bare leg with the back of his hand.

While yet in love with her, Raimbaut died without male heir, and Orange was inherited by his two daughters.

MEDIEVAL LIVES OF THE TROUBADOURS (translated by A Bonner)

A Provençal lovesong .....

> In orchard where the leaves of hawthorn hide,
> The lady holds a lover to her side,
> Until the watcher in the dawning cried.
> *Ah God, ah God, the dawn! it comes how soon.*
>
> 'Ah, would to God that never night must end,
> Nor this my lover far from me should wend,
> Nor watcher day nor dawning ever send!
> *Ah God, ah God, the dawn! it comes how soon.*

Come let us kiss, dear lover, you and I,
Within the meads where pretty song-birds fly;
We will do all despite the jealous eye:
Ah God, ah God, the dawn! it comes how soon.

Sweet lover come, renew our lovemaking
Within the garden where the light birds sing,
Until the watcher sound the severing.
Ah God, ah God, the dawn! it comes how soon.

Through the soft breezes that are blown from there,
From my own lover, courteous, noble and fair,
From his breath have I drunk a draught most rare.
Ah God, ah God, the dawn! it comes how soon.'

Gracious the lady is, and debonaire,
For her beauty a many look at her,
And in her heart is loyal love astir.
Ah God, ah God, the dawn! it comes how soon.

TRADITIONAL . PROVENÇAL (translated by C Coleer Abbott)

Scott Fitzgerald's short story LOVE IN THE NIGHT *was first published in the Saturday Evening Post in 1925.*

THE WORDS THRILLED Val. They had come into his mind sometime during the fresh gold April afternoon and he kept repeating them to himself over and over: 'Love in the night; love in the night.' He tried them in three languages — Russian, French and English — and decided that they were best in English. In each language they meant a different sort of love and a different sort of night — the English night seemed the warmest and softest with a thinnest and most crystalline sprinkling of stars. The English love seemed the most fragile and romantic — a white dress and a dim face above it and eyes that were pools of light. And when I add that it was a French night he was thinking about, after all, I see I must go back and begin over.

Val was half Russian and half American. His mother was the daughter of that Morris Hasylton who helped finance the Chicago World's Fair in 1892, and his father was — see the Almanach de Gotha, issue of 1910 — Prince Paul Serge Boris Rostoff, son of Prince Vladimir Rostoff, grandson of a grand duke — 'Jimberjawed Serge' — and third-cousin-once-removed to the czar. It was all very impressive, you see, on that side — house in St Petersburg, shooting lodge near Riga, and swollen villa, more like a palace, overlooking the Mediterranean. It was at this villa in Cannes that the Rostoffs passed the winter — and it wasn't at all the thing to remind Princess Rostoff that this Riviera villa, from the marble fountain — after Bernini — to the gold cordial glasses — after dinner — was paid for with American gold.

The Russians, of course, were gay people on the Continent in the gala days before the war. Of the three races that used Southern France for a pleasure ground they were easily the most adept at the grand manner. The English were too practical, and the Americans, though they spent freely, had no tradition of romantic conduct. But the Russians — there was a people as gallant as the Latins, and rich besides! When the Rostoffs arrived at Cannes late in January the restaurateurs telegraphed north for the Prince's favorite labels to paste on their champagne, and the jewelers put incredibly gorgeous articles aside to show to him — but not to the princess — and the Russian Church was swept and garnished for the season that the Prince might beg orthodox forgiveness for his sins. Even the Mediterranean turned obligingly to a deep wine color in the spring evening, and fishing boats with robin-breasted sails loitered exquisitely offshore.

In a vague way young Val realized that this was all for the benefit of him and his family. It was a privileged paradise, this white little city on the water, in which he was free to do what he liked because he was rich and young and the blood of Peter the Great ran indigo in his veins. He was only seventeen in 1914, when this history begins, but he had already fought a duel with a young man four years his senior, and he had a small hairless scar to show for it on top of his handsome head.

But the question of love in the night was the thing nearest his heart. It was a vague pleasant dream he had, something that was going to happen to him some day that would be unique and incomparable. He could have told no more about it than that there was a lovely unknown girl concerned in it, and that it ought to take place beneath the Riviera moon.

The odd thing about all this was not that he had this excited and yet almost spiritual hope of romance, for all boys of any imagination have such hopes, but that it actually came true. And when it happened, it happened so unexpectedly; it was such a jumble of impressions and emotions, of curious phrases that sprang to his lips, of sights and sounds and moments that were here, were lost, were past, that he scarcely understood it at all. Perhaps its very vagueness preserved it in his heart and made him forever unable to forget.

There was an atmosphere of love all about him that spring — his father's loves, for instance, which were many and indiscreet, and which Val became aware of gradually from overhearing the gossip of servants, and definitely from coming on his American mother unexpectedly one afternoon, to find her storming hysterically at his father's picture on the salon wall. In the picture his father wore a white uniform with a furred dolman and looked back impassively at his wife as if to say 'Were you under the impression, my dear, that you were marrying into a family of clergymen?'

Val tiptoed away, surprised, confused — and excited. It didn't shock him as it would have shocked an American boy of his age. He had known for years what life was among the Continental rich, and he condemned his father only for making his mother cry.

Love went on around him — reproachless love and illicit love alike. As he strolled along the seaside promenade at nine o'clock, when the stars were bright enough to compete with the bright lamps, he was aware of love on every side. From the open-air cafés, vivid with dresses just down from Paris, came a sweet pungent odor of flowers and chartreuse and fresh black coffee and cigarettes — and mingled with them all he caught another scent, the mysterious thrilling scent of love. Hands touched jewel-sparkling hands upon the white tables. Gay dresses and white shirt fronts swayed together, and matches were held, trembling a little, for slow-lighting cigarettes. On the other side of the boulevard lovers less fashionable, young Frenchmen who worked in the stores of Cannes, sauntered with their fiancées under the dim trees, but Val's young eyes seldom turned that way. The luxury of music and bright colors and low voices — they were all part of his dream. They were the essential trappings of Love in the night.

But assume as he might the rather fierce expression that was expected from a young Russian gentleman who walked the streets alone, Val was beginning to be unhappy. April twilight had succeeded March twilight, the season was almost over, and he had found no use to make of the warm spring evenings. The girls of sixteen and seventeen whom he knew, were chaperoned with care between dusk and bedtime — this, remember, was before the war — and the others who might gladly have walked beside him were an affront to his romantic desire. So April passed by — one week, two weeks, three weeks —

He played tennis until seven and loitered at the courts for another hour, so it was half past eight when a tired cab horse accomplished the hill on which gleamed the façade of the Rostoff villa. The lights of his mother's limousine were yellow in the drive, and the princess, buttoning her gloves, was just coming out the glowing door. Val tossed two francs to the cabman and went to kiss her on the cheek.

'Don't touch me,' she said quickly. 'You've been handling money.'

'But not in my mouth, mother,' he protested humorously.

The princess looked at him impatiently.

'I'm angry,' she said. 'Why must you be so late tonight? We're dining on a yacht and you were to have come along too.'

'What yacht?'

'Americans.' There was always a faint irony in her voice when she mentioned the land of her nativity. Her America was the Chicago of the nineties which she still thought of as the vast upstairs to a butcher shop. Even the irregularities of Prince Paul were not too high a price to have paid for her escape.

'Two yachts,' she continued; 'in fact we don't know which one. The note was very indefinite. Very careless indeed.'

Americans. Val's mother had taught him to look down on Americans, but she hadn't succeeded in making him dislike them. American men noticed you, even if you were seventeen. He liked Americans. Although he was thoroughly Russian he wasn't immaculately so — the exact proportion, like that of a celebrated soap, was about ninety-nine and three-quarters per cent.

'I want to come,' he said, 'I'll hurry up, mother. I'll — '

'We're late now.' The princess turned as her husband appeared in the door. 'Now Val says he wants to come.'

'He can't,' said Prince Paul shortly. 'He's too outrageously late.'

Val nodded. Russian aristocrats, however indulgent about themselves, were always admirably Spartan with their children. There were no arguments.

'I'm sorry,' he said.

Prince Paul grunted. The footman, in red and silver livery, opened the limousine door. But the grunt decided the matter for Val, because Princess Rostoff at that day and hour had certain grievances against her husband which gave her command of the domestic situation.

'On second thought you'd better come, Val,' she announced coolly. 'It's too late now, but come after dinner. The yacht is either the Minnehaha or the Privateer.' She got into the limousine. 'The one to come to will be the gayer one, I suppose — the Jacksons' yacht — '

'Find got sense,' muttered the Prince cryptically, conveying that Val would find it if he had any sense. 'Have my man take a look at you 'fore you start. Wear tie of mine 'stead of that outrageous string you affected in Vienna. Grow up. High time.'

As the limousine crawled crackling down the pebbled drive Val's face was burning.

2

It was dark in Cannes harbour, rather it seemed dark after the brightness of the promenade that Val had just left behind. Three frail dock lights glittered dimly upon innumerable fishing boats heaped like shells along the beach. Farther out in the water there were other lights where a fleet of slender yachts rode the tide with slow dignity, and farther still a full ripe moon made the water's bosom into a polished dancing floor. Occasionally there was a swish! creak! drip! as a rowboat moved about in the shallows, and its blurred shape threaded the labyrinth of hobbled fishing skiffs and launches. Val, descending the velvet slope of sand, stumbled over a sleeping boatman and caught the rank savor of garlic and plain wine. Taking the man by the shoulders he shook open his startled eyes.

'Do you know where the Minnehaha is anchored, and the Privateer?'

As they slid out into the bay he lay back in the stern and stared with vague discontent at the Riviera moon. That was the right moon, all right. Frequently, five nights out of seven, there was the right moon. And here was the soft air, aching with enchantment, and here was the music, many strains of music from many orchestras, drifting out from the shore. Eastward lay the dark Cape of Antibes, and then Nice, and beyond that Monte Carlo, where the night rang chinking full of gold. Some day he would enjoy all that, too, know its every pleasure and success — when he was too old and wise to care.

But tonight — tonight, that stream of silver that waved like a wide strand of curly hair toward the moon; those soft romantic lights of Cannes behind him, the irresistable ineffable love in this air — that was to be wasted forever.

'Which one?' asked the boatman suddenly.

'Which what?' demanded Val, sitting up.

'Which boat?'

He pointed. Val turned; above hovered the gray, sword-like prow of a yacht. During the sustained longing of his wish they had covered half a mile.

He read the brass letters over his head. It was the Privateer, but there were only dim lights on board, and no music and no voices, only a murmurous k-plash at intervals as the small waves leaped at the sides.

'The other one,' said Val; 'the Minnehaha.'

'Don't go yet.'

Val started. The voice, low and soft, had dropped down from the darkness overhead.

'What's the hurry?' said the soft voice. 'Thought maybe somebody was coming to see me, and have suffered terrible disappointment.'

The boatman lifted his oars and looked hesitatingly at Val. But Val was silent, so the man let the blades fall into the water and swept the boat out into the moonlight.

'Wait a minute!' cried Val sharply.

'Good-by,' said the voice. 'Come again when you can stay longer.'

'But I am going to stay now,' he answered breathlessly.

He gave the necessary order and the rowboat swung back at the foot of the small companionway. Someone young, someone in a misty white dress, someone with a lovely low voice, had actually called to him out of the velvet dark. 'If she has eyes,' Val murmured to himself. He liked the romantic sound of it and repeated it under his breath — 'If she has eyes.'

'What are you?' She was directly above him now; she was looking down and he was looking up as he climbed the ladder and as their eyes met they both began to laugh.

She was very young, slim, almost frail, with a dress that accentuated her youth by its blanched simplicity. Two wan dark spots on her cheeks marked where the colour was by day.

'What are you?' she repeated, moving back and laughing again as his head appeared on the level of the deck. 'I'm frightened now and I want to know.'

'I am a gentleman,' said Val, bowing.

'What sort of gentleman? There are all sorts of gentlemen. There was a — there was a coloured gentleman at the table next to ours in Paris, and so —' She broke off. 'You're not American, are you?'

'I'm Russian,' he said, as he might have announced himself to be an archangel. He thought quickly and then added, 'And I am the most fortunate of Russians. All this day, all this spring I have dreamed of falling in love on such a night, and now I see that heaven has sent me to you.'

'Just one moment!' she said, with a little gasp. 'I'm sure now that this visit is a mistake. I don't go in for anything like that. Please!'

'I beg your pardon.' He looked at her in bewilderment, unaware that he had taken too much for granted. Then he drew himself up formally.

'I have made an error. If you will excuse me I will say good night.'

He turned away. His hand was on the rail.

'Don't go,' she said, pushing a strand of indefinite hair out of her eyes. 'On second thoughts you can talk any nonsense you like if you'll only not go. I'm miserable and I don't want to be left alone.'

Val hesitated; there was some element in this that he failed to understand. He had taken it for granted that a girl who called to a strange man at night, even from the deck of a yacht, was certainly in a mood for romance. And he wanted intensely to stay. Then he remembered that this was one of the two yachts he had been seeking.

'I imagine that the dinner's on the other boat,' he said.

'The dinner? Oh, yes, it's on the Minnehaha. Were you going there?'

'I was going there — a long time ago.'

'What's your name?'

He was on the point of telling her when something made him ask a question instead.

'And you? Why are you not at the party?'

'Because I preferred to stay here. Mrs Jackson said there would be some Russians there — I suppose that's you.' She looked at him with interest. 'You're a very young man, aren't you?'

'I am much older than I look,' said Val stiffly. 'People always comment on it. It's considered rather a remarkable thing.'

'How old are you?'

'Twenty-one,' he lied.

She laughed.

'What nonsense! You're not more than nineteen.'

His annoyance was so perceptible that she hastened to reassure him. 'Cheer up! I'm only seventeen myself. I might have gone to the party if I'd thought there'd be anyone under fifty there.'

He welcomed the change of subject.

'You preferred to sit and dream here beneath the moon.'

'I've been thinking of mistakes.' They sat down side by side in two canvas deck chairs. 'It's a most engrossing subject — the subject of mistakes. Women very seldom brood about mistakes — they're much more willing to forget them than men are. But when they do brood — '

'You have made a mistake?' inquired Val.

She nodded.

'Is it something that cannot be repaired?'

'I think so,' she answered. 'I can't be sure. That's what I was considering when you came along.'

'Perhaps I can help in some way,' said Val. 'Perhaps your mistake is not irreparable, after all.'

'You can't,' she said unhappily. 'So let's not think about it. I'm very tired of my mistake and I'd much rather you'd tell me about all the gay, cheerful things that are going on in Cannes tonight.'

They glanced shoreward at the line of mysterious and alluring lights, the big toy banks with candles inside that were really the great fashionable hotels, the lighted clock in the old town, the blurred glow of the Café de Paris, the pricked-out points of villa windows rising on slow hills toward the dark sky.

'What is everyone doing there?' she whispered. 'It looks as though something gorgeous was going on, but what it is I can't quite tell.'

'Everyone there is making love,' said Val quietly.

'Is that it?' She looked for a long time, with a strange expression in her eyes. 'Then I want to go home to America,' she said. 'There is too much love here. I want to go home tomorrow.'

'You are afraid of being in love then?'

She shook her head.

'It isn't that. It's just because — there is no love here for me.'

'Or for me either,' added Val quietly. 'It is sad that we two should be at such a lovely place on such a lovely night and have — nothing.'

He was leaning toward her intently, with a sort of inspired and chaste romance in his eyes — and she drew back.

'Tell me more about yourself,' she inquired quickly. 'If you are Russian where did you learn to speak such excellent English?'

'My mother was American,' he admitted. 'My grandfather was American also, so she had no choice in the matter.'

'Then you're American too!'

'I am Russian,' said Val with dignity.

She looked at him closely, smiled and decided not to argue. 'Well then,' she said diplomatically, 'I suppose you must have a Russian name.'

But he had no intention now of telling her his name. A name, even the Rostoff name, would be a desecration of the night. They were their own low voices, their two white faces — and that was enough. He was sure, without any reason for being sure but with a sort of instinct that sang triumphantly through his mind, that in a little while, a minute or an hour, he was going to undergo an initiation into the life of romance. His name had no reality beside what was stirring in his heart.

'You are beautiful,' he said suddenly.

'How do you know?'

'Because for women moonlight is the hardest light of all.'

'Am I nice in the moonlight?'

'You are the loveliest thing that I have ever known.'

'Oh.' She thought this over. 'Of course I had no business to let you come on board. I might have known what we'd talk about — in this moon. But I can't sit here and look at the shore — forever. I'm too young for that. Don't you think I'm too young for that?'

'Much too young,' he agreed solemnly.

Suddenly they both became aware of new music that was close at hand, music that seemed to come out of the water not a hundred yards away.

'Listen!' she cried. 'It's from the Minnehaha. They've finished dinner.'

For a moment they listened in silence.

'Thank you,' said Val suddenly.

'For what?'

He hardly knew he had spoken. He was thanking the deep low horns for singing in the breeze, the sea for its warm murmurous complaint against the bow, the milk of the stars for washing over them until he felt buoyed up in a substance more taut than air.

'So lovely,' she whispered.

'What are we going to do about it?'

'Do we have to do something about it? I thought we could just sit and enjoy —'

'You didn't think that,' he interrupted quietly. 'You know that we must do something about it. I am going to make love to you — and you are going to be glad.'

'I can't,' she said very low. She wanted to laugh now, to make some light cool remark that would bring the situation back into the safe waters of a casual flirtation. But it was too late now. Val knew that the music had completed what the moon had begun.

'I will tell you the truth,' he said. 'You are my first love. I am seventeen — the same age as you, no more.'

There was something utterly disarming about the fact that they were the same age. It made her helpless before the fate that had thrown them together. The deck chairs creaked and he was conscious of a faint illusive perfume as they swayed suddenly and childishly together.

3

Whether he kissed her once or several times he could not afterward remember, though it must have been an hour that they sat there close together and he held her hand. What surprised him most about making love was that it seemed to have no element of wild passion — regret, desire, despair — but a delirious promise of such happiness in the world, in living, as he had never known. First love — this was only first love! What must love itself in its fullness, its perfection be! He did not know that what he was experiencing then, that unreal, undesirous medley of ecstasy and peace, would be unrecapturable forever.

The music had ceased for some time when presently the murmurous silence was broken by the sound of a rowboat disturbing the quiet waves. She sprang suddenly to her feet and her eyes strained out over the bay.

'Listen!' she said quickly. 'I want you to tell me your name.'

'No.'

'Please,' she begged him. 'I'm going away tomorrow.'

He didn't answer.

'I don't want you to forget me,' she said. 'My name is — '

'I won't forget you. I will promise to remember you always. Whoever I may love I will always compare her to you, my first love. So long as I live you will always have that much freshness in my heart.'

'I want you to remember,' she murmured brokenly. 'Oh, this has meant more to me than it has to you — much more.'

She was standing so close to him that he felt her warm young breath on his face. Once again they swayed together. He pressed her hands and wrists between his as it seemed right to do, and kissed her lips. It was the right kiss, he thought, the romantic kiss — not too little or too much. Yet there was a sort of promise in it of other kisses he might have had, and it was with a slight sinking of his heart that he heard the rowboat close to the yacht and realized that her family had returned. The evening was over.

'And this is only the beginning,' he told himself. 'All my life will be like this night.'

She was saying something in a low quick voice and he was listening tensely.

'You must know one thing — I am married. Three months ago. That was the mistake that I was thinking about when the moon brought you out here. In a moment you will understand.'

She broke off as the boat swung against the companionway and a man's voice floated up out of the darkness.

'Is that you, my dear?'

'Yes.'

'What is this other rowboat waiting?'

'One of Mrs Jackson's guests came here by mistake and I made him stay and amuse me for an hour.'

A moment later the thin white hair and weary face of a man of sixty appeared above the level of the deck. And then Val saw and realised too late how much he cared.

4

When the Riviera season ended in May the Rostoffs and all the other Russians closed their villas and went north for the summer. The Russian Orthodox Church was locked up and so were the bins of rarer wine, and the fashionable spring moonlight was put away, so to speak, to wait for their return.

'We'll be back next season,' they said as a matter of course.

But this was premature, for they were never coming back any more. Those few who straggled south again after five tragic years were glad to get work as chambermaids or *valets de chambre* in the great hotels where they had once dined. Many of them, of course, were killed in the war or in the revolution; many of them faded out as spongers and small cheats in the big capitals, and not a few of them ended their lives in a sort of stupefied despair.

When the Kerensky government collapsed in 1917, Val was a lieutenant on the eastern front, trying desperately to enforce authority in his company long after any vestige of it remained. He was still trying when Prince Paul Rostoff and his wife gave up their lives one rainy morning to atone for the blunders of the Romanoffs — and the enviable career of Morris Hasylton's daughter ended in a city that bore even more resemblance to a butcher shop than had Chicago in 1892.

After that Val fought with Denikin's army for a while until he realized that he was participating in a hollow farce and the glory of Imperial Russia was over. Then he went to France and was suddenly confronted with the astounding problem of keeping his body and soul together.

It was, of course, natural that he should think of going to America. Two vague aunts with whom his mother had quarreled many years ago still lived there in comparative affluence. But the idea was repugnant to the prejudices his mother had implanted in him, and besides he hadn't sufficient money left to pay for his passage over. Until a possible counter-revolution should restore to him the Rostoff properties in Russia he must somehow keep alive in France.

So he went to the little city he knew best of all. He went to Cannes. His last two hundred francs bought him a third-class ticket and when he arrived he gave his dress suit to an obliging party who dealt in such things and received in return money for food and bed. He was sorry afterward that he had sold the dress suit, because it might have helped him to a position as a waiter. But he obtained work as a taxi driver instead and was quite as happy, or rather quite as miserable, at that.

Sometimes he carried Americans to look at villas for rent, and when the front glass of the automobile was up, curious fragments of conversation drifted out to him from within.

' — heard this fellow was a Russian prince.' ..... 'Sh!' ..... 'No, this one right here.' ..... 'Be quiet, Esther!' — followed by subdued laughter.

When the car stopped, his passengers would edge around to have a look at him. At first he was desperately unhappy when girls did this; after a while he didn't mind any more. Once a cheerfully intoxicated American asked if it were true and invited him to lunch, and another time an elderly woman seized his hand as she got out of the taxi, shook it violently and then pressed a hundred-franc note into his hand.

'Well, Florence, now I can tell 'em back home I shook hands with a Russian prince.'

The inebriated American who had invited him to lunch thought at first that Val was a son of the czar, and it had to be explained to him that a prince in Russia was simply the equivalent of a British courtesy lord. But he was puzzled that a man of Val's personality didn't go out and make some real money.

'This is Europe,' said Val gravely. 'Here money is not made. It is inherited or else it is slowly saved over a period of many years and maybe in three generations a family moves up into a higher class.'

'Think of something people want — like we do.'

'That is because there is more money to want with in America. Everything that people want here has been thought of long ago.'

But after a year and with the help of a young Englishman he had played tennis with before the war, Val managed to get into the Cannes branch of an English bank. He forwarded mail and bought railroad tickets and arranged tours for impatient sightseers. Sometimes a familiar face came to his window; if Val was recognized he shook hands; if not he kept silence. After two years he was no longer pointed out as a former prince, for the Russians were an old story now — the splendor of the Rostoffs and their friends was forgotten.

He mixed with people very little. In the evenings he walked for a while on the promenade, took a slow glass of beer in a café, and went early to bed. He was seldom invited anywhere because people thought that his sad, intent face was depressing — and he never accepted any how. He wore cheap French clothes now instead of the rich tweeds and flannels that had been ordered with his father's from England. As for women, he knew none at all. Of the many things he had been certain about at seventeen, he had been most certain about this — that his life would be full of romance. Now after eight years he knew that it was not to be. Somehow he had never had time for love — the war, the revolution and now his poverty had conspired against his expectant heart. The springs of his emotion which had first poured forth one April night had dried up immediately and only a faint trickle remained.

His happy youth had ended almost before it began. He saw himself growing older and more shabby, and living always more and more in the memories of his gorgeous boyhood. Eventually he would become absurd, pulling out an old heirloom of a watch and showing it to amused young fellow clerks who would listen with winks to his tales of the Rostoff name.

He was thinking these gloomy thoughts one April evening in 1922 as he walked beside the sea and watched the never-changing magic of the awakening lights. It was no longer for his benefit, that magic, but it went on, and he was somehow glad. Tomorrow he was going away on his vacation, to a cheap hotel farther down the shore where he could bathe and rest and read; then he would come back and work some more. Every year for three years he had taken his vacation during the last two weeks in April, perhaps because it was then that he felt the most need for remembering. It was in April that what was destined to be the best part of his life had come to a culmination under a romantic moonlight. It was sacred to him — for what he had thought of as an initiation and a beginning had turned out to be the end.

He paused now in front of the Café des Étrangers and after a moment crossed the street on impulse and sauntered down to the shore. A dozen yachts, already turned to a beautiful silver color, rode at anchor in the bay. He had seen them that afternoon, and read the names painted on their bows — but only from habit. He had done it for three years now, and it was almost a natural function of his eye.

'Un beau soir,' remarked a French voice at his elbow. It was a boatman who had often seen Val here before. 'Monsieur finds the sea beautiful?'

'Very beautiful.'

'I too. But a bad living except in the season. Next week, though, I earn something special. I am paid well for simply waiting here and doing nothing more from eight o'clock until midnight.'

'That's very nice,' said Val politely.

'A widowed lady, very beautiful, from America, whose yacht always anchors in the harbor for the last two weeks in April. If the Privateer comes tomorrow it will make three years.

5

All night Val didn't sleep — not because there was any question in his mind as to what he should do, but because his long stupefied emotions were suddenly awake and alive. Of course he must not see her — not he, a poor failure with a name that was now only a shadow — but it would make him a little happier always to know that she remembered. It gave his own memory another dimension, raised it like those stereopticon glasses that bring out a picture from the flat paper. It made him sure that he had not deceived himself — he had been charming once upon a time to a lovely woman, and she did not forget.

An hour before train time next day he was at the railway station with his grip, so as to avoid any chance encounter in the street. He found himself a place in a third-class carriage of the waiting train.

Somehow as he sat there he felt differently about life — a sort of hope, faint and illusory, that he hadn't felt twenty-four hours before. Perhaps there was some way in the next few years in which he could make it possible to meet her once again — if he worked hard, threw himself passionately into whatever was at hand. He knew of at least two Russians in Cannes who had started over again with nothing except good manners and ingenuity and were now doing surprisingly well. The blood of Morris Hasylton began to throb a little in Val's temples and made him remember something he had never before cared to remember — that Morris Hasylton, who had built his daughter a palace in St Petersburg, had also started from nothing at all.

Simultaneously another emotion possessed him, less strange, less dynamic but equally American — the emotion of curiosity. In case he did — well, in case life should ever make it possible for him to seek her out, he should at least know her name.

He jumped to his feet, fumbled excitedly at the carriage handle and jumped from the train. Tossing his valise into the check room he started at a run for the American consulate.

'A yacht came in this morning,' he said hurriedly to a clerk, 'an American yacht — the Privateer. I want to know who owns it.'

'Just a minute,' said the clerk, looking at him oddly. 'I'll try to find out.'

After what seemed to Val an interminable time he returned.

'Why, just a minute,' he repeated hesitantly. 'We're — it seems we're finding out.'

'Did the yacht come?'

'Oh, yes — it's here all right. At least I think so. If you'll just wait in that chair.'

After another ten minutes Val looked impatiently at his watch. If they didn't hurry he'd probably miss his train. He made a nervous movement as if to get up from his chair.

'Please sit still,' said the clerk, glancing at him quickly from his desk. 'I ask you. Just sit down in that chair.'

'I'll miss my train,' he said impatiently. 'I'm sorry to have given you all this bother — '

'Please sit still! We're glad to get it off our hands. You see, we've been waiting for your inquiry for — ah — three years.'

Val jumped to his feet and jammed his hat on his head.

'Why didn't you tell me that?' he demanded angrily.

'Because we had to get word to our — our client. Please don't go! It's — ah, it's too late.'

Val turned. Someone slim and radiant with dark frightened eyes was standing behind him, framed against the sunshine of the doorway.

'Why — '

Val's lips parted, but no words came through. She took a step toward him.

'I — ' She looked at him helplessly, her eyes filling with tears. 'I just wanted to say hello,' she murmured. 'I've come back for three years just because I wanted to say hello.'

Still Val was silent.

'You might answer,' she said impatiently. 'You might answer when I'd — when I'd just about begun to think you'd been killed in the war.' She turned to the clerk. 'Please introduce us!' she cried. 'You see, I can't say hello to him when we don't even know each other's names.'

It's the thing to distrust these international marriages, of course. It's an American tradition that they always turn out badly, and we are accustomed to such headlines as: 'Would Trade Coronet for True American Love, Says Duchess,' and 'Claims Count Mendicant Tortured Toledo Wife.' The other sort of headlines are never printed, for who would want to read: 'Castle is Love Nest, Asserts Former Georgia Belle,' or 'Duke and Packer's Daughter Celebrate Golden Honeymoon.'

So far there have been no headlines at all about the young Rostoffs. Prince Val is much too absorbed in that string of moonlight-blue taxi cabs which he manipulates with such unusual efficiency, to give out interviews. He and his wife only leave New York once a year — but there is still a boatman who rejoices when the Privateer steams into Cannes harbor on a mid-April night.   F SCOTT FITZGERALD (1896-1940)

Poet, novelist and mythologist Robert Graves here allies a traditional tale to a personal plea.

I'm Through With You For Ever

The oddest, surely, of odd tales
    Recorded by the French
Concerns a sneak thief of Marseilles
    Tried by a callous Bench.

His youth, his innocency, his tears —
    No, nothing could abate
Their sentence of 'One hundred years
    In galleys of the State.'

Nevertheless, old wives affirm
    And annalists agree,
He sweated out the whole damned term,
    Bowed stiffly, and went free.

Then come, my angry love, review
    Your sentence of today.
'For ever' was unjust of you,
    The end too far away.

Give me four hundred years, or five —
    Can rage be so intense? —
And I will sweat them out alive
    To prove my impenitence.

      ROBERT GRAVES (1895 -)

Here is one of Katherine Mansfield's most romantic letters to John Middleton Murry.

Thursday 4 March

THIS IS THE kind of thing that happens at 1.30. A big car arrives. We go in from our coffee and liqueurs on the balcony. May is waiting to dress me — I wear 'somebody's' coat — 'anybody's' — we get in, there are rugs, cushions, hassocks, and yesterday the tea basket, and away we go. Yesterday we went to La Turbie ..... It's up, up, high, high on the tops of the mountains. It's a tiny ancient Roman town, incredibly ancient! with old bits with pillars and capitals — Oh, dear — it is so lovely. The road winds and winds to get there round and round the mountains. I could hardly bear it yesterday. I was so much in love with you. I kept seeing it all, for you — wishing for you — longing for you. The rosemary is in flower (our plant it is). The almond

Villa Isola Bella : Katherine Mansfield

trees, pink and white; there are wild cherry trees and the prickly pear white among the olives. Apple trees are just in their first rose and white — wild hyacinths and violets are tumbled out of Flora's wicker ark and are *everywhere*. And over everything, like a light, are the lemon and orange trees glowing. If I saw one house which was *ours*, I saw twenty. I know we shall never live in such houses, but still they are ours — little houses with terraces and a verandah — with bean fields in bloom with a bright scatter of anemones all over the gardens. When we reached the mountain tops we got out and lay on the grass, looking down, down — into the valleys and over Monaco .....

We stayed there about 2 hours and then dropped down by another road to Monte — the light and the shadow were divided on the hills, but the sun was still in the air, all the time — the sea very rosy with a pale big moon over by Bordighera. We got home by 6.30 and there was my fire, the bed turned down — hot milk — May waiting to take off all my things. 'Did you enjoy it, Madam?' Can you imagine such a coming back to Life?

KATHERINE MANSFIELD (1888-1923)

Many of Petrarch's love poems were preoccupied with old age and death.

Giovene donna sotto un verde lauro

A girl under a green laurel
I saw, whiter and more cold than snow
Untouched by the sun numberless years.
Her speaking, the grace of her look, her hair
So moved my pleasure, that I have them before my eyes,
Standing now on this shore.

When my thought of her reaches its last shore
Black leaves will hang on the laurel;
When my heart quiets, joy covers my eyes,
And frozen fire lives in burning snow.
I could not yet number my hair;
Nor could I count the days I would wait for such a year.

The time runs out. You see years
Vanish. Death rides against this shore,
My vigorous brown, white hair
In an instant. And I trace the shadow of the laurel
Through the sun's heat as it rides on snow,
Until the last day will close my eyes.

I never saw such gentle eyes,
In any year,
That draw me into water as the sun melts snow;
And I follow the sad shore
As love leads me to the foot of the cruel laurel,
Whose diamond branches carry golden hair.

You will not recognize my face. My hair
Will change, before pity lives in those eyes.
I have carved an idol of the green laurel.
Today is the marking of the seventh year
My walk takes me along this shore
In the bright nights, in this hot mist of snow.

Fire the core, surrounded with white snow,
Alone in these thoughts, my hair
Whitened also — I will weep on this shore,
Will make pity come to the eyes
Of some gentle person to be born a thousand years
Hence. It will be standing here still, the great laurel.

Gold topaz in sun and snow,
This bright hair conquered my eyes.
My years stand at their final shore.

FRANCESCO PETRARCH (1 3 0 4 - 1 3 7 4) (translated by N Kilmer)

Café Terrasse in Arles : Vincent Van Gogh

CHAPTER NINE

Food
and Wine

Recognised as more than a cook-book writer, culinary historian Elizabeth David here talks about the food of Provence.

P R O V E N C E I S A country to which I am always returning, next week, next year, any day now, as soon as I can get on to a train. Here in London it is an effort of will to believe in the existence of such a place at all. But now and again the vision of golden tiles on a round southern roof, or of some warm, stony, herb-scented hillside will rise out of my kitchen pots with the smell of a piece of orange peel scenting a beef stew. The picture flickers into focus again. Ford Madox Ford's words come back, 'somewhere between Vienne and Valence, below Lyons on the Rhône, the sun is shining and south of Valence Provincia Romana, the Roman Province, lies beneath the sun. There there is no more any evil, for there the apple will not flourish and the brussels sprout will not grow at all.'

It is indeed certain, although the apple of discord can hardly be said to have been absent from the history of Provence, which is a turbulent and often ferocious one, that the sprout from Brussels, the drabness and dreariness and stuffy smells evoked by its very name, has nothing at all to do with southern cooking. But to regard the food of Provence as just a release from routine, a fierce wild riot of flavour and colour, is to oversimplify it and grossly to mistake its nature. For it is not primitive food; it is civilized without being over-civilized. That is to say, it has natural taste, smell, texture, and much character. Often it looks beautiful, too. What it amounts to is that it is the rational, right and proper food for human beings to eat.

Madame Léon Daudet, who, under the pen-name of Pampille, published many years ago a little collection of regional recipes called *Les Bons Plats de France,* goes so far as to say that 'the cooking of Provence seems to me the best of all cooking; this is not said to hurt the feelings of other provinces, but it is the absolute truth.' Whether or not one agrees with Madame Daudet's wonderfully sweeping statement one should on no account be deceived by the often clumsy attempts of London restaurateurs to reproduce Provençal dishes. To them Provence is a name, a symbol to display to their customers; the string of garlic hanging on the wall is something like the equivalent of an inn sign. Nor must some ostentatious meal in a phoney Provençal 'oustalou' whose row of medals stands for price rather than true taste or quality be taken as representative. Provence does not consist only of the international playground of the coast. Northern and western Provence, the departments of the Vaucluse and the Basses Alpes, are still comparatively unsophisticated, and the cooking has retained much of its traditional character, the inhabitants relying on their own plentiful resources of vegetables, fruit, meat, game, and cheese rather than on the imports from other provinces and from Algeria which supplement the more meagre resources of the coastal area.

Provençal food is perhaps best considered in terms of a meal such as that described, again, by Madame Daudet: 'I know of nothing more appetizing,' she says, 'on a very hot day, than to sit down in the cool shade of a dining-room with drawn Venetian blinds, at a little table laid with black olives, *saucisson d'Arles,* some fine tomatoes, a slice of water melon and a pyramid of little green figs baked by the sun. One will scarcely resist the pleasure of afterwards tasting the anchovy tart or the roast of lamb cooked on the spit, its skin perfectly browned, or the dish of tender little artichokes in oil ..... but should one wish, one could make one's meal almost exclusively of the hors-d'oeuvre and the fruit. In this light air, in this fortunate countryside, there is no need to warm oneself with heavy meats or dishes of lentils. The midi is essentially a region of carefully prepared little dishes.'

This was written in 1919, but these little dishes of Provence are still to be found in country restaurants where they aren't falling over backwards to provide local colour; places where you may perhaps have the routine Sunday grilled or roast chicken but with it an interesting anchovy sauce, or a mayonnaise made unmistakably with real Provençal olive oil; or a *rôti de porc* with *pommes mousseline,* the interest lying in the fact that the purée of potatoes will be good enough to serve as a separate course because the aromatic juices from the roast have been poured over it. It may be an hors-d'oeuvre of anchovies and eggs, a salad of chick peas, a *pot-au-feu* or a beef stew which will be different from the *pot-au-feu* and the beef stew of other regions because of the herbs and the wine that have gone into it, even because of the pot it has cooked in. There will be vegetable dishes, too. The *haricots verts* are remarkable, although of course you won't get them on the crowded coast in August. Provence is now a great market garden centre, and from Cavaillon and Pertuis come melons, asparagus, artichokes, lettuces, courgettes, aubergines, peaches, and cherries to enrich our own English markets. The little town of Le Thor supplies France with great quantities of table grapes; Carpentras is the centre of a lively trade in the local black truffles. The natural caves round about the astonishing red and ochre village of Roussillon are used for a large-scale cultivation of mushrooms; Apt provides peach jam and bitter cherry jam and most of the crystallized apricots we ourselves buy at Christmas time. It is also one of the few places hereabouts where you can still find the old traditional earthenware *gratin* dishes, saucepans and cooking pots of Provence.   E L I Z A B E T H   D A V I D   (1 9 1 3 -)

An interesting note on attitudes to food in the 13th and 14th Centuries .....

I N   1 2 4 6   T H E Statutes of Avignon classified the flesh of sick animals and those killed by Jews on the same level. In 1306 the Statutes of Charles II described it as unhealthy, and in 1339 at St Rémy such flesh was called sordid. In 1293 the Statutes of Salon forbade Jews, prostitutes and lepers to handle any fish, fruit, bread, meats other than those they were going to buy.

L O U I S   S T O U F F   (1 9 7 0) (translated by J Karslake)

Louis Stouff, the French historian, has analysed the diet and food rations in the Papal College of Trets as described in the 14th Century documents from the Vatican archives. This diet was probably fairly similar to that eaten by most people in the region at that time.

T H E S E   R A T I O N S   W E R E intended for about 120 pupils aged from 12-18 years. The document outlines the provisions stocked annually: the quantity of grain, wine, meat, salted meat, salt, vegetables. Then from June 1364-1365 it shows the quantities of wheat, wine, oil, fresh and salted meat consumed daily. The amount of cheese, fresh fruit and salted fish is not given, but the existence of these commodities on the masters' or students' tables is always noted even if they came from the school's own garden ..... .

149 days are fast days when fresh or salt fish (tunny fish, grey or red mullet) and eggs were eaten.

217 days were set aside for meat. The consumption of mutton was overwhelming. 160 days were assigned to mutton, beef only appeared 5 times, kid and pork once, salt pork 55 times.

..... salt pork played an important part since it appears on the table more than one day in six and in the guise of cooking fat more than 200 days a year.

The document does not say whether meat appears at both meals. It gives the impression that it is incorporated into the soup which was served to the students twice a day .....

Vegetables always seem to be served cooked which is one of the disadvantages of this diet and to that must be added the minor role played by fruit. Only walnuts, figs and plums were bought and served .....

To complete the picture olive oil was consumed on about 150 days; it was used on fast days for cooking fish or eggs. We note finally that the consumption of cheese was meagre and unequally divided between the pupils (1.8 Kl a year) and staff (4.8 Kl per year). Cheese appears to be a luxury.

LOUIS STOUFF (1 9 7 0) (translated by J Karslake)

Another document from the Vatican Archives shows the annual quantities of food consumed by the Archbishopric of Arles in 1429.

A D A Y B Y day account of food bought for the household of the Archbishop of Arles in 1429 shows: mutton on 191 days, lamb on 34 days, goat on 7, ewe on 2, beef on 68, fresh pork on 7, chicken on 6 etc. 151 days were given to fish and eggs.

These foods appeared on the table twice a day. On 19 May 8½ lbs of mutton and half a hind quarter of lamb were prepared in the kitchen for mid-day; for the evening meal 4 lbs of mutton and a hind quarter of goat.

The amount of vegetables in the diet remains obscure. A garden and vegetable garden certainly existed; we do not know what contribution they played in daily meals. As in other establishments cabbage, leeks, spinach, marrows, onions, lettuces and herbs must have appeared on menus frequently. The purchase of broad beans, peas, celeriac and parsnips is mentioned. The commissariat also acquired off the premises, cherries, apples, pears, plums, figs, walnuts, hazelnuts and even oranges. In June for example oranges were bought three times, a dozen, fifty and a hundred.   LOUIS STOUFF (1 9 7 0) (translated by J Karslake)

Plutarch tells of Antony's meagre rations when fleeing from Caesar in Modena, over the Alps to Provence.

A N T O N Y , I N H I S flight, was overtaken by distresses of every kind, and the worst of all of them was famine. But it was his character in calamities to be better than at any other time.

~~~~~~

Antony, in misfortune, was most nearly a virtuous man. It is common enough for people, when they fall into great disasters, to discern what is right, and what they ought to do; but there are but few who in such extremities have the strength to obey their judgment, either in doing what it approves or avoiding what it condemns; and a good many are so weak as to give way to their habits all the more, and are incapable of using their minds. Antony, on this occasion, was a most wonderful example to his soldiers. He, who had just quitted so much luxury and sumptuous living, made no difficulty now of drinking foul water and feeding on wild fruits and roots. Nay, it is related they ate the very bark of trees, and, in passing over the Alps, lived upon creatures that no one before had ever been willing to touch.

<div style="text-align:right">PLUTÀRCH (c AD 70) (translated by A H Clough)</div>

Jean-l'ont-pris describes his parents' wedding feast in the 14th Century .....

NEVER, MY LORD, could there ever have been such an expensive wedding in Solorgues. However, the poor devils were to regret it later! My father, God rest his soul, saddled a couple of donkeys and went to Nîmes to fetch the food and other necessaries for the feast. He arrived back with four baskets and a sack full of things. For himself, there was a serge jacket from Cádiz, a fine pair of stockings from Saint-Marsot, a pair of grey linen knee-breeches with good, strong garters, yellow ribbons, leather gaiters and new tin buckles. For his betrothed, he brought a fine apron from Saint-Jean, a serge petticoat, a large brass cross and chain, a flannelette jacket with chamois-leather fronts and the wedding-ring, which, if it had been gold, would certainly have weighed half a pound.

The rest was to gorge themselves: tell me if there wasn't enough to feast all the friends and relations! Ah, my lord, look how people talk! How generous people may become when they are in love, for their damned weddings! For you have heard nothing yet of what I have still to tell you and which all Solorgues would confirm. Would you believe, my lord, that on the wedding-day, either on their way to the church or coming back or during the meal that was given, the four baskets of provisions that my father had brought back disappeared? But I'm not surprised. They cast food about in all directions, like seed. People in the street caught at least four pounds of hazelnuts, which my father threw to them, not to mention all the handfuls of hackberries that my mother threw to left and right as she raised her leg.

As if that were not enough, as soon as they had returned home for the feast, my wasteful grandmother — I wonder what sudden madness took hold of her, what came over the old bitch — took it into her head to stand in front of the door and throw at least twenty packets of matches into the street; and if I said twenty-two, I would certainly not be lying! Judge for yourself, my lord, judge for yourself if those who were sitting at the table would go short!

It is said that during the meal they consumed two large pots of girdle-cakes, another pot full of frogs, a *roussette* weighing nine pounds, half a dozen magpies, plus a magnificent fox that the hunter of La Boissière had killed the night before in the Garrigue de Mus and that he had not sold for under 12 sous without the skin. All this was followed by four panfuls of chestnuts, sloes, cornel-berries, arbutus-berries, mulberries and the devil knows what else ..... Plus a four-*setier* butt of wine. Oh, I'm sure your lordship will agree that poor folk who give themselves such airs of greatness cannot reign. That belongs to noblemen like yourself, and even, in the end, it would not be a miracle to see you drowned head over heels .....

The first to say that when the feast is over the fool remains certainly knew a thing or two; he had understood what would become of my parents' affairs, as though he had read it turning the tamis sieve. They found themselves without bread, without wine, without food, without leather, without sulphur, without money ..... and my mother, nine days after the wedding, had the good grace to give forth a fine boy who now has the honour of speaking to you. As if they didn't have enough trouble as it was!

ABBÉ J-B CASTOR FABRE (14th century) (translated by A Sheridan)

WHEN LOUIS XIV visited Toulon in 1660 that gold and that silver still shone in those well-endowed gardens; the knight Paul scored a great success with the King and his Court by inviting them to pluck crystallised oranges, deftly intermingled with the natural ones in his garden. A chronicler reported that some of the ladies were so struck with amazement they almost thought oranges grew like that in Provence.

CHARLES DE RIBBE (1898) (translated by J Karslake)

An engraving after Féraud of the arrival of the English in Toulon, August 1793

〰〰〰〰〰〰〰〰〰〰〰〰〰〰〰〰〰〰〰〰

Antoine Godeau, born in Dreux, was made Bishop of Grasse and Vence by Richelieu. He was also a successful writer and in this poem describes his see.

> J'habite des rochers, mais que d'heureux destins
> Ont partout parsemés de roses, de jasmin,
> Des pieds jusqu' au sommet des arbres les tapissent,
> Les riches orangers dans les plaines fleurissent;
> L'émeraude en leur feuille étale sa couleur,
> L'or brille sur le fruit, et l'argent sur la fleur.

> I live among rocks, which happy fate
> Has sprinkled liberally with roses and with jasmin,
> Trees carpet them from foothill to summit,
> Rich orange groves blossom in the plains;
> The emerald in their leaves reveals its hue,
> On the fruit shines gold, and silver on the flower.

A G O D E A U (1 6 0 5 - 1 6 7 2) (translated by J Karslake)

Tobias Smollett describes the food of Nice.

I N T H E T O W N of Nice, you will find no ready-furnished lodgings for a whole family. Just without one of the gates, there are two houses to be let, ready-furnished, for about five loui'dores per month. As for the country houses in this neighbourhood, they are damp in winter, and generally without chimnies; and in summer they are rendered uninhabitable by the heat and the vermin. If you hire a tenement in Nice, you must take it for a year certain; and this will cost you about twenty pounds sterling. For this price, I have a ground floor paved with brick, consisting of a kitchen, two large halls, a couple of good rooms with chimnies, three large closets that serve for bed-chambers, and dressing-rooms, a butler's room, and three apartments for servants, lumber or stores, to which we ascend by narrow wooden stairs. I have likewise two small gardens, well stocked with oranges, lemons, peaches, figs, grapes, corinths, sallad, and pot-herbs. It is supplied with a draw-well of good water, and there is another in the vestibule of the house, which is cool, large, and magnificent. You may hire furniture for such a tenement for about two guineas a month: but I chose rather to buy what was necessary; and this cost me about sixty pounds. I suppose it will fetch me about half the money when I leave the place. It is very difficult to find a tolerable cook at Nice. A common maid, who serves the people of the country, for three or four livres, will not live with an English family under eight or ten. They are all slovenly, slothful, and unconscionable cheats. The markets at Nice are tolerably well supplied. Their beef, which comes from Piedmont, is pretty good, and we have it all the year. In the winter we have likewise excellent pork, and delicate lamb; but the mutton is indifferent. Piedmont, also, affords us delicious capons, fed with maize; and this country produces excellent turkeys, but very few geese. Chickens and pullets are extremely meagre. I have tried to fatten them, without success. In summer they are subject to the pip, and die in great numbers. Autumn and winter are the seasons for game; hares, partridges, quails, wild-pigeons, woodcocks, snipes, thrushes, beccaficas, and ortolans. Wild-boar is sometimes found in the mountains: it has a delicious taste, not unlike that of the wild hog in Jamaica; and would make an excellent barbecue, about the beginning of winter, when it is in good case: but, when meagre, the head only is presented at tables. Pheasants are very scarce. As for the heath-game, I never saw but one cock, which my servant bought in the market, and brought home; but the commandant's cook came into my kitchen, and carried it off, after it was half plucked, saying, his master had company to dinner. The hares are large, plump, and juicy. The partridges are generally of the red sort; large as pullets, and of a good flavour: there are also some grey partridges in the mountains; and another sort of a white colour, that weigh four or five pounds each. Beccaficas are smaller than sparrows, but very fat, and they are generally eaten half raw. The best way of dressing them is to stuff them into a roll, scooped of its crum; to baste them well with butter, and roast them, until they are brown and crisp. The ortolans are kept in cages, and crammed, until they die of fat, then eaten as dainties. The thrush is presented with the trail, because the bird feeds on olives. They may as well eat the trail of a sheep, because it feeds on the aromatic herbs of the mountain. In the summer, we have beef, veal, and mutton, chicken, and ducks; which last are very fat, and very flabby. All the meat is tough in this season, because the excessive heat, and great number of flies, will not admit of its being kept any time after it is killed. Butter and milk, though not very delicate, we have all the year. Our tea and fine sugar come from Marseilles, at a very reasonable price.

Nice is not without variety of fish; though they are not counted so good in their kinds as those of the ocean. Soals, and flat fish in general, are scarce. Here are some mullets, both grey and red. We sometimes see the dory, which is called St Pierre; with rock fish, bonita, and mackarel. The gurnard appears pretty often; and there is plenty of a kind of large whiting, which eats pretty well; but has not the delicacy of that which is caught on our coast. One of the best fish of this country, is called *le loup,* about two or three pounds in weight; white, firm, and well-flavoured. Another, no way inferior to it, is the *moustel,* about the same size; of a dark-grey colour, and short, blunt snout; growing thinner and flatter from the shoulders downwards, so as to resemble a soal at the tail. This cannot be the *mustela* of the antients, which is supposed to be the sea lamprey. Here too are found the *vyvre,* or, as we call it, weaver; remarkable for its long, sharp spines, so dangerous to the fingers of the fishermen. We have abundance of the *sæpia,* or cuttle-fish, of which the people in this country make a delicate ragout; as also of the *polype de mer,* which is an ugly animal, with long feelers, like tails, which they often wind about the legs of the fishermen. They are stewed with onions, and eat something like cow-heel. The market sometimes affords the *ecrivisse de mer,* which is a lobster without claws, of a sweetish taste; and there are a few rock oysters, very small and very rank. Sometimes the fishermen find under water, pieces of a very hard cement, like plaister of Paris, which contain a kind of muscle, called *la datte,* from its resemblance to a date. These petrifactions are commonly of a triangular form, and may weigh about twelve or fifteen pounds each; and one of them may contain a dozen of these muscles, which have nothing extraordinary in the taste or flavour; though extremely curious, as found alive and juicy, in the heart of a rock, almost as hard as marble, without any visible communication with the air or water. I take it for granted, however, that the enclosing cement is porous, and admits the finer parts of the surrounding fluid. In order to reach the muscles, this cement must be broke with large hammers; and it may be truly said, the kernal is not worth the trouble of cracking the shell. Among the fish of this country, there is a very ugly animal of the eel species, which might pass for a serpent: it is of a dusky, black colour, marked with spots of yellow, about eighteen inches, or two feet long. The Italians call it *murena;* but whether it is the fish which had the same name among the antient Romans, I cannot pretend to determine. The antient *murena* was counted a great delicacy, and was kept in ponds for extraordinary occasions. Julius Caesar borrowed six thousand for one entertainment: but I imagine this was the river lamprey. The *murena* of this country is in no esteem, and only eaten by the poor people. Craw-fish and trout are rarely found in the rivers among the mountains. The sword-fish is much esteemed in Nice, and called *l'empereur,* about six or seven feet long: but I have never seen it. They are very scarce; and when taken, are generally concealed, because the head belongs to the commandant, who has likewise the privilege of buying the best fish at a very low price. For which reason, the choice pieces are concealed by the fishermen, and sent privately to Piedmont or Genoa. But, the chief fisheries on this coast are of the sardines, anchovies and tunny. These are taken in small quantities all the year; but spring and summer is the season when they mostly abound. In June and July, a fleet of about fifty fishing-boats puts to sea every evening about eight o'clock, and catches anchovies in immense quantities. One small boat sometimes takes in one night twenty-five rup, amounting to six hundred weight; but it must be observed, that the pound here, as well as in other parts of Italy, consists but of twelve ounces. Anchovies, besides their making a considerable article in the commerce of Nice, are a great resource in all families. The noblesse and burgeois sup on sallad and anchovies, which are eaten on all their meagre days. The fishermen and mariners all along this coast have scarce any other food but dry bread, with a few pickled anchovies in immense quantities. One small boat sometimes takes in one night twenty-five more delicious than fresh anchovies fried in oil; I prefer them to the smelts of the Thames. I need not mention, that the sardines and anchovies are caught in nets; salted, barrelled, and exported into all the different kingdoms and states of Europe. The sardines, however, are largest and fattest in the month of September. A company of adventurers have farmed the tunny-fishery of the king, for six years; a monopoly, for which they pay about three thousand pounds sterling. They are at a very considerable expence for nets, boats, and attendance. Their nets are disposed in a very curious manner across the small bay of St Hospice, in this neighbourhood, where the fish chiefly resort. They are never removed, except in the winter, and when they want repair: but there are avenues for the fish to enter, and pass, from one inclosure to another. There is a man in a boat, who constantly keeps watch. When he perceives they are fairly entered, he has a method for shutting all the passes, and confining the fish to one apartment of the net, which is lifted up into the boat, until the prisoners are taken and secured. The tunny-fish generally runs from fifty to one hundred weight; but some of them are much larger. They are immediately gutted, boiled, and cut in slices. The guts and head afford oil: the slices are partly dried, to be eaten occasionally with oil and vinegar, or barrelled up in oil, to be exported. It is counted a delicacy in Italy and Piedmont, and tastes not unlike sturgeon. The famous pickle of the ancients, called garum, was made of the gills and blood of the tunny, or thynnus.   TOBIAS   SMOLLETT   (1721-1771)

19th-century engraving of Promenade des Anglais, Nice

The Countess of Blessington found that the dairy products of Aix were not particularly to her taste.

W E H A V E H A D nothing to complain of at Aix, except the impossibility of procuring either cream or butter, or, at least, any that is palatable. There is only one cow in the town, which is the property of an English family settled here; and goats, of which there are an abundant stock, serve but as sorry substitutes; their milk destroying the flavour of tea and coffee. The inhabitants of Aix are quite satisfied with goat's milk, proclaim that it is far more wholesome, and quite as agreeable; but in the latter assertion I cannot coincide with them. The butter is brought from a distance, and is abominable; but to its bad quality habit has inured the people here; and our landlady seemed to think us very fastidious when we desired it to be removed from the table, where its odour was really offensive.

COUNTESS   OF   BLESSINGTON   (1789-1849)

━━

This charming picture of breakfast in Cannes was written at the turn of the century.

CANNES IS THE first important town of the Riviera that the gourmet flying south comes to, and at Cannes he will find a typical Riviera restaurant. The Réserve at Cannes consists of one glassed-in shelter and another smaller building on the rocks, which juts out into the sea from the elbow of the Promenade de la Croisette. The spray of the wavelets set up by the breeze splash up against the glass, and to one side are the Iles des Lerins, St Marguerite, and St-Honorat, where the liqueur Lerina is made, shining on the deep blue sea, and to the other the purple Montagnes de l'Esterel stand up with a wonderful jagged edge against the sky. Amongst the rocks on which the building of the restaurant stand are tanks, and in these swim fish, large and small, the fine lazy *dorades* and the lively little sea-gudgeon. One of the amusements of the place is that the breakfasters fish out with a net the little fishes which are to form a *friture,* or point out the bigger victim which they will presently eat for their meal. The cooking is simple and good, and with fish that thirty minutes before were swimming in the green water, an omelette, a simple dish of meat, and a pint of Cerons, or other white wine, a man may breakfast in the highest content looking at some of the sunniest scenes in the world. There is always some little band of Italian musicians playing and singing at the Réserve, and though in London one would vote them a nuisance, at Cannes the music seems to fit in with the lazy pleasure of breakfasting almost upon the waves, and the throaty tenor who has been singing of Santa Lucia gets a lining of francs to his hat. Most of the crowned heads who make holiday at Cannes have taken their breakfast often enough in the little glass summer-house, but the prices are in no way alarming. The ladies gather at tea-time at the white building, where Mme Rumplemayer sells cakes and tea and coffee; and the Gallia also has a *clientèle* of tea-drinkers, for whose benefit the band plays of an afternoon.

LIEUT-COL NEWNHAM DAVIS and ALGERNON BASTARD (1903)

Bouillabaisse, the great fish dish, is always associated with Marseilles, although The Bouillabaisse of Thackeray's famous ballad was eaten in Paris. The actual recipe varies from chef to chef, both in the types of fish used and the quantities used, although there is generally agreement on a few basic points. The main fish generally used are traditionally Rascasse, grondin and Congre (Conger eel) which are cooked in a bouillon with herbs and served with rouille, a paste of Spanish peppers. Over the years a rich variety of legends have grown up around the origin of Bouillabaisse.

THE BEST BOUILLABAISSE that I can recall eating on the Riviera I had at the Voile d'Or in Saint-Jean-Cap-Ferrat; but the best in my entire eating career was served me, not on the Riviera, and not even in France, but, however extraordinary it may seem, in New York — at the Restaurant du Midi, before society discovered it, when it was still a rendezvous for French sailors.

Marseilles can hardly claim *bouillabaisse* on the ground that it originated there unless it changes the account of its origin that the Marseillais will tell you quite unblushingly (Marseilles is a city of tall stories). According to this legend, *bouillabaisse* would have to be considerably older even than Marseilles, with its twenty-five hundred years of existence. It is based on the superstition that fish chowder made with saffron is a soporific (it is not, but any food taken in on the gargantuan scale that *bouillabaisse* encourages is likely to make the eater sleepy). The story goes that *bouillabaisse* was invented by Venus to put her husband Vulcan to sleep when she had a rendezvous with Mars. Possibly the Marseillais see in this story a chance to claim the dish by inheritance, as their city, long held by the Greeks, may look upon itself as the heir of Greek divinity. In any case, one may sympathize with the contention that *bouillabaisse* is divine.

More prosaic accounts also give the dish a Greek origin, pointing out that ancient Greek literature contains references to fish soups resembling *bouillabaisse*. Perhaps the Greeks who founded Marseilles did bring with them the ancestor of *bouillabaisse*. We know that they did introduce the olive into Provence, thus providing at least one important ingredient of the soup. However, whether the Greeks imported the first *bouillabaisse* or not, it would have been almost inevitable for Marseilles to have developed some such dish, even without outside inspiration.

WAVERLEY ROOT (1903-)

Waverley Root, American historian who also writes about French food and now resides in Paris here describes Cassoulet, the famous bean stew, traditionally from West of Provence and very popular inland in the Languedoc.

THERE ARE THREE main types of *cassoulet,* those of Castelnaudary, Carcassonne, and Toulouse, of which the first seems to have been the original dish. It is therefore, in principle at least, the simplest, combining with the beans only fresh pork, ham, a bit of pork shoulder, sausage, and fresh pork crackling. Carcassonne starts with this, and adds hunks of leg of mutton to the mixture (in season, there may also be partridge in this *cassoulet)*. Toulouse also starts out with the Castelnaudary base, but adds to it not only mutton (in this case from less expensive cuts), but also bacon, Toulouse sausage, and preserved goose. The last ingredient may sometimes be replaced by preserved duck, or there may even be samples of both.

This would seem to make everything plain — Castelnaudary, only pork; Carcassonne, distinguished by mutton; Toulouse, distinguished by goose. However, an authority I have just consulted,which lays down these distinctions very sternly, then goes on to give two recipes for *cassoulet de Castelnaudary;* one of them contains mutton and the other contains goose. The conclusion that must be drawn is that *cassoulet* is what you find it.

WAVERLEY ROOT (1903-)

There are probably some 500 miles of vineyards in the Southern Rhône Valley and Provence. However not everybody is impressed with the quality of wine produced.

TO THE EAST of the Bouches-du-Rhône a few just drinkable wines are made in the outskirts of Marseilles, such as Séon, Château-Gombert, Lançon, Rognac, Saint-André and Sainte-

Marthe. A few miles to the east of it, near Ciotat on the Mediterranean coast, is Cassis, where a very dry, almost gritty white wine is made from Muscat grapes. This, which is much esteemed locally with shellfish, must not be confused with the blackcurrant liqueur of the same name from Dijon. Red wine is also made there (Clos Calendal), as also at Trévaresse: poor enough growths in all conscience but much appreciated by the Marseillais. In the Basses-Alpes the red wine of Peyruis-les-Mées, near Digne, and the heady white growth of Chabrières once boasted some celebrity. In the coastal region the rather undistinguished white wine of Bellet, near Nice, enjoys much local esteem. Saint-Laurent-du-Var, once the frontier of France, still grows the Muscat wines which were mentioned by Smollett. The mountains overhanging the gulfs of Fréjus and Tropez produce ordinary wines, some of the white being passable. Of the wines of the Var, Vidauban, La Gaule, Château-des-Meaulx, Le Castellet (Château La Rouvière), Pelayon, Pierrefeu, Bandol, Cagnes-sur-Mer, La Malgue and the Vins de Taude of Vence the kindest thing that can be said is that they are the best of a poor enough lot. A good deal of *vin cuit* is, or till lately was, made in Provence, in the same way as is *vino cotto* in Italy.

MORTON SHAND (1960)

By the 1880s the Hotel de Paris in Monte Carlo had become too small for the growing stream of glittering guests. So in 1898 the palatial Hermitage opened. Here is one of their typical dinner menus.

Saumon Fumé de Hollande
Ox-tail Clair en Tasse
Velouté de Homard au Paprika
Truite Saumonée à la Chambord
Tourte de Ris-de-Veau Brillat-Savarin
Selle d'Agneau de Lait Polignac
Pommes Dauphin   Petits Pois Fine-Fleur
Caille de Vigne à la Richelieu
Sorbet au Clicquot
Poularde Soufflée Impériale
Pâté de Foie Gras d'Alsace
Salade Aida
Asperges d'Argenteuil Sauce Mousseline
Buisson d'Ecrevisses à la Nage
Crêpes Flambées au Grand Marnier
Ananas Givré à l'Orientale
Coffret de Friandises
Corbeille de Fruits   Café   Liqueurs

Tobias Smollett discusses the wines of the region.

ANOTHER CONSIDERABLE ARTICLE in housekeeping is wine, which we have here good and reasonable. The wine of Tavelle in Languedoc is very near as good as Burgundy, and may be had at Nice, at the rate of sixpence a bottle. The sweet wine of St Laurent, counted equal to that of Frontignan, costs about eight or ninepence a quart: pretty good Malaga may be had for half the money. Those who make their own wine choose the grapes from different vineyards, and have them picked, pressed, and fermented at home. That which is made by the peasants, both red and white, is generally genuine: but the wine-merchants of Nice brew a balderdash, and even mix it with pigeons dung and quick-lime. It cannot be supposed, that a stranger and sojourner should buy his own grapes, and make his own provision of wine: but he may buy it by recommendation from the peasants, for about eighteen or twenty livres the charge, consisting of eleven rup five pounds; in other words, of two hundred and eighty pounds of this country, so as to bring it for something less than threepence a quart. The Nice wine, when mixed with water, makes an agreeable beverage. There is an inferior sort for servants drank by the common people, which in the cabaret does not cost above a penny a bottle. The people here are not so nice as the English, in the management of their wine. It is kept in flacons, or large flasks, without corks, having a little oil at top. It is not deemed the worse for having been opened a day or two before; and they expose it to the hot sun, and all kinds of weather, without hesitation. Certain it is, this treatment has little or no effect upon its taste, flavour, and transparency.

The brandy of Nice is very indifferent: and the liqueurs are so sweetened with coarse sugar, that they scarce retain the taste or flavour of any other ingredient.

TOBIAS SMOLLETT (1721-1771)

CHÂTEAUNEUF-DU-PAPE was, as its name implies, an old pontifical summer residence, almost a hill station, dating from the era of the seventy-years 'Babylonish Captivity' of the Popes at Avignon in the fourteenth century. The actual construction of this pleasaunce, which was called the 'Château neuf' to distinguish it from the old château, the fortress-palace of the Popes at Avignon, was begun in 1309 by the wine-loving Clement V — the same *Pape Clément* who planted the vineyard that still bears his name hard by the gates of Bordeaux on the Bayonne Road. Though this Bordelais pope, who boldly took the iniative in depriving Rome of the seat of the Papacy, has been described by the Provençal poet, Félix Gras, as passing his life serenely:

..... assetoun sus sa muïlo

S'envaï veire sa vigno amount à Casteù-Nou

it seems clear that it was Clément's successor, Jacques Duèze, John XXII, who created the actual vineyard, the 'twenty salmées of vines and olive-groves' of this Papal Simla, in 1316. It was into the mouth of one of those Babylonish Popes, and more probably John XXII's, that the ribald drinking song has been put:

Je veux vous chanter, mes amis,
Ce vieux Châteauneuf que j'ai mis
    Pour vous seuls en bouteille:
    Il va faire merveille!

Quand de ce vin nous serons gris,
Vénus applaudira nos ris:
    J'en prends à temoin Lise,
    La chose est bien permise!

MORTON SHAND (1960)

Memories of the Ballets Russes – Mr and Mrs J M S / Serge Diaghilev : Jean Cocteau

La Treille Muscate : Dunoyer de Segonzac

CHAPTER TEN

Endings

The troubadour Peire Vidal accompanied Richard Coeur de Lion on the Third Crusade (1189-1192), long before writing this lament for inaction.

I'm getting old, — threescore today,
And all my life in dust and mire
I've labored hard, yet found no way
To satisfy my great desire;
I see 't is folly here below
Full happiness to count upon;
My prayer unanswered is to go, —
I have not seen fair Carcassonne.

PEIRE VIDAL (1 1 7 5 - 1 2 1 5) (translated by J Rutherford)

H E W A S E V E N busier at Cagnes than in Paris; in the country, when the weather was good, he liked to work out of doors as much as possible. At Essoyes, where there were almost no automobiles, he went out in his wheel-chair along the road, or by the river's edge. At Cagnes, which is overrun with automobiles, he had himself carried in an arm-chair to various points on his property, to the patch of rose-bushes, the plots full of mandarin and orange-trees, the grape-vines, the Terrain Fayard with its medlar-trees from Japan, the cherry-orchard, and, dominating *Les Collettes,* the olive-trees all in silver.

'I have the right now to idle a little,' Renoir liked to say. From his care-free wanderings came many extraordinary landscape sketches; for it goes without saying that the model always followed with the colour-box.

While he was doing the portrait of Madame de Galéa, which required fifty or more sittings and which interested him to such an extent that he kept at it without interruption up to the end, the weather was exceptionally hot, and he remarked one day: 'I pay dearly for the pleasure I get from this canvas; but it is so satisfying to give in entirely to the sheer pleasure of painting.'

And then when the weather began to grow cold and his goatskin jacket was not a sufficient protection for work out of doors, he had his motor-car to fall back on. Antibes especially had an irresistible attraction for him. When he went round the Corniche, and the neighbouring hills, the sweet penetrating atmosphere gave him an ever-renewing sensation of tranquillity.

'I must stay here at least two months more and paint!' he cried one day when particularly intoxicated by the charm of the landscape. And, quite forgetting that it was necessary for him to live in a special 'incubator' house on account of his rheumatism, he ordered the chauffeur to stop every time he saw 'Villa to Let.'

The doctor himself advised Renoir to be out of doors as much as possible. 'Nothing is better for cleansing the lungs than plenty of fresh air,' he said to his patient. Whenever the doctor ordered something to his liking, Renoir would follow the prescription to the letter.

One day the family had planned to go to Nice to eat a bowl of *bouillabaisse;* it was raining in torrents, but Renoir insisted: 'Bah! The doctor said that I breathe better out of doors than in the house. Here I am, past seventy-five years old, and I don't intend being ordered about like a child any more. Now send for the car!'

When Renoir bought *Les Colletts,* he did not at first have a motor-road built to the house. His wife would roll his wheel-chair to the bottom of the hill, and Renoir would be lifted in and out of the car in an arm-chair. 'It's a little inconvenient perhaps,' he would say, 'but the people who like me for myself will take the trouble to come to see me; as for the rest, the fence ought to be high enough to stop them.'

But when the Parisian arrives in the Midi, he is soon so bored that he is ready to climb any fence, no matter how high, just to kill time. As soon as Renoir had moved in at *Les Collettes,* the whole swarm of faithful bores from Paris descended upon him, with many new members to boot.

I recall the day I saw Renoir under the big lime-tree in the garden, with a long stick in his hand, dictating volumes to the sculptor who was executing his *Venus Victorious.*

'I'm at my statue at last! With this fine weather, I will be able to work out of doors all afternoon!'

'If you're not interrupted,' I suggested.

'So far as that goes, I'd like to see anyone with nerve enough to ..... ' He had not finished his sentence, when an automobile drove up, bringing three strange ladies.

'The porter at the Hotel du Palais at Nice,' one of them explained, 'told us that we could see Renoir's studio at Cagnes — '

Another of the visitors struck in, trying to be agreeable: 'But if the Master is busy, we can wait a bit.'

Renoir was working away, when other visitors arrived: Monsieur Z, a seed merchant, accompanied by a young woman. By this time Renoir had given up trying to work. One of the three ladies from Nice remarked that she had a literary and artistic circle at Paris. 'If the Master would like to come to one of my days,' she said, 'I could arrange a little talk on painting beforehand.'

'Why don't you say something too?' said Monsieur Z's companion in his ear, but loud enough for me to overhear.

'I'm trying to think of something ..... ' He finally found it, and, turning to Renoir, he said:

'Master, if you did water-colours instead of oil you'd have everything you need for preparing your colours, with all the rain that's fallen the past week.'

As Renoir wagged his head, he continued: 'You must be sick of it in this hole!'

Renoir: I have my painting .....

Monsieur Z: Painting! I know what that is; I paint myself ....

Everyone had gone, and Renoir's eyes were beginning to close, for a visit tired him more than a model posing. Just then the postman brought a letter.

Renoir was reading it rather indifferently, when all of a sudden he cried: 'There's a friend for you! He's interested enough to ask if Jean's dog has been found. ..... His daughters have started knitting a spread for me ..... ' Then his face darkened. 'It's not me he cares about, it's my painting. He asks me about some pictures that he wants ..... '

And with a deep sadness in his voice, he went on:

'I have arrived more definitely than any other painter during his lifetime; honours shower upon me from every side; artists pay me compliments on my work; there are many people to whom my position must seem enviable ..... But I don't seem to have a single real friend!'

AMBROISE VOLLARD (1 9 2 5) (translated by Van Doren and Weaver)

In November 1897 the celebrated English illustrator Aubrey Beardsley moved, on his doctor's advice, to Menton, where, a few months later, aged twenty-six, he died.

Hôtel Cosmopolitain,
Menton, Nov 29th.

MY DEAREST BROTHER

I have quite recovered from my fatigue, & am prospering in this wonderful sunshine. I can't tell how grateful I feel to have got better again. The pains in my lungs have left me & my cough is much less troublesome. I sleep without any distress & eat quite heartily. Even in this short time the people here have noticed an improvement in me.

I am able to be out almost all day, & there are such beautifully sheltered spots in the grounds of this hotel where I can sit all the morning if I am too tired to get down to the sea.

The little town here is so gay & amusing.

There are several churches. The old Cathedral of S Michel, the Penitents Blancs & Penitents Noirs & quite near me a little chapel which I shall always attend. Père Calixte is in charge of it. He seems very kind & serious. I shall make my confessions to him. You would like the chapel so much, it is dedicated to S Roch. The quête is made in a shell.

I am much happier & more peaceful than when I wrote to you last. I do hope I shall be able to send you more & more satisfactory accounts of myself.

The mistral has not blown yet.

With much love

Always your very affectionate

AUBREY BEARDSLEY (1 8 7 2 - 1 8 9 8)

In this letter to a friend, the Russian novelist Leo Tolstoy recounts the death of his brother Nikolay from consumption in a hotel in the resort of Hyères.

To A A FET

Hyères, 17/29 October 1860

I THINK YOU already know what has happened. On 20 September, our style, he died, literally in my arms. Nothing in life has made such an impression on me. He was telling the truth when he said that there is nothing worse than death. And if you really think that death is after all the end of everything, then there's nothing worse than life either. What's the point of struggling and trying, if nothing remains of what used to be N N Tolstoy? He didn't say that he felt death approaching, but I know he followed its every step, and surely knew what still remained to him of life. A few minutes before he died, he dozed off, then suddenly came to and whispered with horror: 'What does it all mean?' He had seen it — this absorption of the self in nothingness. And if he found nothing to cling to, what shall I find? Even less. And then it's most unlikely that I or anyone else would struggle with it up to the last minute quite as he did. A couple of days before, I said to him: 'We'll have to put a chamber pot in your room.' — 'No,' he said, 'I'm weak, but not as weak as that yet: we'll struggle on a bit longer.'

Up to the last minute he didn't give in to it; he did everything himself, continually tried to occupy himself, wrote, asked me about my writing, gave me advice. But I felt that he was no longer doing all this from any inner desire, but on principle. One thing remained for him to the end — nature. The night before he died he went into his bedroom to [.....] and fell exhausted on the bed by the open window. I came in. With tears in his eyes he said: 'How I've enjoyed this whole last hour.' From the earth you came and to the earth you will return. The one thing that remains is the vague hope that there, in nature, of which you will become a part in the earth, something will remain and be discovered. All who knew and saw his last minutes say: 'How wonderfully calmly and peacefully he died', but I know how frightfully agonising it was, for not a single feeling escaped me. I said to myself a thousand times: 'Let the dead bury their dead'; you must put the powers you still have to some use, but you can't persuade a stone to fall upwards instead of down, the way it's attracted. You can't laugh at a joke you find boring, you can't eat when you don't want to. What's the point of everything, when tomorrow the torments of death will begin, with all the abomination of meanness, lies, and self-deceit, and end in nothingness, in the annihilation of the self. An amusing trick! Be useful, be virtuous, be happy while you're alive, people have said to each other for centuries — we as well — and happiness and virtue and usefulness are truth; but the truth that I've taken away from my 32 years is that the situation in which someone has placed us is the most terrible fraud and crime, for which words would have failed us (us liberals) had it been one man who had placed another man in that situation. Praise be to Allah, to God, to Brahma. What a benefactor! 'Take life as it is', 'It's not God who has placed you in this situation, but you yourselves!'. Nothing of the sort! I do accept life as it is, as a most mean, detestable and false condition. And the proof that it was not I who placed myself in this situation is the fact that for centuries we have been trying to believe that it's very fine; but as soon as man reaches a higher stage of development and ceases to be stupid, it becomes clear to him that everything is rubbish and a fraud, and that the truth which he nevertheless loves more than anything else is a terrible truth. So that when you see it clearly and truly, you come to, and say with horror like my brother: 'What does it all mean?'

Well, of course, while there is the desire to eat, you eat, to [s .....], you [s .....]; while there is the unconscious, stupid desire to know and speak the truth, you try to know and speak it. That's the one thing left to me from the world of morality, higher than which I've been unable to rise; it's the one thing that I'll go on doing, only not in the form of your art. Art is a lie, and I can no longer love a beautiful lie. I'm spending the winter here for the simple reason that I am here, and it makes no difference where I live.

Please write to me. I love you just as my brother loved you and remembered you up to the last minute.　　　　　　　　　　LEO TOLSTOY (1828-1910) (translated by R F Christian)

Lament

Thou all-loving Father, how sadly I pray
The days of the past to my heart might return;
For the dear happy hours of the long summer day,
And the friends of the past, so wistful I yearn.
Will the moment ere come when, like bird on the wing,
Once more I'll fly back, and in liberty sing?

In the house of my father how happy I heard,
From the red wheat uprising, the song of the bird,
The chant of the thrush as it poured out its lay,
Then fled to its nest 'neath the hawthorn spray.
Dear ones that I love — ah! I bade you adieu,
But the eyes of my heart are still looking to you!

19th-century engraving of Cimiez

Ah! how often at night I hear in my dream
The rippling so sweet of the crystalline stream;
The joy of my home, never wearied my heart;
Oh, why then could I from its portals depart?
Alas! thought dear father, 'twill make his life fair,
To carve out his lot in the city of care.

Ah! how my heart wept as I saw pass away
The house of my people on that cruel day;
Its smiling fields vanish as I rode sad along,
Where — where — in this city amid all the throng
Can I find a dear mother my heart to console,
Or brother, or sister, so dear to my soul?

Farewell, elm shadows! weeping willow, farewell!
Farewell, ye sweet linnets, that wild notes outswell!
Ye murmurs of river, and thrushes' wild strain;
Ye friends I lament for, with sorrow and pain;
Alas! ye loved ones, I have whispered adieu,
But the eyes of my heart are still looking to you!

The city of fogs and smoke clouds so drear
I love not; my heart cannot bear to rest here.
Oh, house of my father, shall I e'er see again
Thy red tiles, sun-flashing amid the green plains?
The loved ones once more clasp with joy to my heart,
And never again from the old house depart?

There's a Father's House still, tho' I never see more
The home I have left by the river's sweet shore;
There's a mansion above which I hope soon to gain,
When I'm done with my sorrow and this wild aching pain,
I hear His voice whisper from the Heaven so blue,
My child, it is waiting — yes, waiting for you.

Soon I'll leave this dark city for Zion on high,
These mist clouds below for the amethyst sky;
The wild bird's sweet note for the angel song's strain;
The sorrow below, for the land of no pain;
From my Father's House I never shall roam,
But tearless e'er dwell in my Father's blest home.

ANONYMOUS (translated by J Duncan Craig)

The end of a beautiful holiday ..... This extract is taken from the novel A N O T H E R
C O U N T R Y *by the American James Baldwin. The author now lives near Vence.*

E R I C S A T N A K E D in his rented garden. Flies buzzed and boomed in the brilliant heat,
and a yellow bee circled his head. Eric remained very still, then reached for the cigarettes
beside him and lit one, hoping that the smoke would drive the bee away. Yves' tiny black-and-
white kitten stalked the garden as though it were Africa, crouching beneath the mimosas like
a panther and leaping into the air.

The house and the garden overlooked the sea. Far down the slope, beyond the sand of the
beach, in the thunderous blue of the Mediterranean, Yves' head went under, reappeared, went
under again. He vanished entirely. Eric stood up, looking out over the sea, almost poised to
run. Yves liked to hold his breath under water for as long as possible, a test of endurance which
Eric found pointless and, in Yves' case, frightening. Then Yves' head appeared again, and his
arm flashed. And, even from this distance, Eric could see that Yves was laughing — he had
known that Eric would be watching from the garden. Yves began swimming toward the beach.
Eric sat down. The kitten rushed over and rubbed itself against his legs.

It was the end of May. They had been in this house for more than two months. Tomorrow
they were leaving. Not for a long time, perhaps never again, would Eric sit in a garden watching
Yves in the water. They would take the train for Paris in the morning and, after two days there,
Yves would put Eric on the boat for New York. Eric was to get settled there and then Yves was
to join him.

Now that it had all been decided and there could be no turning back, Eric felt a sour and
savage apprehension. He watched as Yves stepped out of the water. His brown hair was bleach-
ing from the sun and glowed about his head; his long, wiry body was as brown as bread. He
bent down to lift off the scarlet bikini. Then he pulled on an old pair of blue jeans which he
had expropriated from Eric. They were somewhat too short for him, but no matter — Yves was
not very fond of Americans, but he liked their clothes. He stalked up the slope, toward the
house, the red cloth of the bikini dangling from one hand.

J A M E S B A L D W I N (1 9 2 4 -)

---

*At the end of the 1880s Paul Gauguin moved into Van Gogh's house in Arles with a view to
starting an artists' colony in the South. Later Gauguin described this traumatic time and the
beginnings of Vincent's madness.*

I A R R I V E D I N Arles very early in the morning and I awaited daylight in an all-night café.
The patron looked at me and said: 'You're the chum; I recognise you.' A portrait of myself that
I had sent to Vincent was sufficient to explain the exclamation of this man. Showing him the
portrait, Vincent had explained to him that it was a friend who was shortly coming.

Neither too late, nor too early, I went to wake Vincent. The day was given over to getting
myself installed, to a great deal of gossiping, to a walk for the purpose of admiring the beauties
of Arles and the Arlésiennes, for whom, as a matter of fact, I was never able to become very
enthusiastic.

I remained therefore some weeks before clearly understanding the rough savour of Arles and its surroundings, which did not prevent us from working hard, particularly Vincent. Two beings, he and myself, the one a volcano and the other boiling also. But inside in some way a struggle was preparing itself.

To begin with I found in everything and with everything a disorder that shocked me. His box of colours was scarcely large enough to contain all the squeezed tubes which were never closed, and in spite of all this disorder, this mess, something rumbled in his canvases; in his words also. Daudet, de Goncourt, and the Bible burned through his Dutch brain. He had forgotten even how to write Dutch, and as one has been able to see from the publication of his letters to his brother he only wrote in French, and that admirably with an infinity of 'in so far as's.'

In spite of all my efforts to unravel in his disorderly mind a logical reasoning in his critical opinions, I was not able to explain to myself all the contradiction that there was between his painting and his opinions. Thus, for example, he had an unbounded admiration for Meissonnier and a profound hatred for Ingres. Degas made him despair and Cézanne was only a dauber. Thinking of Monticelli made him cry.

One of the things that annoyed him was to have to allow me great intelligence whereas I had too small a forehead, a sign of imbecility. And among all this a great tenderness or rather a saintly altruism.

From the first month, I saw our joint finances take on the same aspects of disorder. What was to be done? The situation was delicate, the cash-box being modestly provisioned by his brother employed by Goupil's; on my side in combination with an exchange into pictures. It was necessary to speak, and to risk blundering against his great touchiness. It was therefore only with great precaution and much coaxing, little compatible with my character, that I touched on the question. I must admit, I succeeded much more easily than I had thought. In a box [was put] so much for nocturnal and hygienic promenading, so much for tobacco, so much also for impromptu expenses, including the rent. On top, a piece of paper and a pencil for the honest noting down of what each took out of the cash-box. In another box, the rest of the sum divided into four parts for the expenses of food for each week. Our little restaurant was suppressed, and with the help of a little gas oven I did the cooking while Vincent did the shopping, without going very far from the house. Once, however, Vincent wanted to make a soup, but I don't know how he made his mixtures. Probably like the colours in his pictures. It remains that we could not eat it. At which Vincent laughed, saying: 'Tarascon! The cap of *père* Daudet.' On the wall he wrote in chalk:

Je suis Saint-Esprit.
Je suis sain d'esprit.

How long did we remain together? I could not say, having totally forgotten. In spite of the rapidity with which the catastrophe happened; in spite of the fever for working that had got hold of me, all this time appears to me as a century. In spite of what the public may think two men did tremendous work there, useful to both of them; possibly to others. Certain things bear fruit.

Vincent, at the time of my arrival at Arles, was up to the ears in the post-Impressionist School, and he was making a nice mess of it, which made him suffer; not that this school, like all schools, was bad, but because it did not correspond with his nature, so little patient and so independent. With all his yellows on violets, all this work with complementary colours, a disorderly work on his part, he only arrived at soft, incomplete and monotonous harmonies; the sound of the bugle was lacking. I undertook the task of explaining things to him which was easy for me, for I found rich and fruitful ground. Like all original natures marked with the seal of personality, Vincent had no fear of his neighbour and no obstinacy. From that day my friend, Van Gogh, made astonishing progress; he seemed to catch a glimpse of everything that he had in him, and hence all that series of sunflowers on sunflowers in the brilliant sunshine .....

It would be idle here to enter into details of technique. This has been related in order to tell you that Van Gogh, without losing an inch of his originality, found in me a fruitful preceptor. And every day he was grateful to me for it. And this is what he meant when he wrote to Monsieur Aurier that he owed much to Paul Gauguin. When I arrived at Arles Vincent was trying to find himself, whilst I, much older, was a completed man. I am indebted to Vincent for something, which is, with the knowledge of having been useful to him, the strengthening of my previous pictural ideas: then in very difficult moments remembering that there are some more unfortunate than oneself. When I read this statement — *Gauguin's drawing recalls a little that of Van Gogh* — I smile.

During the latter part of my stay, Vincent became excessively brusque and noisy, then silent. On some evenings I surprised Vincent, who had got up, in the act of coming over to my bed. To what should I attribute my waking up at those moments? At all events it was sufficient to say to him very seriously: 'What is wrong with you, Vincent?' for him to get back to bed without saying a word, and sleep solidly. I had the idea of doing his portrait while he was painting the *nature morte* that he was so fond of with the sunflowers. And when the portrait was finished he said to me: 'It is certainly I, but I gone mad.'

The same evening we went to the café. He ordered a weak absinthe. Suddenly he threw the glass and its contents at my head. I avoided it, and taking him under the arm I left the café, crossed the Place Victor Hugo, and a few minutes later Vincent found himself in his bed where in a few seconds he went to sleep and did not wake again until the morning. When he woke, very calm, he said to me: 'My dear Gauguin, I have a vague remembrance that I offended you last evening.' 'I forgive you willingly and delightedly, but yesterday's scene might happen again, and if I were hit I might not remain master of myself, and strangle you. Allow me, therefore, to write to your brother to announce my return.' What a day! Good God!

When the evening came, I swallowed my dinner and felt the need of going alone to take some air where the laurels were in flower. I had already almost entirely crossed the Place Victor Hugo when I heard behind me a well-known little step, rapid and jerky. I turned round at the very moment when Vincent was on the point of throwing himself on me with an open razor in his hand. My look must have been very powerful at that moment for he stopped and lowering his head he returned running to the house.

Was I cowardly at that moment and ought I not to have disarmed him and tried to pacify him? Often I have questioned my conscience and I have made myself no reproaches. He who likes may cast his stone at me. In a very short time I was at a good hotel in Arles where, after having asked the time, I took a room and went to bed. Being very upset I could only get to sleep towards three in the morning and I woke up rather late, about seven-thirty.

Arriving at the square I saw a large crowd assembled. Near our house some *gendarmes* and a little man in a bowler hat who was the police commissioner. This is what had taken place.

Van Gogh went back to the house and immediately cut off an ear close to the head. He must have taken a certain time to stop the force of the bleeding, for the next day numerous damp towels were spread out on the flagstones of the two ground-floor rooms. The blood had dirtied the two rooms and the little staircase that led up to our bedroom.

When he was in a condition to go out, his head enveloped in a completely pulled down *béret basque* he went straight to a house where, lacking a sweetheart, one makes an acquaintance, and gave the person in charge his ear, well cleaned and enclosed in an envelope. 'Here,' he said, 'in remembrance of me,' then he ran out and went home where he went to bed and to sleep. He took the precaution, however, of closing the shutters and of putting a lighted lamp on a table near the window.

Ten minutes later the whole street reserved to the women was in movement and the happening was being discussed.

I was far from knowing anything of all that when I presented myself on the doorstep of our house, and when the man with the bowler hat said to me point-blank in a more severe tone: 'What have you done, sir, to your friend?'

'I don't know .....'

'Of course ..... you know very well ..... he is dead.'

I wish no one such a moment, and several long minutes were necessary before I was capable of thinking and restraining the beating of my heart.

Anger, indignation, pain also and shame before all the glances that were tearing my whole body were suffocating me and I could only stutter: 'Very well, sir, let us go upstairs and we shall discuss that there.' Vincent was lying in the bed completely covered with the sheets, crouching like a retriever: he seemed dead. Softly, very softly, I touched the body whose warmth certainly assured life. It was for me the resumption of all my senses and energy.

Almost in a whisper I said to the police commissioner: 'Kindly, sir, wake this man with great tact, and if he asks for me tell him that I have left for Paris: the sight of me might perhaps be fatal to him.' I must admit that from that moment the police commissioner was as pleasant as possible, and he sent, intelligently, for a doctor and a carriage.

Once he was awake, Vincent asked for his friend, his pipe and his tobacco, even thought of asking for the box that was downstairs and that contained our money — a suspicion, no doubt, that glanced off me for I was already armed against all suffering.

Vincent was taken to the hospital where, as soon as he had arrived, his brain began again to become unbalanced.

All the rest is known in those circles where that is of interest and it is useless to speak of it, unless it be of the extreme suffering of a man who, looked after in an asylum, found himself at monthly intervals sufficiently in possession of his senses to understand his condition and to paint with passion the admirable pictures that one knows.

The last letter that I had was dated from Auvers, near Pontoise. He told me that he had hoped to be sufficiently cured to come to look me up in Brittany, but that now he was obliged to recognise the impossibility of a cure:

'Dear Master (the only time that he used this word), it is better, after having known you and given you trouble, to die in a good state of mind than in a state that is degrading.'

He shot himself in the stomach, and it was a few hours afterwards only, lying in his bed and smoking his pipe, that he died, having complete lucidity of mind, with love for his art and without hatred for anyone.　　　　PAUL GAUGUIN (1848-1903) (translated by R Burnett)

Shortly after the actor Dirk Bogarde moved into his house near Grasse he invited his former agent and close friend Robin together with his wife Angela to stay. Robin was suffering from a fatal cancer.

AS SEPTEMBER STARTED to ease towards October, as the sun sank earlier each evening, the dew became thicker every morning, the days still blazed; and Robin gained strength. Sometimes he was well enough to come down and eat on the terrace, even though walking was a hazard because he kept falling over, which, in a man of some height, elegance and enormous pride, was wounding to see, though we all laughed as we hurried to help him up. But the days became happier, Angela braver. There were times now when it felt almost like the past, when we had sat together so often in England or in Italy, discussing, arguing, reading bits to each other from newspapers or books, listening to music, being together. All perfectly all right. A time switch. Each evening, about six o'clock, Angela went to her room to 'preen a bit' as she called it, and would shortly re-appear fresh, crisp, groomed; pearls, a different dress, a cloud of scent about her. Immensely encouraging, and a swift reminder to oneself to change from the mucky garb of the day. It is something I have always admired tremendously in women, the extraordinary ability, which some possess, of being able to illuminate a room, lift morale, turn the edge of evening into an event, by nothing more, it would seem, than the changing of a skirt, a cotton dress, a quick brushing of the hair, a touch of scent, a stroke of lipstick all within, apparently, moments. Angela did this supremely well, charging the evenings with a brisk normality in which we could all function.

And then the mistral arrived.

I have lived here long enough now to know the warning signs; then I was quite unaware that there were any. I don't really think that I ever knew what a mistral was, except that it was a wind and blew sand into your eyes on the beach and sent the sea roaring. But just a wind, that's all.

The sudden appearance one morning of a shoal of slender cigar-shaped clouds drifting across the intensity of the late September sky gave me no cause for alarm. I accepted them as amusing and unusual and recommended everyone to come and admire them. We stood, that day, Robin supported by Angela, and watched with pleasure as the little silver zeppelins idled above us towards the sea. To us it was all a part of being 'abroad', and 'abroad' had a different sort of cloud; it also had a very different sort of wind, as we were shortly to discover.

First a zephyr. Nothing more. A breath which rustled suggestively, uneasily, in the vine and then went scurrying across the land whispering among the trees, swaying them, scattering fallen leaves across the terrace, sweeping dust into suddenly spiralling, eye-stinging, eddies. Then, gaining strength, it took off, and wrestled, tossing the trees like feather dusters, racing through the big oaks high behind the house with such force that they beat and swung, twisting, lurching, writhing, like a host of crazed Rackham witches, howling and rending.

Deck-chairs clattered, bowled over and over into the tossing scrubland, dustbins spun through the air and were lost to sight, shutters slammed, wrenched open, slammed again: dust and sticks, small branches, scatterings of grapes beat all about us until, unable to stand upright, we managed to drag Robin, and indeed ourselves, into the house.

Standing in bewildered disarray, the dog cowering in a far corner, I saw a large potted fern, recently bought, career past the open door and explode into smithereens as it crashed into the side of the stone laundry-tanks, the water in which foamed and boiled like small Atlantics. It was all very impressive. I wondered how many tiles there would be left on the roof as they clattered down to shatter on the stones below. Not many, was the obvious answer to that. The roaring and screaming was such that we had to shout to be heard, and I then remembered the elderly builder who had told me that when the mistral came it would hit the house dead centre. He was absolutely right.

The only one of us who really enjoyed it all was Robin: he begged to be helped out again, notwithstanding shards of singing tile whipping about like shrapnel, and hung on to the orange tree by the door with both arms round its straining trunk, his head thrown back, eyes closed, mouth wide, gulping in the roaring air as it buffeted and bullied him, and far across the valley, high up on the mountains ahead, clear in the wind-washed air, I saw smoke.

At first I thought that perhaps it was scudding cloud, but in a second I knew that it was smoke streaming away in the wind towards the sea, for at its base, in the brilliance of the scoured morning light, there was a sudden leap of vermilion light.

The fires had started.

By nightfall more than half the long mountain range before us was alight. Acres and acres of pine and scrub, of mimosa and oak, blazed. Silently we watched the sudden shafts of yellow fire streak upwards when a great tree caught and burned, or the sudden bursts of billowing smoke from a house. And then we waited, dry-mouthed, for the explosion we knew must follow as the gas-tanks burst asunder, barrelling tumbling flames high into the crimson sky.

By morning the fires had reached almost to the sea, and they burned unabated for three days, until suddenly the wind dropped, trailed lazily off to Africa, and left the devastated land smoking in great clouds which curled silently into the high copper sky from a ten-mile ridge of black dust and cinders; the once pure air acrid with ash and the scent of burnt wood and earth.

Aware of Dr Poteau's strict advice, we had, on the first night, arranged that if by chance the wind should change and blow towards us from the fires, we would get Robin down to the coast by ambulance. But the wind stayed on its course and never veered. For days the mountains were blotted out in the thick haze of dust and ash, and the sun smouldered wanly in the sky like an umber disc.

And then, after all that, I caught a cold. Nothing much; a cold. A head cold. But enough to alert us to fear. It was time for Robin to leave.

'You know,' he said on the morning he was flying to London, 'I'm going because I *want* to go, not because of the fire and the smoke, or because of your cold; not for those reasons.' He was sitting in a big armchair in the long room, a beer in his hand, which he could hardly hold but which he steadied from time to time with the other. 'I want to go because I'm not going to die in your house.'

'You're not going to die anyway.'

'I'm not frightened of that. Bloody angry at fifty-six, but not frightened. But I'm not going to die here, in your new house, and leave you that memory, you're starting a new life. You aren't going to start it with a death.'

At the airport, Angela pushed him through the barrier at International in a wheel-chair, he raised a hand, blew a kiss to the dog.

I never saw him again.

DIRK BOGARDE (1921-)

Song of the Nizzard Conscript in Lombardy

Oh, Nice, so fair to me,
   To thee in thought I fly;
'Neath rows of olive trees
   My red-tiled home descry.
     Pleasures my sad heart fill
     A thousand mem'ries thrill.
     And happy years come back to me
     Of childish life and glee.

When through the meadows bounding
   I leaped the brook resounding;
The butterfly on flower besprinkled tree,
   Or sparrows chirp, were ecstasy to me —
     Like to some little wanderer on I stray,
     Laughing and strong the happy summer's day.
Oh, happy hours! Oh, Nice, so fair, so sweet!
   To thee I fly in many a longing dream;
Thy red-tiled roofs in fancy oft I greet,
   And orange groves that fair for ever seem.

Lettice Sandford

I hail each mountain brow
  Which wears an eternal smile;
I feel thy sea breeze now,
  Blue skies my thoughts beguile.
    Unto my home in reverie I turn
    There, there's the stove — the aged copper urn —
    The kneading trough — the table that has stood
    Inside so long, of carven olive wood.
    I see the cart — I mark the iron hoe,
    The axe I've swung for many a woodland blow,
    And hear my very dog, who waileth forth his woe!
    In yonder corner see my cradle lie,
    I hear the sound of mother's lullaby;
    Oh, little one, she cries, with soothing tone,
    Sleep on, my babe, sleep on!

Oh, happy home! Oh, Nice, so fair, so sweet,
  To thee I fly in many a longing dream;
Thy red-tiled roof in reverie I greet,
  And orange groves that fair for ever seem.

EUGENE EMMNUEL (19th Century) (translated by J Duncan Craig)

≈≈

After many years of wandering D H Lawrence finally died in Vence aged 45. Aldous Huxley (1894-1963), who spent much of his time on the Riviera wrote to his brother Julian a few days later.

Vence
3 March, 1930

M Y D E A R J,

As you will have seen by the papers, DHL died yesterday. We had just got back from Villefranche, where we had been seeing the Nicholses over the weekend, and found him very weak and suffering much pain and strangely *égaré,* feeling that he wasn't there — that he was two people at once. We got the doctor up at nine, who stuck some morphia into him, and he settled off to sleep — to die quietly at 10.15. The heart had begun to go and the intestines were badly affected — general intoxication, I suppose — and he seemed to have hardly any lungs left to breathe with. It had been most distressing, the two or three times we saw him during the past week — he was such a miserable wreck of himself and suffering so much pain. Morever the illness had reduced him to an appalling state of emaciation. So that it was a great comfort really that he went when he did — and went so quietly at the last. The funeral takes place tomorrow at Vence.

After it's over we shall go back to Cannes and thence along the coast to Toulon and Marseilles to see if we can find a nice house. On this part of the Riviera there is nothing — the whole thing is one vast and sordid suburb, the suburb of all Europe, from Mentone to Cannes — indescribably ugly and mingy and very expensive. This is a nice place and if we can find nothing by the sea, it may be we'll come back to Vence.

Frieda bears up well. She proposes to live with her daughter now. I hope she won't be too lost.

I hope all goes well with you. Love from us both to you all.

A L D O U S   H U X L E Y   (1 8 9 4 - 1 9 6 3)

---

28 November

Il fait beau, aujourd'hui. I am sitting in my long chair on the terrace. The wind of the last days has scattered almost the last of the fig leaves and now through those candle-shaped boughs I love so much there is a beautiful glimpse of the old town. Some fowls are making no end of a noise. I've just been for a walk on my small boulevard and looking down below at the houses all bright in the sun and housewives washing their linen in great tubs of glittering water and flinging it over the orange trees to dry. Perhaps all human activity is beautiful in the sunlight. Certainly these women lifting their arms, turning to the sun to shake out the wet clothes were supremely beautiful. I couldn't help feeling — and after they have lived they will die and it won't matter. It will be all right .....

Wander with me 10 years — will you, darling? Ten years in the sun. It's not long — only 10 springs.

You are coming quite soon now — aren't you, Boge?

K A T H E R I N E   M A N S F I E L D   (1 8 8 8 - 1 9 2 3)

An engraving after Ozanne of the Port of Antibes 1776

La bella donna che cotanto amavi

The lady whom you have loved so deeply
Has left us without warning.
So kind and gentle were her actions, I must
Think her in heaven.

While she lived, she held both keys to your heart.
It is time to recover them, and to follow her.
Strip the world's weight from you.

The first great chain being broken,
Others will fall with ease.
You will be a pilgrim, and weightless.

You have seen everything created running toward its death.
The soul must keep poverty for the dangerous journey.

F R A N C E S C O   P E T R A R C H   (1 3 0 4 - 1 3 7 4) (translated by N Kilmer)

BIBLIOGRAPHY

A

Abbott, C Colleer, *Early Medieval French Lyrics,* Constable & Co, London 1932

Agulhon, Maurice, *Pénitents et Francs-Macons de l'ancien Provence,* Fayard 1968

Alexander, Sidney, *Marc Chagall,* Cassells, New York 1979

Allen, Percy, *Impressions of Provence,* Francis Griffiths 1910

Aragon, Louis, translated by William Alwyn, *An Anthology of Twentieth Century French Poetry,* Chatto & Windus 1979

B

Baldwin, James, *Another Country,* Michael Joseph 1962

Barr, Alfred, *Henri Matisse: his Art and his Public,* M.O.M.A., New York 1951

Beardsley, Aubrey, *Last Letters of Aubrey Beardsley,* Longman's Green & Co 1904

Belloc, Hilaire, *Hills and the Sea,* Methuen & Co 1906

Bennett, Arnold, *Sketches for an Autobiography,* London

Berenger-Feraud, *Les Provençaux à travers les Ages,* Paris

Berlioz, Hector, *Memoirs of Hector Berlioz,* Victor Gollancz 1969

Bernen, Robert, *In the Heat of the Sun,* Hamish Hamilton 1981

Bishop, Morris, *Petrarch and His World,* Chatto & Windus 1964

Blessington, Countess of, *The Idler in Italy,* Henry Colburn 1839

Bogarde, Dirk, *An Orderly Man,* Chatto & Windus 1983

Bonaparte, Napoleon, *Letters to Josephine,* J M Dent & Sons

Bonner, A, *Songs of the Troubadours,* Allen & Unwin 1973

Bradby, E D, *A Short History of the French Revolution,* Clarendon Press 1926

Brion, Marcel, *Provence,* Nicholas Kaye 1956

Brougham, Lord, *Statesmen of the Time of George II,* London 1848

Burnett, R, *The Life of Paul Gauguin,* Cobden Sanderson 1936

Byron, Lord, *Complete Poetical Works,* Oxford University Press 1980

C

Cali, F, *Provence: Land of Enchantment,* Allen & Unwin 1965

Cameron, Roderick, *The Golden Riviera,* Weidenfeld & Nicolson 1975

Campbell, Roy, *The Collected Poems of Roy Campbell,* The Bodley Head 1961

Cézanne Paul, *Letters,* Bruno Cassirer 1941

Cocteau, Jean, *Cocteau's World,* Peter Owen 1972

Colette, *Letters from Colette,* Farrar, Straus & Giroux, New York 1980

Coward, Noel, *The Noel Coward Diaries,* Weidenfeld & Nicolson 1982

D

Daudet, Alphonse, *Letters from My Windmill,* Penguin 1982

Daudet, Alphonse, *Port Tarascon,* Sampson Low 1892

David, Elizabeth, *French Provincial Cooking,* Michael Joseph 1965

Dickens, Charles, *Pictures from Italy,* London 1856

Dumas, Alexandre, *Pictures of Travels in the South of France,* Offices of the National Illustrated Library 1956

Durrell, Lawrence, *Vega & Other Poems,* Faber & Faber 1973

E

Evelyn, John, *The Diary of John Evelyn,* Oxford University Press 1983

F

Farnell, I, *The Lives of the Troubadours,* David Knutt 1896

Fielding, Xan, *The Money Spinner,* Weidenfeld & Nicolson 1977

Fitzgerald, Scott, *Bits of Paradise,* The Bodley Head 1973

Fleming, Ian, *Thrilling Cities,* Jonathan Cape 1963

Ford, Ford Madox, *Provence,* Allen & Unwin 1938

G

Gascoyne, David, *Collected Verse Translations,* Oxford University Press 1970

Gide, André, *The Journals of André Gide,* Secker & Warburg 1949

Girdlestone, C M, *Dreamer and Striver,* Methuen & Co 1937

Gould, Baring, *A Book of the Riviera,* W H Allen 1896

Grant, J Duncan, *Miejour or The Land of the Félibre,* James Nisbett & Co 1877

Graves, Charles, *The Rich Man's Guide to Europe,* Prentice-Hall Inc 1966

Graves, Robert, *Collected Works,* Cassell 1958

H

Hare, Augustus, *The Riviera,* London

Haskell, Arnold, *Ballet Russe,* Weidenfeld & Nicolson 1968

Hennessy, James Pope, *Aspects of Provence,* Hogarth Press 1961

Huxley, Aldous, *The Letters of Aldous Huxley,* Chatto & Windus 1969

J

Johnson, W Branch, *Folktales of Provence,* Chapman & Hall 1927

K

Kanin, Garson, *Remembering Mr Maugham,* Hamish Hamilton 1966

L

Ladurie, Emmanuel Leroi, *Love, Death and Money in the Pays d'Oc*, Penguin 1984

Lawrence, D H, *Collected Letters*, William Heinemann 1962

Lear, Edward, *The Book of Nonsense and More Nonsense*

Lee, Laurie, *I Can't Stay Long*, Andre Deutsch 1975

Lentheric, C, *The Riviera Ancient and Modern*, T Fisher Unwin, London 1895

Longfellow, H Wadsworth, *The Collected Works of H W Longfellow*, London 1883

M

Macaulay, Rose, *The Pleasure of Ruins*, Thames & Hudson 1984

Mack, Gerstle, *Paul Cézanne*, Jonathan Cape 1935

MacNeice, Louis, *Collected Poems*, Faber & Faber 1966

Mansfield, Katherine, *Passionate Pilgrimage*, Michael Joseph 1976

Merimée, Prosper, *Notes d'un Voyage dans le Midi de France*, Paris 1835

Moorehead, Alan, *Incorrigible Marseilles*, from *Abroad*, edited by J Evans, Methuen 1970

Morgan, Ted, *Somerset Maugham*, Jonathan Cape 1980

N

Nabokov, Vladimir, *Poems & Problems*, Weidenfeld & Nicolson 1972

Newnham-Davis, Lt-Col, *A Gourmet's Guide to Europe*, Grant Richards 1903

Nietzsche, F W, *Unpublished Letters*, Peter Owen 1960

P

Pagnol, Marcel, *The Days Were Too Short*, Hamish Hamilton 1960

Petrarch, Francesco, *Songs & Sonnets from Laura's Lifetime*, Anvil Press 1980

de Polnay, Peter, *A Door Ajar*, Robert Hale 1959

Polybius, *Histories*, Macmillan & Co 1889

Pound, Ezra, *Collected Shorter Poems*, Faber & Faber 1984

Q

Quennell, Peter, *The Sign of the Fish*, Collins 1960

R

Ribbe, *La Société Provençale à la Fin du Moyen Age*, Paris 1898

Rigby, Dr Edward, *Dr Rigby's Letters in 1879*, Longman Green & Co

Root, Waverley, *The Food of France*, Macmillan

Ross, Alan, *Poems 1942-1967*, Eyre & Spottiswode 1967

Runciman, Steven, *A History of the Crusades, Vol III*, Cambridge University Press 1954

Ruskin, John, *Praeterita Vol XXXV*, George Allen 1908

S

Sansom, William, *Blue Skies, Brown Studies*, Hogarth Press 1961

Santayana, George, *The Letters of George Santayana*, Constable 1956

Scott, Sir Walter, *Anne of Geierstein*, London 1928

Service, Robert, *The Complete Poems of Robert Service*, Dodd, Mead & Co 1949

Shand, P Morton, *A Book of French Wines*, Jonathan Cape 1960

Sitwell, Osbert, *Laughter in the Next Room*, Gollancz

Smith, J H, *The Troubadours at Home*, Gordon Press, New York

Smollet, Tobias, *Travels Through France and Italy*, London 1776

Steinman, D B, *Bridges and their Builders*, Putnam's Sons 1941

Stendhal, *Travels in the South of France*, Calder & Boyers 1971

Stevenson, R L, *The Works of Robert Louis Stevenson Vol XIV*, Chatto & Windus 1912

Stouff, Louis, *Ravitaillement et Alimentation en Provence au XIV — XV Siècles*, Mouton & Co, Paris 1970

Strabo, *The Geography of Strabo*, Henry G Bohn 1891

Swinburne, Henry, *Travels through Spain in the Years 1775 & 1776*, London 1778

T

Tassart, François, *Recollections of Guy de Maupassant*, John Lane 1912

Tate, Allen, *The Swimmers & Other Poems*, Oxford University Press 1970

Tennyson, Lord Alfred, *Collected Works*

Thirion, Jacques, *Alpes Romanes*, Zodiaque, Paris 1970

Tolstoy, Leo, *Letters*, Athlone Press 1978

Tomlinson, Charles, *Collected Poems*, Oxford University Press 1985

Turnbull, Andrew, *Scott Fitzgerald*, The Bodley Head 1962

Twain, Mark, *Innocents Abroad*, New York 1869

Tylor, Charles, *The Camisards*, London 1893

Van Gogh, Vincent, *Collected Letters of Vincent Van Gogh*, New York Graphic Society, 1978

Vollard, Ambrose, *Renoir: An Intimate Record*, Alfred A Knopf, New York 1925

W

Watson, S R, *Bridges and their Builders*, Putnam's Sons 1941

West, Rebecca, *The Thinking Reed*, Hutchinson 1936

Wilde, Oscar, *Selected Letters of Oscar Wilde*, edited by Rupert Hart-Davies, Oxford University Press 1979

Wilson, Sandy, *The Boyfriend*, Andre Deutsch 1955

Woolf, Virginia, *A Writer's Diary*, Hogarth Press 1975

Young, Arthur, *Travels in France during the Years 1787, 1788, 1789*, Bell & Hyman 1892

INDEX

ACKNOWLEDGEMENTS

Grateful acknowledgement is made to the following for permission to reprint copyright material in this anthology.

C Colleer Abbott: Translation by C Colleer Abbott from *Early Medieval French Lyrics*. Reprinted by permission of Constable Publishers.

Sidney Alexander: Excerpt from *Marc Chagall* by Sidney Alexander, originally published by Cassell & Co. Copyright 1978. Reprinted by permission of Roslyn Targ Agency, 105 West 13th Street, New York 10011.

Louis Aragon: 'A Very Small Chagall' by Louis Aragon, translated by William Alwyn. Reprinted by permission of William Alwyn.

James Baldwin: Excerpt from *Another Country* by James Baldwin. © 1962, 1963 by James Baldwin. Reprinted by permission of James Baldwin.

Alfred Barr: Excerpt from *Matisse: His Art and His Public* by Alfred Barr Jr. Copyright © 1951, renewed 1979 The Museum of Modern Art, New York. All rights reserved. Reprinted by permission.

Hilaire Belloc: Excerpt from *The Hills and the Sea* by Hilaire Belloc. Reprinted by permission of A D Peters & Co Ltd.

Hector Berlioz: Excerpt from *The Memoirs of Hector Berlioz* translated by David Cairns. © 1969 by David Cairns. Reprinted by permission of Alfred A Knopf Inc.

Morris Bishop: Excerpts from *Petrarch and His World* by Morris Bishop. Reprinted by permission of Indiana University Press.

Dirk Bogarde: Excerpt from *An Orderly Man* by Dirk Bogarde. © 1963 by Labofilms SA. Reprinted by permission of Alfred A Knopf Inc.

Anthony Bonner: Excerpts from *Songs of the Troubadours* by Anthony Bonner. Copyright © 1972 by Schocken Books Inc. Reprinted by permission of Schocken Books Inc.

Marcel Brion: Excerpts from *Provence* by Marcel Brion. Reprinted by permission of William Heinemann Ltd.

Roderick Cameron: Excerpt from *The Golden Riviera* by Roderick Cameron. Reprinted by permission of George Weidenfeld & Nicolson Ltd.

Roy Campbell: 'Fishing Boats in Martigues', 'Horses on the Camargue' and 'Felibre' by Roy Campbell. Reprinted by permission of A D Donker, Johannesburg.

Paul Cézanne: Excerpt from the *Letters of Paul Cézanne,* edited by John Rewald. Reprinted by permission of Bruno Cassirer and John Rewald.

Jean Cocteau: Excerpt from *Cocteau's World* by Jean Cocteau, translated by Margaret Crosland. Reprinted by permission of Peter Owen Ltd, London.

Noel Coward: Excerpts from *The Noel Coward Diaries* by Noel Coward. Reprinted by permission of Little, Brown and Company.

Alphonse Daudet: Excerpts from *Letters From My Windmill* by Alphonse Daudet, translated by Frederick Davies (Penguin Classics, 1978). Copyright © Frederick Davies, 1978. Reprinted by permission of Penguin Books Ltd.

Elizabeth David: Excerpts from *French Provincial Cooking* by Elizabeth David.
Reprinted by permission of Elizabeth David and Michael Joseph.

Lawrence Durrell: 'Mistral' and 'Avignon' from *Collected Poems 1931-1974* by Lawrence Durrell. Copyright © 1973 by Lawrence Durrell. Reprinted by permission of Viking Penguin Inc.

John Evelyn: Excerpts from *The Diary of John Evelyn,* edited by John Bowle (1983). Reprinted by permission of Oxford University Press.

Xan Fielding: Excerpts from *The Money Spinner* by Xan Fielding. Reprinted by permission of George Weidenfeld & Nicolson Ltd.

F Scott & Zelda Fitzgerald: 'Love in the Night' from *Bits of Paradise* by F Scott and Zelda Fitzgerald. Copyright © 1973 Mrs F Scott Fitzgerald Smith. Reprinted with permission Charles Scribner's Sons.

Ian Fleming: Excerpt from *Thrilling Cities* by Ian Fleming. Reprinted by permission of Glidrose Publications Ltd. Copyright © 1963 by Glidrose Publications Ltd.

Ford Madox Ford: Excerpt from *Provence* by Ford Madox Ford. Reprinted by permnission of Allen & Unwin and David Higham Associates Ltd.

David Gascoyne: 'Georges Braque' by Paul Eluard. Reprinted from *Collected Verse Translations* by David Gascoyne (1970)

ILLUSTRATIONS